Communion with God

John Owen

Communion with God

The present edition is a reproduction of previous publication of this classic work. Minor typographical errors may have been corrected without note, however, for an authentic reading experience the spelling, punctuation, and capitalization have been retained from the original text.

ISBN: 978-1-61895-769-6

TABLE OF CONTENTS

Part 1. Communion with the Father

Part 2. Communion with the Son Jesus Christ

Part 3. Communion with the Holy Spirit

iii

PART I. COMMUNION WITH THE FATHER

CHAPTER I.

THE SAINTS HAVE COMMUNION WITH GOD –

In 1John 1:3, the apostle assures those to whom he wrote that the fellowship of believers "is with the Father, and with his Son Jesus Christ." The expression he uses speaks with such force that we have rendered it, "*Truly* our fellowship is with the Father, and with his Son Jesus Christ."

The outward appearance and condition of the saints in those days was paltry and contemptible. Their leaders were considered the scum of the earth, the offscouring of all things. Inviting others to fellowship with them, and to participate in the precious things that they enjoyed, evoked a number of awkward encounters and objections: "What benefit is there in communion with them? All it brings is sharing their troubles, reproaches, scorns, and all kinds of evils." To prevent or remove these and similar objections, the apostle lets the believers know in earnest, that despite all the disadvantages of their fellowship, at least to a carnal view, in truth what they had was very honorable, glorious, and desirable. For "*truly,*" he says, "*our fellowship is with the Father, and with his Son Jesus Christ.*"

This is so earnestly and directly asserted by the apostle, that we may boldly follow him with our affirmation, "That the saints of God have communion with him." And a holy and spiritual communion it is, as I will demonstrate. Why this reference to the Father and the Son is distinct between them, must be fully examined later.

Since sin entered the world, no man has had communion with God because of his sinful nature. He is light; we are darkness; and what communion has light with darkness? (2Cor. 6:14). He is life; we are dead. He is love; we are enmity. What agreement can there be between us? Men in such a condition have neither Christ, nor hope, nor God in the world, Eph. 2:12. "Being alienated from the life of God through their ignorance," chap. 4:18. Now, two cannot walk together unless they are agreed, Amos 3:3. So, while this distance between God and man exists, they cannot walk together in fellowship or communion. Our first interest in God was so lost by sin, that no recovery remained in ourselves. We deprived ourselves of all power to return to him. And God had not revealed that there was any way to regain access to him. Nor did he reveal that sinners could approach him in peace for any reason. Nothing that God made, and no attribute that he revealed, provided the least hint of such a possibility.

The manifestation of God's grace and pardoning mercy is the only door we have to such communion. It is committed only to the one who atoned. He is the one in whom it is evidenced. He is the one by whom grace and mercy was purchased. He is the one through whom it is dispensed, and from whom it is revealed from the heart of the Father. Hence, this communion and fellowship with God is not expressly mentioned in the Old Testament. It is found there, but its clear light, and the boldness of faith contained in it, is discovered only in the gospel of the New Testament. There the Spirit administers it. By the Spirit we have this liberty of communion, 2Cor. 3:17, 18. Abraham was the friend, of God, Isa. 41:8. David was a man after his own heart. Enoch walked with him, Gen. 5:22. All of them enjoyed the substance of this communion and fellowship. But the way into the holiest of holies was not evident while the first tabernacle was still standing, Heb. 9:8. Although they had communion with God, they did not have *parresian* [NT:3954], Eph. 3:12, which is a boldness and confidence in that communion. It came only after our High Priest entered into the most holy place, Heb. 4:16, 10:19. And so, the veil remained on those in the Old Testament. They did not have *eleuterian* [NT:1657], or freedom and liberty in their access to God, 2Cor. 3:15, 16, etc.

But in Christ we now have boldness and confident access to God, Eph. 3:12. The saints of old were not familiar with this. This distance from God is removed by Jesus Christ alone. He has consecrated a new and living way for us "through the veil, that is, his flesh," Heb. 10:20. The old way is sealed. "Through him we have access by one Spirit to the Father," Eph. 2:18. "You who sometimes were far off, are made close by the blood of Christ, for he is our peace...," verses 13, 14. More of this foundation of our communion with God will follow afterward. On this new foundation, by this new and living way, sinners are admitted into communion with God. They have fellowship with him. It is a truly astonishing provision for sinners to have fellowship with God, the infinitely holy God.

Communion relates to things and persons. It means jointly participating in something, whether good or evil, duty or enjoyment, nature or actions. Sharing a common nature means all men have fellowship or communion in that nature. It is said of the elect, in Heb. 2:14, "Those children partook of" (shared or had fellowship with) "flesh and blood" (their common nature with mankind); "and, therefore, Christ likewise shared in the same fellowship."

There is also communion as to our state or condition, whether good or evil, or things internal and spiritual. Such is the communion of saints among themselves, or with regard to their experience of outward

2

things. Christ shared a condition with the two thieves. They were all sentenced to the cross, Luke 23:40. They shared the evil condition they were judged to suffer under. And one of them requested, and obtained, a share in that blessed condition our Savior would enter shortly.

There is also a communion or fellowship in actions, whether those actions are good or evil. Among good actions is the communion and fellowship that the saints enjoy in the gospel, or in performing and celebrating the worship of God that is instituted in the gospel, Phil. 1:5. David rejoices in the same general kind of actions, Ps. 42:4. Among evil actions, there was communion in that cruel act of revenge and murder shared between the brothers Simon and Levi in Gen. 49:5.

Our communion with God is no single one of these; indeed it excludes some of them. It cannot be natural communion. It must be voluntary and by consent. It cannot be communion in a shared state or condition, but in actions. It cannot be communion in shared actions on a third party. It must be shared actions between God and us. The infinite disparity between God and man made the great philosopher conclude that there could be no friendship between them.[1] He could allow some undetermined closeness between friends; but in his understanding, there was no place for closeness between God and man. Another says that while there is a certain fellowship between God and man, it is only the general interaction of providence. Some expressed higher regard for this communion, but they understood nothing of which they spoke. This knowledge is hidden in Christ, as will be made apparent later. It is too wonderful for our sinful and corrupted nature to comprehend. Guessing only leads to terror and fear of death if we were to come into the presence of God. But as was said, we have a new foundation, and a new revelation of this privilege.

Communion is the mutual communication of the good things that those who commune delight in, based on the union that exists between them. This is how it was with Jonathan and David. Their souls clung to one another in love (1Sam. 20:17). There was a union between them based on love. And they mutually communicated all the outpourings of that love. In spiritual things this exchange is more eminent. The outpourings or issues of that union are the most precious and eminent possible.

Our communion with God consists in him communicating himself to us, and us returning to him the things he requires and accepts. These things flow from the union that we have with him in Jesus Christ. This communion is twofold:

1.   A perfect and complete communion. This is the full fruition of all his glory and our total surrender to him, resting in him as our ultimate end. We will enjoy this kind of communion when we see him as he is in eternity.

3

2. An initial and incomplete communion. This consists in the first fruits and the dawning of perfection that we have here and now, in grace. This kind is all that I will handle in this discourse.

I will address the mutual communication that exists between God and the saints while they walk together in a covenant of peace, ratified in the blood of Jesus. By the riches of his grace, the God and Father of our Lord and Savior Jesus Christ has restored us from a state of enmity to a condition of communion and fellowship with himself. I pray that anyone who reads these words of his mercy may taste his sweetness and excellence in doing this, so that he will be stirred to a greater longing for the fullness of his salvation, and his eternal fruition in glory.

CHAPTER 2.

THE SAINTS HAVE DISTINCT COMMUNION WITH THE FATHER, SON, AND SPIRIT

The saints have communion with God. What this communion consists of in general was declared in the first chapter. How this communion is carried on, and what it consists of specifically, comes next. In respect to the distinct persons of the Godhead with whom the saints have this fellowship, it is either a distinct and unique relationship with each, or it is obtained and exercised jointly and in common. It must be made clear that the saints have distinct and separate communions each with the Father, and the Son, and the Holy Spirit. It must be made clear how distinct communion with the several persons of the godhead is uniquely appropriated for each.

In 1John 5:7, the apostle tells us, "There are three that bear record in heaven: the Father, the Word, and the Holy Spirit." They are in heaven and bear witness to us. What is it that they bear witness to? To the sonship of Christ, and the salvation of believers in his blood. He discusses how that is carried on, both by blood and water, which is our justification and sanctification. And how do they distinctly bear witness to this? When God witnesses concerning our salvation, surely it is incumbent on us to accept his testimony. As he bears witness, so we are to receive it. The Father, the Son, and the Holy Spirit each bear witness distinctly, because they are three distinct witnesses. That, then, is how we are to receive their several testimonies: distinctly. In doing so, we have communion with them severally, because this giving and receiving of testimony is no small part of our fellowship with God. What their distinct witnessing consists of will be declared later.

In 1Cor. 12:4-6, the apostle distinctly ascribes to the several persons of the godhead the distribution of gifts and graces to the saints. "There are diversities of gifts, but the same Spirit," "that one and the self same Spirit;" that is, the Holy Spirit in verse 11. "And there are differences of administrations, but the same Lord," that is, the same Lord Jesus in verse 5. "And there are diversities of operations, but it is the same God....," which is the Father, Eph. 4:6. So graces and gifts are bestowed distinctly, and that is how they are received.

The same distinction applies not only in the emanation of grace from God, and the passing of the Spirit to us, but also in our access to God. "For through Christ we have access by one Spirit to the Father," Eph. 2:18. Our access to God (in which we have communion with him) is "dia Christou," "through Christ," "en Pneumati," "in the Spirit," and

5

"pros ton Patera," "to the Father." The persons of the godhead are distinctively engaged in accomplishing the will of God as revealed in the gospel.

Sometimes express mention is made only of the Father and the Son, as in John 1:3, "Our fellowship is with the Father, and with his Son Jesus Christ." The particle "and" is both distinguishing and uniting. Also in John 14:23, "If a man loves me, he will keep my words: and my Father will love him, and we will come to him, and make our abode with him." It is in this fellowship, or communion, that the Father and Son make their abode with the soul.

Sometimes only the Son is mentioned in this communion. 1Cor. 1:9, "God is faithful, by whom you were called to the fellowship of his Son Jesus Christ our Lord." And in Rev. 3:20, "If any man hears my voice, and opens the door, I will come in to him, and will sup with him, and he with me."

Sometimes the Spirit alone is mentioned. "The grace of the Lord Jesus Christ, and the love of God, and the communion of the Holy Spirit be with you all," 2Cor. 13:14. This distinct communion, then, of the saints with the Father, the Son, and the Spirit, is very plain in the Scripture. Even so, it can be demonstrated further. I must give this caution beforehand: whatever is affirmed in pursuit of this truth, is done in relation to the explanation given in the beginning of the next chapter.

Their spiritual and holy activities are the means by which the saints enjoy communion with God in Christ. It is found in the exercise of those graces that comprise the moral and instituted worship of God. Faith, love, trust, joy, etc., are what comprise the natural or moral worship of God. These are the means by which the saints have communion with him. These either act on God immediately, untied to any outward display, or else they are visibly displayed in solemn prayer and praise, according to what God has appointed. In all of these graces, the Scripture distinctly assigns the saints' acts to each person respectively: the Father, the Son, and the Spirit. This is true whether the acts are purely moral, or they are part of instituted worship. I will give further light to this assertion using particular examples:

1. For the Father. The saints uniquely and distinctly yield their faith, love, obedience, etc., to the Father. He uniquely manifests himself and responds to the saints through these graces, which should stimulate the saints to practice them more. He bears witness of his Son, 1John 5:9, "This is the witness of God which he has testified of his Son." In bearing witness, God becomes the object of our belief. And when he gives such testimony, his testimony is received by faith. This is affirmed in verse 10, "He that believes on the Son of God, has the witness in himself." To believe on the Son of God in this passage, is to

6

receive the Lord Christ as the Son. He has been given to us for all the purposes of the Father's love, based on the credibility of the Father's testimony. Therefore, in doing this, our faith immediately makes the Father the object of our belief. So it follows in the next words, "he that does not believe God" (that is, the Father, who bears witness to the Son) "has made him a liar." "You believe in God," says our Savior, John 14:1 – that is, the Father, because he adds, "Believe also in me;" or, "Believe you in God; believe also in me." God, as the prima Veritas [the primary truth], is the primary object of this belief. It is founded on his authority, in which all divine faith is ultimately resolved. Normally, faith is not considered "hupostatikos," distinctly expressing a specific person in the godhead. Instead, it is "ousiodos," comprehending the whole Deity undividedly. But in this particular case, it is the testimony and authority of the Father that we speak of, and it is the Father on whom our faith is distinctly fixed. If this were not so, the Son could not add, "Believe also in me."

The same is also said of love in 1John 2:15, "If any man loves the world, the love of the Father is not in him." This is speaking of the love we give to God, not the love we receive from him. The Father is the object of our love here, in opposition to the world that consumes our affections. The Father denotes the subject and object of our love, not the efficient cause of our love. And this love of him as a Father is what he calls his "honor," Mal. 1:6.

Furthermore, these graces that are acted out in our prayers and praises, or that are part of our instituted worship, are uniquely directed toward the Father. "You call on the Father," 1Pet. 1:17. Eph. 3:14-15, "For this cause I bow my knees to the Father of our Lord Jesus Christ, of whom the whole family in heaven and earth is named." Bowing the knee is the whole worship of God, whether in the universal moral obedience that he requires, or in other ways that he appoints. Isa. 45:23, "To me," says the Lord, "every knee will bow, every tongue will swear." In verses 24 and 25, he declares that this submission consists in acknowledging him as the source of righteousness and strength. In fact, it sometimes seems to include the orderly subjection of the whole creation to his sovereignty. In the Ephesian passage, the apostle has a far more restrained use. It is only a figurative phrase, using the most expressive bodily posture taken during prayer, which is kneeling. He further explains this in Eph. 3:16, 17. There he expands on what his aim was, and what he had in mind in bowing his knees. Thus, the actions of the Spirit in prayer are distinctly directed to the Father as the fountain of the Deity. The Father is the source of all good things that we have in Christ, because he is the "Father of our Lord Jesus Christ." In another place, the apostle expressly joins, and then distinguishes, the Father and the Son in his supplications. 1Thess. 3:11, "God himself even our

Father, and our Lord Jesus Christ, direct our way to you." The same precedent is given in regard to thanksgiving. Eph. 1:3, 4, "Blessed be the God and Father of our Lord Jesus Christ..." I will not add all the other places which agree with the particulars of this divine worship, in which the saints hold communion with God, and distinctly direct it to the Father.

2. This is also true in reference to the Son. John 14:1, "You believe in God," says Christ, "believe also in me." "Believe also," means letting our divine and supernatural faith act distinctly on the Son. It is that faith whereby you believe in God, that is, in the Father. There is also a believing *of* Christ. This belief is accepting that he is the Son of God, the Savior of the world. Neglecting that belief incurs what our Savior threatened the Pharisees with in John 8:24. "If you do not believe that I am he, you will die in your sins." In this sense, faith is not immediately fixed on the Son. It only accepts Christ as the Son by believing the testimony of the Father concerning him. But there is also a believing *on* him. This is called "Believing on the name of the Son of God," 1John 5:13; also John 9:36. Indeed, distinctly affixing our faith, commitment, and confidence on the Lord Jesus Christ, as the Son of God, is frequently pressed. John 3:16, "God" (that is, the Father) "so loved the world, that whoever believes in him" (that is, the Son) "should not perish." The Son that the Father gives must be believed on. "He that believes on him is not condemned," verse 18. " He that believes on the Son has everlasting life," verse 36. "This is the work of God, that you believe on the one whom he has sent," John 6:29, 40; 1John 5:10. The foundation of the whole truth is laid down in John 5:23, "That all men should honor the Son, even as they honor the Father. He who does not honor the Son does not honor the Father who has sent him." As for the love of the Son, I will only add that solemn apostolic benediction from Eph. 6:24, "Grace be with all those who love our Lord Jesus Christ in sincerity," that is, with divine love, or the love of religious worship. This is the only proper love of the Lord Jesus.

The solemn doxology given in Rev. 1:5, 6, makes it abundantly clear that faith, hope, and love, acted out in obedience and appointed worship, are specifically due from the saints, and distinctly directed to the Son. "To him that loved us, and washed us from our sins in his own blood, and has made us kings and priests to God and his Father; to him be glory and dominion forever and ever. Amen." This is stated with even more glory in chap. 5:8, "The four living creatures, and the four and twenty elders fell down before the Lamb, every one of them having harps, and golden vials full of fragrant aromas, which are the prayers of saints." And in verses 13 and 14, "Every creature that is in heaven, and on the earth, and under the earth, and those in the sea, and all that are in them, I heard saying, 'blessing, and honor, and glory, and power, be

8

to him that sits upon the throne, and to the Lamb forever and ever.'" The Father and the Son (he that sits upon the throne, and the Lamb) are held out jointly, yet distinctly, as the adequate object of all divine worship and honor, forever and ever. Therefore, in his solemn, dying invocation, Stephen fixes his faith and hope distinctly on Jesus, Acts 7:59, 60, "Lord Jesus, receive my spirit;" and, "Lord, lay not this sin to their charge." He knew that the son of man had the power to forgive sins. The apostle makes this worship of the Lord Jesus the discriminating character of the saints in 1Cor. 1:2, "With all that in every place call upon the name of Jesus Christ our Lord, both theirs and ours," that is, with all the saints of God. Invocation generally comprises the whole worship of God. This, then, is what is due Christ as our God and as the Son, though not as Mediator.

3. This is also true in reference to the Holy Spirit of grace. The great sin of unbelief is still described as opposing and resisting the Holy Spirit. You have the love of the Spirit distinctly mentioned in Rom. 15:30. The apostle specifically directs his supplication to him in that solemn benediction found in 2Cor. 13:14, "The grace of the Lord Jesus Christ, and the love of God, and the communion of the Holy Spirit, be with you all." Such benedictions were originally supplications. The Holy Spirit is also entitled to all instituted worship. This is understood from the administration of baptism in his name, Matt. 28:19. More will be said about this later.

Now, to sum up what has been said: There is no grace by which our souls reach out to God, no act of divine worship that is yielded to him, no duty or obedience that is performed, that is not distinctly directed to the Father, Son, and Spirit. By these graces and similar means, we hold communion with God, and we have that communion distinctly with each person of the godhead, as described.

This may be clearer if we consider how the persons of the Deity act in communicating those good things in which the saints have communion with God. In the same way that all their spiritual ascensions are assigned to the distinct persons of the Deity, all of God's communications to them are distinct as to their fountain and dispensations. This is declared in two ways:

(1.) It is declared when the same thing, at the same time, is ascribed jointly, distinctly, and respectively to all the persons in the Deity. Grace and peace are jointly and severally ascribed in Rev. 1:4, 5, "Grace be to you, and peace, from him which is, and which was, and which is to come; and from the seven Spirits which are before his throne; and from Jesus Christ, who is the faithful witness..." The seven Spirits before the throne are the Holy Spirit of God. He is considered the perfect fountain of every perfect gift and dispensation. All are joined together here, and yet all are mentioned as distinguished in their

9

communication of grace and peace to the saints. "Grace and peace be to you, from the Father, and from..."

(2.) It is declared when the same thing is attributed severally and singly to each person of the godhead. There is no gracious influence from above, no passing of light, life, love, or grace upon us, that does not proceed in this distinctive dispensation. I will give only one example, which is very comprehensive, and may include all the others. This is teaching. The teaching of God is the real communication of every particular emanation from himself to the saints. The promise that, "They will all be taught of God," wraps in itself the whole mystery of grace as to its actual dispensation to us, to the extent that we may really possess it. This is assigned,

[1.] To the Father. The accomplishment of that promise is specifically referred to the Father in John 6:45, "It is written in the prophets, 'And they will be all taught of God.' Every man therefore that has heard, and has learned of the Father, comes to me." This teaching, by which we are translated from death to life, and brought to Christ to participate in life and love in him, is of and from the Father. From him we hear; of him we learn; by him we are brought into union and communion with the Lord Jesus. This is him drawing us, and reproducing us of his own will, by his Spirit. It is what he employs the ministers of the gospel to do, Acts 26:17, 18.

[2.] To the Son. The Father proclaims from heaven that Christ is the great teacher. This proclamation is in the solemn charge to hear him, which once again came from heaven: "This is my beloved Son; hear him." The Son's entire prophetical office, and a substantial part of his kingly office, consist of this teaching. In this he is said to draw men to himself, as the Father is said to do in his teaching, John 12:32. He does this with such efficacy that "the dead hear his voice and live." The teaching of the Son is a life-giving, spirit-breathing teaching. It is an effectual influence of light by which he shines into darkness. It is a communication of life that quickens the dead. It is an opening of blind eyes, and a changing of hard hearts. It is a pouring out of the Spirit, with all its fruits. Hence, he claims it as his privilege to be the sole master in Matt. 23:10, "One is your Master, even Christ."

[3.] To the Spirit – In John 14:26 it says, "The Comforter will teach you all things." "But the anointing which you have received," says the apostle, "abides in you, and you do not need any man to teach you: but as the same anointing teaches you all things, and is truth, and is no lie, and even as it has taught you, you will abide in him," 1John 2:27. That teaching unction is not only true, but it is truth itself. It can only be the Holy Spirit of God. Being given to us, he

10

teaches us so "that we might know the things that are freely given to us of God," 1Cor. 2:12.

I have chosen this special example because, as I told you, it is comprehensive, and includes most of the particulars that might be enumerated (such as quickening, preserving, etc.). This further drives home the truth that is being demonstrated. Because there is such a distinct communication of grace from the several persons of the Deity to the saints, the saints must have distinct communion with each of them. All that remains is to intimate the basis of this distinction. It is that the Father communicates all grace by original authority; the Son does it by communicating from a purchased treasury; and the Holy Spirit does it by immediate efficacy.

1st. The Father communicates all grace by original authority: He quickens *whom he will*, John 5:21. "*Of his own will* he produced us," James 1:18. Life-giving power is invested in the Father because of his eminence; it respects his original authority. Therefore, in sending the quickening Spirit, Christ is said to do it from the Father, or else the Father does it himself. "But the Comforter, which is the Holy Spirit, whom the Father will send..." John 14:26. "But when the Comforter comes, whom I will send to you from the Father..." John 15:26. He is also said to send the Spirit himself, in John 16:7.

2dly. The Son communicates by giving from a purchased treasury: "We have all received of his fullness, and grace for grace," John 1:16. And where does this fullness come from? "It pleased the Father that in him all fullness should dwell," Col. 1:19. The reason that this fullness has been committed to him is found in Phil. 2:8-11. "When you shall make his soul an offering for sin, he will prolong his days, and the pleasure of the LORD will prosper in his hand. He will see the travail of his soul, and will be satisfied: by his knowledge will my righteous servant justify many; for he will bear their iniquities," Isa. 53:10-11. And with this fullness he also has the authority to communicate it, John 5:25-27; Matt. 28:18.

3dly. The Spirit communicates by immediate efficacy Rom. 8:11, "But if the Spirit of him that raised Jesus from the dead dwells in you, he that raised up Christ from the dead will also quicken your mortal bodies by his Spirit that dwells in you." Here all three persons are included, with their distinct contribution to our quickening. Here is the Father's authoritative quickening, "He raised Christ from the dead, and he will quicken you;" and the Son's mediatory quickening that is done in "the death of Christ;" and we have the Spirit's immediate efficacy, "He will do it by the Spirit that dwells in you." If you want this whole matter further explained, you may consult what I have written elsewhere on this subject. Thus we have both proven and demonstrated this distinct communion.

11

CHAPTER 3

THE DISTINCT COMMUNION WHICH THE SAINTS HAVE WITH THE FATHER –

What remains to further clear up this distinctive communion, is to introduce a number of examples showing what the saints specifically hold in this communion. I will premise that with some observations:

1. When I assign anything as unique in which we distinctly hold communion with any individual person of the godhead, I do not exclude the other persons from communion in the very same thing. I am only saying that it is held principally, immediately, and eminently with that one person. It is held with the others secondarily, and as a consequence of that foundation. This is because any one of the persons, as the person, is not the prime object of divine worship, except as identified with the nature or essence of God. The outward works of God (called " Trinitatis ad extra"), which are usually said to be common and undivided, are either completely works of common providence, or else they are distinguished in respect to their manner of operation. So creation is appropriated to the Father, and redemption to the Son.

2. There is a concurrence in the acts and operations of the whole Deity in the dispensation of the work of our salvation, and in every act of our communion with each singular person. Look at whatever act we hold in communion with any person, and there is an influence from every person in that act. Take the act of faith. The Father bestows it on us. "It is not of yourselves: it is the gift of God," Eph. 2:8. It is the Father that reveals the gospel, and Christ in it, Matt. 11:25. And it is purchased for us by the Son: "To you it is given on behalf of Christ, to believe on him," Phil. 1:29. In him we are "blessed with spiritual blessings," Eph. 1:3. He bestows faith on us, and increases faith in us, Luke 17:5. And the Spirit works it in us. He administers that "exceeding greatness of his power," which he exercises towards those who believe, "according to the working of his mighty power, which he worked in Christ, when he raised him from the dead," Eph. 1:19, 20; Rom. 8:11.

3. When I assign any particular thing that we hold in communion with any single person of the godhead, I do not exclude other mediums of communion. I am only urging a special and eminent example to prove and manifest the general assertion. Otherwise there is no grace or duty in which we do not have communion with God in that way. In everything in which we are made partakers of the divine nature, there is a communication and receiving between God and us, because we are so near to him in Christ.

4. By asserting this distinct communion, I do not intend in the least to restrict all communion with God to these precincts, nor to prejudice that holy fellowship we have with the whole Deity.

These few observations being made, I will now declare what it is, specifically and eminently, in which the saints have communion with the Father. It is love: free, undeserved, and eternal love. The Father specifically fixes this love on the saints. They are to see this immediately in him, to receive it from him, and to return it to him in any way that delights him. This is the great discovery of the gospel. The Father, as the fountain of the Deity, is only known as full of wrath, anger, and indignation against sin. Nor can the sons of men have any other thoughts of him (Rom. 1:18; Isa. 33:13-14; Hab. 1:13; Ps. 5:4-6; Eph. 2:3). Yet here in the gospel he is now revealed specifically as love, and as full of love towards us. The manifestation of this truth is the unique work of the gospel, Tit. 3:4-7.[2]

1. In 1John 4:8 we read, "God is love." It is evident from verse 9 that the name of God is taken personally here. It refers to the person of the Father, and not just his essence. He is distinguished from his only begotten Son whom he sends into the world. He says, "The Father is love." That is, he not only has an infinitely gracious, tender, compassionate, and loving nature, as he proclaimed in Exod. 34:6, 7.[3] He is also the one who eminently and specifically gives himself to us in free love. The apostle presents this fact in subsequent verses. "This is love," he says. "This is what I would have you take notice of in him, that he shows you love in 'sending his only begotten Son into the world, that we might live through him,'" 1John 4:9. The same idea is found in 1John 4:10, "He loved us, and sent his Son to be the propitiation for our sins." The Holy Spirit plainly declares that this love is specifically seen in him. It is displayed prior to sending Christ, and prior to all the mercies and benefits that we receive through him. This love precedes the purchase of Christ, although its entire fruit is revealed in that alone, Eph. 1:4-6.

2. The apostle makes such a distribution of graces in his solemn benediction, 2Cor. 13:14, "The grace of the Lord Jesus Christ, *the love of God*, and the fellowship of the Holy Spirit, be with you all." In ascribing a number of things to the distinct persons, it is love that he specifically assigns to the Father. The fellowship of the Spirit is mentioned with the grace of Christ and the love of God, because it is by the Spirit alone that we have fellowship with Christ in grace, and fellowship with the Father in love. We also have also unique fellowship with the Spirit, as will be declared later.

3. In John 16:26, 27, our Savior says, "I do not say to you, that I will pray the Father for you; for the Father himself loves you." Why does he say, "I do *not* say that I will pray the Father for you," when he

13

said plainly in chap. 14:16, "I *will* pray the Father for you?" The disciples were fully convinced of Christ's dear and tender affections towards them, and of his continued care and kindness. With all the gracious words, the comforting and faithful promises of their Master, and the opening of his heart to them, they knew that he would not forget them when he was gone from them bodily. But now all their thoughts concerned the Father. How would they be accepted by him, and what regard did he have towards them? Our Savior says in essence, "Do not worry about that. You do not need to have me procure the Father's love for you. Instead, know that this is his unique regard for you and what you are in him: 'He himself loves you.' It is true, indeed (as I told you), that I will pray that the Father sends you the Spirit, the Comforter, and with him all the gracious fruits of his love. But as to this love itself, his free and eternal love for you, there is no need to intercede for that. For the Father himself eminently loves you. Be resolved in that, so that you may hold communion with him in that love, and not be troubled about it any more. In fact, if you are troubled about the Father's love, understand that you can no more trouble and burden him than by your unkindness in not believing it." This must be so when sincere love is questioned.

4. The apostle teaches the same thing in Rom. 5:5. "The love of God is shed abroad in our hearts by the Holy Spirit, which is given to us." God, whose love this is, is plainly distinguished from the Holy Spirit, who sheds that love abroad. And in verse 8, he is also distinguished from the Son, because it is from his love that the Son is sent. Therefore, it is the Father of whom the apostle speaks. And what is it that he ascribes to him? Love, which he also commends to us in verse 8. To carry this to its climax, not only is there frequent and specific mention of the love of God the Father, but he is also called "The God of love" in 2Cor. 13:11. And he is said to be "love," so that whoever wants to know him, 1John 4:8, or dwell in him by fellowship or communion, 1John 4:16, must do it *because* he is love."

5. There is a twofold divine love. There is *beneplaciti*, a love of good pleasure and purpose, and *amicitiae*, a love of friendship and approval. They are both specifically and eminently assigned to the Father:

(1.) John 3:16, "God so loved the world, that he gave..." This is the love of his purpose and good pleasure. It is his determinate will to do good. This is distinctly ascribed to him, and laid down as the cause of sending his Son. See also Rom. 9:11-12; Eph. 1:4-5; 2Thess. 2:13-14; 1John 4:8-9.

(2.) In John 14:23, there is mention of that other kind of love. "If a man loves me," says Christ, "he will keep my words: and my Father will love him, and we will come to him, and make our abode with him."

14

The love of friendship and approval is eminently ascribed to him here. Christ says, "We will come," both Father and Son, "to such a one, and dwell with him" by the Spirit. Yet he has us notice that, as to love, the Father has a unique prerogative: "My Father will love him."

6. As this love is uniquely seen in the Father, it should be understood as the fountain of all subsequent gracious dispensations. Christians are often very troubled concerning how the Father thinks of them. They are well persuaded of the good will of the Lord Christ. The difficulty lies in how well they are accepted by the Father. What is his heart towards them? "Show us the Father, and that will be enough for us," John 14:8. Now, his love ought to be looked on as the fountain from which all other sweetness flows. This is how the apostle sets it out in Tit. 3:4. "After that, the kindness and love of God our Savior toward man appeared." It is the Father of whom he speaks, for in verse 6, he tells us that "he sheds that love upon us abundantly, through Jesus Christ our Savior." He makes this love the linchpin on which the great alteration and translation of the saints turns. He says in verse 3, "We too were sometimes foolish, disobedient, deceived, serving diverse lusts and pleasures, living in malice and envy, hateful, and hating one another." Where, then, does our recovery come from? It all arises from this love of God, flowing out as described. For when the kindness and love of God appeared, then this alteration ensued. To make us secure in this, there is nothing in the world of a loving and tender nature that God has not compared himself to. If we remove all their weaknesses and imperfections, great impressions of love must remain. He is like a father, a mother, a shepherd, a hen over her chickens, and the like, Ps. 103:13; Isa. 63:16; Matt. 6:6; Isa. 66:13; Ps. 23:1; Isa. 40:11; Matt. 23:37.

I will not need to add any more proofs. I have demonstrated that there is love in the person of the Father, specifically held out to the saints, in which he holds communion with them.

Now, to complete communion with the Father in love, two things are required of believers: (1.) that they receive it from him and (2.) that they suitably return it to him.

(1.) That they receive it Communion consists in giving and receiving. Until the love of the Father is received, we have no communion with him in that love. How, then, is this love of the Father received so as to hold fellowship with him? By faith. We receive it by believing it. God has so fully, and so eminently revealed his love, that it may be received by faith. "You believe in God," John 14:1, that is, in the Father. And what is it to believe in him? It is to believe in his love, for he is "love," 1John 4:8.

It is true that our faith does not act immediately upon the Father, but by the Son. "He is the way, the truth, and the life. No man comes to

15

the Father but by him," John 14:6. Christ is the merciful high priest over the house of God. By him we have access to the throne of grace. By him we are introduced to the Father. By him we believe in God, 1 Pet. 1:21. When we have access to the Father by and through Christ, then we behold the Father's glory. We see his love that he uniquely bears towards us, and our faith acts on that love. We are to see it, believe it, and receive it, as it exists in him. The issues and fruits of this love are bestowed on us through Christ alone. Though there is no light for us to see except in the beams, yet by its beams we may see the sun, which is its source. Though all of our refreshment actually lies in the streams, yet those streams lead us up to the fountain. Jesus Christ, in respect to the love of the Father, is the beam or the stream in which all of our light and refreshment is actually found. Yet, he leads us to the fountain, the sun of eternal love itself. If believers would exercise themselves in this truth, they would discover a substantial spiritual improvement in their walk with God.

This is what is aimed at. Many dark and disturbing thoughts are apt to arise in this thing. Few believers can carry their hearts and minds to this height by faith, to rest their souls in the love of the Father. They live below this peak, in the troublesome region of hopes and fears, storms and clouds. Everything at the peak is serene and quiet, but they do not know how to reach it. It is the will of God that he may always be seen as benign, kind, tender, loving, and unchangeable in this attribute. Specifically as the Father, he is the great fountain and spring of all gracious communications and fruits of love. This is what Christ came to reveal: God as a *Father*, John 1:18. This is the name that Christ declares to those who are given to him out of the world, John 17:6. And this love of the Father is what he effectually leads us to by himself, because he is the only way of going to God as a Father, John 14:5, 6. By doing so, he gives us the rest of what he promises; for the love of the Father is the only rest for the soul.

It is true, as was said, that we do not formally understand this in the first instant of believing. We believe in God through Christ, 1Pet. 1:21. Faith seeks out rest for the soul. This is presented to the soul by Christ, the mediator, as the only procuring cause. The soul does not remain here. By Christ it has access to the Father, Eph. 2:18, and access into his love. It finds out that he is love, and that he has a design, a purpose of love, and a good pleasure towards us from eternity. The soul finds delight, contentment, and good will in Christ, because all cause of anger and aversion has been taken away. The soul reposes and rests itself there. By faith through Christ and by Christ, the soul has been brought into the heart of God, into a comforting persuasion and spiritual perception and sense of his love. This is the first thing that the saints do in their communion with the

Father. More will be said of how to properly improve this communion later.

(2.) That the saints suitably return this love to him God loves so that he may be beloved. When he commands the return of his received love to complete communion with him, he says, "My son, give me your heart," Prov. 23:26, your affections, your love. "You shall love the Lord your God with all your heart, and with all your soul, and with all your strength, and with all your mind," Luke 10:27. This is the return that he demands. When the soul sees God in his dispensation of love, and it sees that he is love, infinitely lovely and loving, it rests upon and delights in him as such. Then has it communion with him in love. This is love: that God loves us first, and then we love him again. I will not go into a description of divine love now. Generally, love is an affection of union and nearness, with contentment in it. Whenever the Father is looked upon as acting in any other way than with love upon our soul, it breeds dread and aversion in us. Hence the fleeing and hiding of sinners in the Scriptures. But when the Father is considered as a father, acting in love on the soul, it stimulates the soul to love him again. In faith, this is the foundation of all acceptable obedience, Deut. 5:10; Exod. 20:6; Deut. 10:12, 11:1, 13, 13:3.

This is this whole of what is stated by the apostle in Eph. 1:4, "According as he has chosen us in him before the foundation of the world, that we should be holy and without blame before him in love." It begins in God's love for us, and ends in our love for him. That is what the eternal love of God aims at in us, and works us up to do. It is true that our universal obedience falls within the compass of our communion with God. But that communion is with him *as* God. He is our blessed, sovereign, lawgiver and rewarder. We have communion with God *because* he is the Father, our Father in Christ, revealed to us as being love, above and contrary to all the expectations of the natural man. So it is in love that we have this intercourse with him. I am not just referring to that love which is at the heart of all moral obedience, but to a unique delight in the Father, acquiescing in him, which is effectually revealed to the soul as love.

To make this love of God to us and our love to him clearer, I will show two things: [1.] In what they agree, and [2.] In what they differ. This will further uncover the nature of each.

[1.] *They agree in two things:*

1st. They are each a love of rest and contentment.

2nd. The issues and fruits of these loves are communicated only in Christ.

[2.] *There are a number of things in which they differ:*

17

1st. The love of God is a love of bounty; our love to him is a love of duty.

2nd. The love of the Father to us is a prior love; our love to him is a consequential love.

3rd. The love of God is equal, constant, and incapable of augmentation or diminution; our love is unequal, increasing, waning, growing, and declining.

[1.] Things in which they agree:

1st. They are each a love of rest and contentment.

(1) The love of God is such a love. Zeph. 3:17, "The LORD your God in the midst of you is mighty; he will save, he will rejoice over you with joy, he will rest in his love; he will joy over you with singing." Both these things are assigned here to God in his love.

REST and DELIGHT. The words are, *"yacharish be'ahavato"* [OT:2790,160] "He will be silent because of his love." To rest with contentment is expressed by being silent. That is, it is done without whining, and without complaint. God does this because of his own love. It is so full, complete, and absolute, that it will not allow him to complain of anything in those whom he loves. Instead, he is silent because of it. "Rest in his love." That is, he will not remove his love and he will not seek another object for it. His love will make its abode forever with the one on whom it has become fixed.

CONTENTMENT or DELIGHT: "He rejoices with singing" as one who is fully satisfied in that object he has fixed his love on. Here are two words used to express the delight and joy that God has in his love: *yasis* and *yagil* [OT:7797, 1523] The first denotes the inward affection of the mind, and the joy of heart. To indicate the intensity of it, it is said that he will do it *besimchah* [OT:8057], in gladness, or with joy. To have joy of heart in gladness, is the highest expression of delight in love. The latter word denotes not the inward affection, but the outward demonstration of it. It is to exult in an outward demonstration of internal delight and joy. It is to leap as if overcome with some joyful surprise. Therefore, God is said to do this *berinnah* [OT:7440], with a joyful sound, or singing. To rejoice with gladness of heart, to exult with singing and praise, argues that this is the greatest delight and contentment possible.

When he expresses the contrary of this love, he says *"ouk eudokese"* [NT:2106], "he was not well pleased," 1Cor. 10:5. He did not fix his delight or his rest on them. "If any man draws back, the Lord's soul has no pleasure in him," Heb. 10:38; Jer. 22:28; Hos. 8:8; Mal. 1:10. He takes pleasure in those who abide with him. He sings to his church, "A vineyard of red wine: I the LORD keep it," Isa. 27:2, 3;

Ps. 147:11, 149:4. There is rest and contentment in his love. In the Hebrew there is only a transposition of a letter between the word that signifies a love of will and desire ("'ahav" [OT:157] is to love this way), and what denotes a love of rest and acquiescence (which is 'avah [OT:160]). Both are applied to God. He wills good to us, so that he may rest in that will. Some say that *agapain* [NT;25], "to love," is from *agan potestai*, which is to perfectly acquiesce in the thing loved. And when God calls his Son "*agapeton*," "beloved," Matt. 3:17, he adds, as an exposition of it, "*en hoi eudokesa*," "in whom I rest well pleased."

(2) The return of love that the saints make to God – It is returned to complete their communion with him. It holds some analogy to God's love in this matter, for it is also a love of rest and delight. "Return to your rest, my soul," says David, Ps. 116:7. He makes God his rest. That is, his soul rests in God without seeking a more suitable and desirable object. He says, "Whom have I in heaven but you, and there is no one upon earth that I desire besides you," Ps. 73:25. Thus the soul gathers itself from all its wanderings, from all its other loves, to rest in God alone, to satiate and content itself in him, choosing the Father for its present and eternal rest. And this is also done with delight. "Your loving-kindness," says the psalmist, "is better than life; therefore I will praise you," Ps. 63:3. "Than life," "*michayim*" [OT:2416], literally means "before lives." What is meant is the whole of life, with all its concerns, which makes it considerable.

Writing on this passage, Austin [Augustine] reads it "super vitas," extending it to the several seasons of life that men engage in. It at least means life in its entirety, with all its advantages. Seeing himself in the jaws of death, rolling into the grave through innumerable troubles, David found more sweetness in God than in a long life. He preferred God to a life with all the best and noblest possibilities, including with all the enjoyments that make it pleasant and comfortable. The church returns this same kind of love in both these aspects in Hos. 14:3, "Asshur will not save us; we will not ride upon horses: no longer will we say to the work of our hands, 'You are our gods:' for in you the fatherless finds mercy." They reject the best rest and contentment in favor of God. They throw themselves on him as otherwise helpless orphans.

2dly. The love of the Father to us and the love of the saints returned to God are the same in this: the issues and fruits of these loves are communicated only in Christ. The Father communicates no issue of his love to us except through Christ; and we return no love to him but through Christ. He is the treasury in which the Father disposes all the riches of his grace, riches taken from the bottomless mine of his eternal love. Christ is the priest into whose hand we put all the offerings that

19

we return to the Father. Consequently, the Father is said to love the Son first and eminently. He loves him not only as his eternal Son, the delight of his soul before the foundation of the world, Prov. 8:30, but also as our mediator, and as the means of conveying his love to us, Matt. 3:17; John 3:35, 5:20, 10:17, 15:9, 17:24. And we are said to believe in and to have access to God through him.

(1.) The Father loves us, and "chose us before the foundation of the world." But in the pursuit of that love, he "blesses us with all spiritual blessings in heavenly places in Christ," Eph. 1:3, 4. From his love, he sheds or pours out the Holy Spirit richly upon us, through Jesus Christ our Savior, Tit. 3:6. In the pouring out of his love, not one drop falls apart from the Lord Christ. The holy anointing oil was poured all over the head of Aaron, Ps. 133:2; from there it dripped down to the skirts of his clothing. Love is first poured out on Christ, and from him it drips like the dew of Mt. Herman upon the souls of his saints. The Father wants him to have "pre-eminence in all things," Col. 1:18; "it pleased [the Father] that all fullness should dwell in [the Son]," verse 19; that "we might receive from his fullness, grace for grace," John 1:16. The love of the Father's purpose and good pleasure arise from and have their foundation in his mere grace and will. Yet its accomplishment is only in Christ. All its fruits are first given to him, and only in him that they are dispensed to us. Although the saints see an infinite ocean of love in the heart of the Father, they are not to look for one drop from him apart from what comes through Christ. He is the only means of communication. Love in the Father is like honey in the flower. It must be in the comb before we can use it. Christ must extract and prepare this honey for us. He draws this water from the fountain through union, and then he dispenses its fullness. By faith, we draw from the wells of salvation that are in him. This was discussed in part before.

(2.) Our return of love to the Father is completely in Christ and by him. It is good for us that it is. Otherwise, what lame and blind sacrifices we would present to God! Christ bears the iniquity of our offerings, and he adds incense to our prayers. Our love is fixed on the Father, but it is conveyed to him through the Son of his love. He is the only way for our graces, as well as for us, to go to God. Through Christ passes all of our desire, delight, contentment, and obedience. More of this afterward.

[2.] Things in which these two loves differ

1st. The love of God is a love of bounty; our love to him is a love of duty.

(1.) The love of the Father is a love of bounty, a descending love. His love moves him to do good things to us, and great things for

20

us. His love lies at the bottom of all his dispensations towards us. We hardly find any mention of it, but it is the cause and fountain of the free gifts that flow from it. He loves us, and he sends his Son to die for us. He loves us, and he blesses us with all spiritual blessings. Loving is choosing, Rom. 9:11, 12. He loves us and he chastises us. It is a love like the heavens have for the earth, when, being full of rain, they pour forth showers to make the earth fruitful. It is a love like the sea, which communicates its waters to the rivers out of its own fullness; they return to the sea only what they receive from it. It is the love of a spring or a fountain that always communicates. It is a love from which proceeds everything that is lovely. It infuses into and creates goodness in those who are loved. One who loves will do good to those he loves as he is able. God's will and his power are commensurate; what he wills, she works.

(2.) Our love to God is a love of duty, the love of a child. His love descends upon us in bounty and fruitfulness; our love ascends to him in duty and thankfulness. He adds to us by his love; we add nothing to him by ours. Our goodness does not extend to him. Though our love is immediately fixed on him, no fruit of our love immediately reaches him. Though he requires our love, it does not benefit him, Job 35:5-8, Rom. 11:35, Job 22:2, 3. Our love includes four things: rest, delight, reverence, and obedience. By these four things we hold communion with the Father in his love. Hence God calls the love that is due to him as a father "honor." Mal. 1:6, "If I be a father, where is my honor?" It is a deserved act of duty.

2dly. The love of the Father to us is a prior love; our love to him is a consequential love.

(1.) The love of the Father is prior in two respects:

[1.] It is prior in respect to our love. 1John 4:10, "This is love, not that we loved God, but that he first loved us." His love goes before ours. The father loves the child even when the child does not know the father, much less love him. By nature, we are "Teostugeis," Rom. 1:30, haters of God. In his own nature, God is "philanthropos," a lover of men. Surely all mutual love between God and us must begin in his hand.

[2.] It is prior in respect to all other causes of love. It not only precedes our love, but it also precedes anything in us that is lovely. Rom. 5:8, "God commends his love towards us, in that while we were yet sinners Christ died for us." His love and its eminent fruits are showered on us as sinners. Our sin displays all the unloveliness and undesirability that can exist in a creature. The very mention of that sin removes every cause and motivation for love. Yet the Father's love is commended to us by this most signal testimony. It is not only when we have done no good, but while we are still in our blood, that he loves us. It is not because we are better than others, but because he is infinitely good in himself. His kindness appears when we are foolish and disobedient. Hence he is said to "love the world." That is, he loves those who have only what is in and of the world, whose whole being lies in evil.

(2.) Our love is a consequence of his in both these regards:

[1.] In respect to the love of God. No creature would ever turn his affections toward God if the heart of God were not first set on him.

[2.] In respect to the sufficient causes of love. God must be revealed to us as lovely and desirable, as a suitable object for our soul to rest upon, before we can bear any love to him. In this sense, the saints do not love God for nothing, but for his excellence, loveliness, and desirability. As the psalmist says in Ps. 116:1, "I love the LORD, *because!*" Or, as David says in another case, "What have I done now? Is there not a cause?" (1Sam. 17:29). If anyone inquires about our love for God, we may likewise ask, "What have we done now? Is there not a cause?"

3dly. They differ in this also: the love of God is like himself. It is equal, constant, and incapable of augmentation or diminution. Our love is like ourselves. It is unequal, increasing, waning, growing, and declining. His love is like the sun. It is always the same in its light, though a cloud may sometimes interpose. Our love is like the moon. It is sometimes enlarged, sometimes reduced.

(1.) The love of the Father is equal. The one he loves, he loves to the end, and always the same. "The Strength of Israel is not a man, that he should repent," 1Sam 15:29. His love is immutably fixed on the one he loves; it does not grow or diminish at any time. It is an eternal love that had no beginning or end. It cannot be heightened by any act of ours, nor lessened by anything in us. However, there are two regards in which changes may be seen:

[1.] In respect to its fruits. As I said, it is a fruitful love, a love of bounty. Those fruits may sometimes be greater, sometimes less; its communication varies. Who among the saints finds this is not so? What life, what light, what strength, we sometimes have! And again, how dead, how dark, how weak we sometimes are! God is pleased to release or restrain the fruits of his love. All the graces of the Spirit in us, all the sanctified pleasures we have, are fruits of his love. Personal experience abundantly testifies how these are variously dispensed, and how differently and seasonally they may be dispensed to the same person.

[2.] In respect to its manifestations. He "sheds abroad his love in our hearts by the Holy Spirit," Rom. 5:5. He gives us a sense of his love, manifesting it to us. This varies and changes, sometimes more, sometimes less. Now he shines his face upon us, another time he hides it, as necessary for our profit. Our Father will not always chide us, or we may be cast down. He does not always smile, or we may be full and neglect him. Yet, his love in itself remains the same. Even though he may hide his face for a moment, he gathers us with everlasting kindness.

Objection. You may say, "This comes close to blasphemy. You say that God loves his people in their sinning as well as in their strictest obedience. If so, then who will serve him more, or walk with him to be well-pleasing?"

Answer. There are few truths of Christ that someone has not attacked with this. They do not vary in their content. The love of God in itself is the eternal purpose and act of his will. This is no love less changeable than God's. Otherwise, no flesh could be saved. But God's love does not change, and we are not consumed. What then? Does he love his people in their sinning? Yes. He loves his people, but not their sinning. Does he not alter his love towards them? He does not alter the purpose of his will, but he does alter the dispensations of his grace. He rebukes them; he chastens them; he hides his face from them; he strikes them; he fills them with a sense of his indignation. But woe to us if he changes in his love, or removes his kindness from us! Those things that seem to indicate a change in his affections towards us, are as much a demonstration of his love as those kindnesses we prefer. "But will this not encourage people to sin?" No one who ever tasted of the love of God can seriously make this objection. The doctrine of grace may be turned into wantonness, but the principle cannot. I will not wrong the saints by giving a different answer to this objection. Detesting people's sin may well be separate from God's accepting them and designating them to eternal life.

And so our love to God ebbs and flows, wanes and waxes. We lose our first love, and we grow again in love, scarcely a day stands still. What poor creatures we are! How unlike the Lord and his love! "Unstable as water, we cannot excel" (Gen. 49:4). Now it is, "Though all men forsake you, I will not" (Mk. 14:29), but in another place, "I do not know the man" (Mt. 26:74). One day we say, "I will never be moved, my hill is so strong" (Ps. 30:6-7), and the next, "All men are liars, I will perish" (Ps. 116:10-11). Was there ever a time and place that our love was equal towards God?

Thus, these agreements and differences further describe the mutual love of the Father and the saints, in which they hold communion. I will not give other examples of the Father's love, but I will try to improve on this description in the next chapter.

23

CHAPTER 4.

INFERENCES CONCERNING COMMUNION WITH THE FATHER IN LOVE.

Having discovered the nature of the distinct communion we have with the Father, what remains is to give some exhortations, directions, and observations:

1. First is a duty seldom exercised by Christians, which is to hold immediate communion with the Father in love. Our problem and our sin is that we are unacquainted with our mercies and privileges. We do not respond to the voice of the Spirit that is given to us, "that we may know the things that are freely bestowed on us of God" (1Cor. 2:12). This burdens us when we might have rejoiced, and weakens us when we might have been strong in the Lord. How few of the saints experience this privilege of holding immediate communion with the Father in love! Many look upon him with anxious, doubtful thoughts! They fear and question his good will and kindness! At best, they think he has no sweetness towards us, except what was purchased at the high price of Jesus' blood. It is true that Christ's blood alone is the means of communication; but the free fountain and spring of every good thing comes from the heart of the Father. "Eternal life was with the Father, and is manifested to us" (1Jn. 1:2).

(1.) Let us see the Father as love. Do look not at him as a father who is always critical, but as one who is most kind and tender. By faith let us look at him as someone who has had thoughts of kindness towards us from everlasting. Only a misapprehension of God would make someone run from the one who knows him in the least. "Those who know you will put their trust in you" (Ps . 9:10). Men cannot abide with God in spiritual meditations. They lose his company by lacking this insight into his love. They fix their thoughts only on his terrible majesty, severity, and greatness, and so their spirits are not endeared to him. If they would focus on his everlasting tenderness and compassion, his thoughts of kindness towards them from eternity, and his present gracious acceptance of them, then they could not bear an hour's absence from him. Now, perhaps, they cannot watch with him for even one hour (Mt. 16:40). Let this be the saints' first notion of the Father. He is one who is full of eternal, free love towards them. Let their hearts and thoughts break through any discouragement that lies in the way of this idea. To raise us to that level, let us consider,

24

[1.] Whose love it is. It is the love of God. He is self-sufficient, infinitely satiated with himself and with his own glorious excellence and perfection. He has no need to pursue others with his love, nor to seek an object for his love outside himself. He could rest there with delight and contentment for all eternity. He is sufficient in his own love. He also has his Son, his eternal Wisdom, in whom he can rejoice and delight from all eternity, Prov. 8:30. This might consume and satiate the whole delight of the Father; but he loves his saints also. It is such a love, that he does not seek just his own satisfaction in it, but our good as well. It is the love of a God, and the love of a Father. Its proper effects are kindness and bounty.

[2.] Let us also consider what kind of love it is –

1. *Eternal.* It was fixed on us before the foundation of the world. Before we had done the least good, his thoughts were upon us, his delight was in us, and the Son rejoiced in the thoughts of fulfilling his Father's delight in him, Prov. 8:30. The delight of the Father in the Son is not so much his absolute delight in him as the express image of himself and the brightness of his glory. In the Son he might behold all his own excellence and perfection. But it is with regard to the Son's love and his delight in the sons of men. So the order of the words requires us to understand it: "I was his delight daily," and, "My delights were with the sons of men" (Prov. 8:30-31). That is, his delight was in thoughts of kindness and redemption for them, and in that he was his Father's delight. From eternity he laid in his own heart a design for our happiness. The very thought of this is enough to make all that is within us leap for joy, like the babe in the womb of Elizabeth. A sense of it will prostrate our soul in humble, holy reverence, and make us rejoice before him with trembling.

2. *Free* He loves us because he wants to. It is his will. There was and is nothing in us for which we should be loved. If we did deserve his love, it would lower its valuation. Things of debt are seldom a matter for thankfulness. But what exists eternally, prior to our being, is necessarily free as they relate to our well-being. This gives his love life and being. It is the reason for it, and it sets a price on it, Rom. 9:11; Eph. 1:3, 4; Titus 3:5; James 1:18.

3. *Unchangeable* Though we change every day, his love does not change. If any kind of provocation could turn it away, it has long since ceased to do so. Its unchangeableness is what prompts the Father to that infinite patience and forbearance without which we would die or perish, 2Pet. 3:9, and which he exercises towards us.

4. *Distinguishing* He has not loved the whole world:

25

"Jacob have I loved, but Esau have I hated" (Rom. 9:13). Why should he fix his love on us, and pass by millions whose nature is the same as ours? Why should he let us share in that love, and all its fruits, which most of the great and wise men of the world are excluded from?

Let the soul frequently focus on the love of the Father and these considerations. All of them are soul-conquering and endearing.

(2.) Eye his love with the intent to receive it. Unless this is added, everything else will fail to gain us communion with God. We do not hold communion with him in anything, until his love is received by faith. This is what I would provoke the saints of God to. They need to believe this love of God for themselves. They must believe that such is the heart of the Father towards them, and accept his witness to that fact. The sweetness of his love is not ours until we receive it this way. Continually and actively think of God with faith as loving you, as embracing you with the eternal free love described before. When the Lord is presented as such to you by his word, let your mind know it, and assent to it. Let your will embrace it as being true, and let all your emotions be filled with it. Set your whole heart to it. Bind it with the cords of this love. If the King is bound in the galleries with your love, will you not be bound in heaven with his?

(3.) Let the Father's love have its proper fruit and effect on your heart by returning that love to him. That is how we will walk in the light of God's countenance, and hold holy communion with him all day long. Let us not deal unkindly with him, and return disrespect for his good will. Let no heart deal so thanklessly with our God.

2. Now, to help us in the daily practice of this duty, I will add one or two considerations that may be of importance.

(1.) It is very acceptable to God our Father to hold communion with him in his love. Through this communion we receive him as one who is full of love, tenderness, and kindness towards us. In our flesh, we are apt to think that he is always angry, even implacable. We may feel that poor creatures like us are not to draw close to him. We may even think that it is more desirable to never come into his presence. "Who among us will dwell with the devouring fire? Who among us will dwell with everlasting burnings?" ask the sinners in Zion (Isa. 33:14). "I knew you were a harsh man," says the evil servant in the gospels (Mt. 25:24). There is nothing more grievous to the Lord, nor more helpful to Satan's design, than thoughts like these. Satan applauds when he is able to fill our soul with such thoughts of God. It satisfies all his desires. This has been his design and his way from the beginning. The first blood that murderer shed was by this means. He led our first parents into these severe thoughts of God: "Has God said so? Has he threatened you with death? He knows well enough it will be better with you;" (Gen. 3:1). With this war engine he battered and overthrew all mankind in one step. Remembering his ancient conquest, he readily uses the same weapons today that he so successfully used then.

It grieves the Spirit of God to be slandered this way in the hearts of those whom he dearly loves. How he remonstrates Zion! "What iniquity have you seen in me?" he demands. "Have I been a wilderness to you, or a land of darkness?" "Zion said, The LORD has forsaken me, and my Lord has forgotten me. Can a woman..." The Lord takes nothing worse at the hands of his own people than such hard thoughts of him. He knows full well what it is like to bear the fruit of this bitter root. He knows the alienation of the heart that it produces, the drawing back, and the unbelief and apostasy in our walk with him. A child is so unwilling to come into the presence of an angry father! Consider receiving the Father as he holds out his love, giving him the honor he aims for, which is exceedingly acceptable to him. He often sets out his love in an eminent manner, that it may be received in an eminent way: "He commends his love toward us," Rom. 5:8. "Behold, what manner of love the Father has bestowed upon us!" 1John 3:1. Where, then, does this folly of ours come from? Why are men afraid to have good thoughts of God? They think it is audacity to see God as good, gracious, tender, kind, and loving. I am speaking of the saints. For the other side, they too can judge God as hard, austere, severe, almost implacable, and fierce. But these are the very worst emotions of the very worst men, who most hate God, Rom. 1:31; 2Tim. 3:3. They think they do well. Does this soul-deceit not come from Satan? Was it not his design from the beginning to inject such thoughts of God into men? Assure yourself, then, that there is nothing more acceptable to the Father, than to lift our hearts to him as the eternal fountain of all that rich grace which flows out to sinners in the blood of Jesus.

(2.) This will very effectively endear your soul to God, causing you to delight in him and to make your abode with him. Many saints have no greater burden in their lives than recognizing that their hearts do not constantly delight and rejoice in God. Their spirit is still indisposed to walking closely with him. What is at the bottom of this? Is it not their lack of skill, or neglect of duty, in holding communion with the Father in love? We will delight in him only to the extent that we see God's love. Without this, every other revelation of God will only make us fly from Him. But once the heart realizes the eminence of the Father's love, it cannot help being overpowered, conquered, and endeared to him. If nothing else, this will work on us to make our abode with him. If the love of a father will not make a child delight in

27

him, what will? Put this to the test. Ponder the eternal, free, and fruitful love of the Father, and see if your heart isn't stimulated to delight in him. I dare say believers will find it as thriving a course as they ever pitched on in their lives. Sit down for a little while at the fountain, and you will quickly discover the sweetness of the streams. If you have run from him in the past, you will not be able to keep your distance for a moment.

Objection 1. Some may ask, "How will I hold communion with the Father in love? I do not know whether he loves me or not. Should I risk casting myself upon his love? What if I am not accepted? Would I not perish for my presumption, rather than find sweetness in his heart? I see God only as a consuming fire with everlasting burning. I dread to look up to him."

Answer 1. I do not know what others understand by "knowing the love of God." It is exercised by spiritual sense and experience, and received purely by believing. Knowing it means believing it, as it is revealed. "We have known and believed the love that God has for us. God is love," 1John 4:16. This is the assurance you may have of this love at the very start of your walk with God. The one who is truth itself has said it. Ignore what your heart says, or Satan says. Unless you accept this as God's promise, you are calling God a liar, 1John 5:10.

Objection 2. "I can believe that God is love to others, because he has said he is love. But I see no reason for him to love me. There is no cause, and no reason in the world, why he should turn one thought of love or kindness towards me. Therefore, I dare not depend on that to hold communion with him in his special love."

Answer 2. He has spoken of his love as particularly to you as he has to anyone else in the world. As for the cause of his love, he has as much reason to fix it on you as he does on any of the other children of men. I will make speedy work with this objection. No one from the foundation of the world, who believed such love existed in the Father, and returned that love to him, was ever deceived. Nor will anyone be deceived to the world's end. In this, you are on a most secure foundation. If you believe and receive the Father's love, he will infallibly love you, though others may fall under his severity.

Objection 3. "I cannot find my heart returning God's love to him. If I were fixed upon him, then I could believe that he delights in me."

Answer 3. This is the most preposterous course that your thoughts can take. It is a good way to rob God of his glory. "This is love," says the Holy Spirit, "not that we loved God, but that he first loved us," 1John 4:10, 11. You would invert this order, and say, "This is love, not that God loved me, but that I loved him first." This takes God's glory from him. He loves us without a cause in ourselves, and we have all the cause in the world to love him. Yet, you would have the contrary

28

be true. Something needs to be in you for God to love you, even if it is your love for him. You think that you should love God before you know whether he loves you or not. This is the flesh speaking. It will never bring glory to God, or peace to your soul. Lay down your reasoning. Take up the love of the Father as a pure act of believing. That will release your soul to the Lord in the communion of love.

To further reveal this truth, let us discover the eminence and privilege of the saints of God. Whatever low opinion the sons of men may have of them, it appears that the saints have meat to eat that the world does not know of (Jn. 4:32). They have close communion and fellowship with the Father, interchanging their love with him. Men are generally respected according to the company they keep. It is an honor to stand in the presence of princes, even as servants. What an honor it is, then, for all the saints to boldly stand in the presence of the Father, and there enjoy his heart's love! What a blessing the queen of Sheba pronounced on the servants of Solomon who stood before him and heard his wisdom! How much more blessed, then, are those who stand continually before the God of Solomon, hearing his wisdom and enjoying his love! Others have fellowship with Satan and their own lusts, making provision for them and receiving perishing refreshments from them. They are the ones "whose end is destruction, whose god is their belly, and whose glory is in their shame, who mind earthly things." But the saints have this sweet communion with the Father.

Moreover, what a safe and sweet retreat the saints have from all the scorns, reproaches, scandals, and misrepresentations that they undergo in the world. When strangers abuse a child in the streets, he runs with speed to the heart of his father. There he makes his complaint and is comforted. In all the hardy censures and tongue-persecutions which the saints meet with in the streets of the world, they may run to their Father, and be comforted. "As one whom his mother comforts, so will I comfort you," says the Lord, Isa. 66:13. The soul may say, "If I have hatred in the world, I will go where I am sure of love. Though all others are harsh to me, my Father is tender and full of compassion. I will go to him and satisfy myself in him. Here in the world I am considered vile, frowned on, and rejected. But I have honor and love with the Father, whose kindness is better than life itself. There with him I have all the things in the fountain that others have only in the drops. In my Father's love there is everything desirable, the sweetness of all mercies, and I have them fully and durably."

Evidently, then, the saints are the most misunderstood men in the world. If they say, "Come and have fellowship with us" men are ready to say, "Why? What are you but a sorry company of seditious, factious people. We despise your fellowship. When we leave our fellowship with all honest men, and men of worth, then will we come to

29

you." But, how mistaken these men are! *Truly, the fellowship of the saints is with the Father*. Let men think what they please; the saints have close, spiritual, heavenly refreshing in their mutual communication of love with the Father himself. The apostle declares how the saints are generally misperceived "as deceivers, and yet true; as unknown, and yet well known; as dying, and, behold, we live; as chastened, and not killed; as sorrowful, yet always rejoicing; as poor, yet making many rich; as having nothing, and yet possessing all things," 2Cor. 6:8-10. The saints are looked on as poor, low, despicable persons, when indeed they are the only great and noble people in the world. Consider the company they keep: it is with the Father; who else is so glorious? The merchandise they trade in is love; what is more precious? Doubtless "they are the excellent on the earth," Ps. 16:3.

To further illustrate a major difference between the saints and empty professors of the faith, consider this: In performing their duties, and enjoying outward privileges, fruitless professors often walk hand in hand with the saints. But when we look at what they do in private, what a difference there is! The saints hold communion with God, while hypocrites hold communion with the world and their own lusts, conversing and communicating with them. They listen attentively to what they hear and accommodate it. Meanwhile, the saints are sweetly wrapped in the heart of their Father's love. It is almost impossible for believers, in outward appearance, to go beyond those who have very rotten hearts. But they have this meat that those others do not know of. They have this refreshment in the banquet house that others have no share in. The comfort they receive from God their Father refreshes their souls and fills their minds.

Now, if these things are true, "what manner of men ought we to be, in all manner of holy living?" 2Pet. 3:11. Especially when "our God is a consuming fire." What communion is there between light and darkness? Will sin and lust dwell in those thoughts that receive love from the Father and return it to him? Holiness is forever appropriate in his presence. An unclean spirit cannot draw close to him; an unholy heart cannot make an abode with him. A wicked person will not desire to hold fellowship with a self-controlled man. Will a man with a proud and foolish mind dwell with the most holy God and hold communion with him? Any consideration of this love will be a powerful incentive to holiness; it will lead us there. When he finds salvation in God, Ephraim says, "What have I to do any more with idols?" Communion with the Father is completely inconsistent with an immoral walk. "If we say that we have fellowship with him, and walk in darkness, we lie, and do not exercise the truth," 1John 1:6. "He that says, I know him" (i.e. I have communion with him), "and does not keep his commandments, is a liar, and the truth is not in him," chap. 2:4. Pretending to be acquainted with the Father, without holiness and obedience to his commandments, only proves that pretenders are liars. The love of the world, and the love of the Father, do not dwell together.

If this is so, so many who call themselves Christians come short of the truth of it! Most professors of Christ are unacquainted with the mystery of this communion and its fruits! Many obviously hold communion with their lusts and with the world instead of God; and yet they want to be thought of as having a portion and inheritance among those who are sanctified! They have neither a new name nor a white stone (Rev. 2:17), and yet they want to be called the people of the Most High. It would more correct to say that God is not in their thoughts at all, than to say that they have communion with him. May the Lord open the eyes of men so they may see that walking with God is a matter of power, not form!

This concludes this part of unique communion with the Father in love. "He is also faithful who has called us to the fellowship of his Son Jesus Christ our Lord," which is the next topic.

PART 2. COMMUNION WITH THE SON JESUS CHRIST

CHAPTER 1.

THE FELLOWSHIP WHICH THE SAINTS HAVE WITH THE SON OF GOD –

I will do two things here: I. Declare that we have such fellowship with the Son of God. II. Show what that fellowship or communion consists of:

I. For the first part, I will only produce a few passages of Scripture to confirm it:

1Cor. 1:9, "God is faithful, by whom you were called to the fellowship of his Son Jesus Christ our Lord." This fellowship is what all the saints are called to, and they will be preserved in it by the faithfulness of God. We are called of God the Father, as the Father, in pursuit of his love, to commune with the Son as our Lord.

Rev. 3:20, "Behold, I stand at the door, and knock: if any man hears my voice, and opens the door, I will come in to him, and will sup with him, and he with me." Certainly this is fellowship, or else I do not know not what fellowship is. Christ will sup with believers: he refreshes himself with his own graces in believers, by his Spirit who is bestowed on them. The Lord Christ is greatly delighted in tasting the sweet fruits of the Spirit in the saints. This is reflected in that prayer of the spouse that she may have something for his entertainment when he comes to her, Cant. 4:16, "Awake, O north wind, and come, you south wind. Blow upon my garden, that its spices may flow out. Let my Beloved come into his garden, and eat his pleasant fruits." The souls of the saints are the garden of Jesus Christ, the good ground, Heb. 6:7; they are a garden for delight. He rejoices in them for, "his delights are with the sons of men," Prov. 8:31; and he "rejoices over them," Zeph. 3:17. The believers are a garden for pleasant fruit. Cant. 4:12-14, "An enclosed garden is my sister, my spouse; a spring shut up, a fountain sealed. Your plants are an orchard of pomegranates, with pleasant fruits, camphire with spikenard, spikenard and saffron, calamus and

32

cinnamon, with all trees of frankincense, myrrh, and aloes, and all the chief spices."

Whatever is sweet and delicious to the taste, whatever is savory and fragrant, whatever is useful and medicinal, is in this garden. There are all kinds of spiritual refreshments in the souls of the saints for the Lord Jesus. For this reason, the spouse is earnest in her prayer for an increase of these things, that her Beloved may sup with her as he has promised. "Awake, O north wind..." It is as if to pray, "O that the breathing and workings of the Spirit of all grace might arouse all his gifts and graces in me, that the Lord Jesus, the beloved of my soul, may have fit and acceptable entertainment from me." God complains of a lack of fruit in his vineyard in Isa. 5:2; Hos. 10:1. The lack of good food for Christ's entertainment is what the spouse fears, and what she labors to prevent. A barren heart is not fit to receive him. The delight that he takes in the fruit of the Spirit is unspeakable. He expresses this at large in Cant. 5:1, "I am come," says he; "I have eaten, I am refreshed." He calls it *periy megadim* [OT:6529,4022], "the fruit of his sweetnesses" or what is most pleasant to him. Moreover, as Christ sups with his saints, they will sup with him to complete their fellowship with him. Christ provides for their entertainment in a most eminent way. Beasts are killed, wine is mingled, and a table is furnished, Prov. 9:2. He calls the spiritual delicacies that he has for them a "feast," a "wedding," "a feast of sumptuous things, wine on the lees" [finishing it to its dregs], etc. The fatted calf is killed for their entertainment. This is the mutual entertainment of Christ and his saints in that communion.

Cant. 2:1-7, "I am the rose of Sharon, and the lily of the valleys. As the lily among thorns, so is my love among the daughters. As the apple-tree among the trees of the wood, so is my Beloved among the sons. I sat down under his shadow with great delight, and his fruit was sweet to my taste..."

In the two first verses you have the description that Christ gives, first of himself, and then of his church. In verse 1 he describes what he is to his spouse: "I am the rose of Sharon, and the lily of the valleys." The Lords Christ is compared to all things of eminence in the whole creation. In the heavens, he is the sun and the bright morning star. Among the beasts, he is the lion of Judah. Among the flowers of the field, he is the rose and the lily. These two are eminent in their savory sweetness and colorful beauty, the rose in its sweetness, and the lily in its beauty. "Solomon in all his glory was not arrayed like one of these." Further, he is "the rose of *Sharon*." This is a fruitful plain, where the choicest herds were fed, 1Chron. 27:29. It is so eminent, that it is promised to the church that she will be given the excellence of Sharon, Isa. 35:2. This fruitful place undoubtedly produced the most precious roses. Christ, in the savor of his love, and in his righteousness, is like this excellent rose. He draws and allures the hearts of his saints to him. The rose is like the garment in which Jacob received his blessing, giving forth an aroma like the smell of a pleasant field, Gen. 27:27. God smelled a sweet savor from the blood of Christ's atonement, Eph. 5:2. From the graces with which he is anointed for them, his saints receive a refreshing, cherishing savor, Cant. 1:3. A sweet savor expresses what is acceptable and delightful, Gen. 8:21.

Christ is also "the lily of the valleys," which of all the flowers is the most beautiful, Matt. 6:29. He is most desirable for his personal attractiveness and perfection. He is incomparably fairer than the children of men (more of this later). He abundantly satiates all their spiritual senses. He is their refreshment, their adornment, their delight, and their glory. In the next verse he tells us what they are to him: "As the lily among thorns, so is my beloved among the daughters." Christ and his church are described the same way (as the lily). This is because of their union by the indwelling of the same Spirit. It is from the conformity and likeness that exists between them, and to which the saints are appointed. The church is a lily, and she is very beautiful to Christ "as the lily among thorns." As the lily excels the thorns, so the saints excel all others in the eye of Christ. The remainder of the world is "pricking briers and grieving thorns to the house of Israel," Ezek. 28:94. "The best of them is like a brier, the most upright is sharper than a thorn hedge," Mic. 7:4. This is how the saints appear among the daughters. There cannot be any greater exaltation of excellence. So, then, this is how Christ is to them in verse 1. And that is how the saints are in his esteem in verse 2.

That is also how he is in their esteem in verse 3. "As the apple-tree among the trees of the wood, so is my Beloved among the sons. I sat down under his shadow with great delight, and his fruit was sweet to my taste." To carry on this intercourse, the spouse begins to reveal her thoughts of him, and to show her delight in the Lord Christ. As he compares her to the lily among the thorns, so she compares him to the apple-tree among the trees of the wood. And she adds this reason for it. He has the two things that the others do not: fruit for food and shade for refreshment. She eats of the one, and rests under the other, both with great delight. All other sons are the fruitless, leafless trees of the forest, which will yield neither food nor refreshment to a hungry, weary soul. This is true of the angels, who are the sons of God by creation, Job 1:6, 38:7, and of the best of the sons of Adam, called daughters in verse 2. "In Christ," she says, "there is fruit, fruit sweet to the taste." "His flesh is meat indeed, and his blood is drink indeed," John 6:55. Moreover, he has produced that everlasting righteousness which will abundantly satisfy any hungry soul, especially after it has gone to many

34

a barren tree for food and has found none. Besides, he abounds in precious and pleasant graces of which I may eat. In fact, he calls me to eat of them and to do so abundantly (Mt. 26:26; Lk. 9:17; Jn. 6:53-58). These are the fruits that Christ bears.

They speak of a tree that brings forth all things that are necessary for life, in food and raiment. Christ is that tree of life that has brought forth all things that are necessary for eternal life. In him is the righteousness that we hunger for. In him is the water of life. Whoever drinks of it will thirst no more. Oh, how sweet are the fruits of Christ's mediation to the faith of his saints! Someone who can find no relief in mercy, pardon, grace, acceptance by God, holiness, sanctification, etc., is an utter stranger to these things that are prepared for believers. Also, the believer has shades for refreshment and shelter. He has shelter from wrath without, and refreshment from weariness within. The first benefit of the shade is to keep us from the heat of the sun, as Jonah's gourd did for him. When the heat of wrath is ready to scorch the soul, Christ interposes himself and bears it all. Under the shadow of his wings we sit down steadfastly, quietly, safely, putting our trust in him, and we do this with great delight. Who can express the joy of a soul that is safe, shadowed from wrath under the cover of the righteousness of the Lord Jesus! There is also refreshment in being shaded from weariness. He is "as the shadow of a great rock in a weary land," Isa. 32:2. In him there is quiet, rest, and repose from the power of corruptions, the trouble of temptations, and the distress of persecutions, Matt. 11:27, 28.

It is apparent that Christ and believers cannot be anything but delighted in their mutual fellowship and communion. In the next verses that describe their communion, I will briefly observe four things in it: (1.) Sweetness. (2.) Delight. (3.) Safety. (4.) Comfort.

(1.) **Sweetness**: "He brought me to the banquet-house," or "house of wine." This expresses the greatest sweetness and most delicious refreshment, flagons, apples, wine, etc. "*He* entertains me," says the spouse, "as some great personage." Great personages and great entertainment are had in the banquet-house the house of wine and delicacies. These are types of the preparations we find in grace and mercy. They are love, kindness, resources that are revealed in the gospel, declared in the assemblies of the saints, and exhibited by the Spirit. This "love is better than wine," Cant. 1:2; it is "not meat and drink, but righteousness, and peace, and joy in the Holy Spirit" (Rom. 14:17). Gospel delicacies are sweet refreshments, whether these "houses of wine" are the Scriptures, the gospel, the ordinances dispensed in the assemblies of the saints, or the exquisite manifestations of his special love. Banqueting is not an everyday affair, nor are these preparations used in ordinary entertainment. What is promised at this banquet is wine that cheers the heart of man, that makes him forget his misery, Prov. 31:6-7, that gives him a cheerful look and countenance, Gen. 49:12. The grace exhibited by Christ in his ordinances is refreshing, strengthening, comforting, and full of sweetness to the souls of the saints. Pity those foul souls who loathe these honey-combs! But in the ways described, Christ makes all the assemblies of his saints love banquet-houses, and there he gives them entertainment.

(2.) *Delight*: The spouse is quite ravished with the sweetness of this entertainment. She finds there the love, care, and kindness that are bestowed by Christ in the assemblies of the saints. Hence she cries out, Cant. 2:5, "Keep me with flagons, comfort me with apples, for I am sick with love." On discovering the excellence and sweetness of Christ in the banquet-house, the soul is instantly overpowered, and cries out to partake of its fullness. She is "sick with love." She is not (as some assume) fainting for lack of love and fearing wrath. After she has once tasted of the sweetness of Christ in the banquet-house, she becomes sick, faint, overcome, with the mighty impact of that divine affection. Her desire being deferred makes her heartsick. Therefore she cries, "Keep me..." Her plea is this: "I have seen a glimpse of the 'King in his beauty,' tasted of the fruit of his righteousness; my soul melts in longing for him. Oh! Keep and sustain my spirit with his presence in his ordinances, those 'flagons and apples of his banquet-house,' or I will sink and faint! Oh, what you have done, blessed Jesus! I have seen you, and my soul has become like the chariots of Amminadib. Let me have something from you to support me, or I will die." When a person us fainting, two things are to be done: strength is used to support him so that he will not sink to the ground; and comforting things are applied to refresh his spirits. These two things are what the soul prays for when it is overpowered and fainting with the force of its own love, which is increased by a sense of Christ's love. It wants strengthening grace to support it in this condition, so that it may be able to attend to its duty. And it wants the consolation of the Holy Spirit to content, revive, and satiate it, until it can fully enjoy Christ. Thus sweetly, and with delight, this communion is carried on.

(3.) *Safety*: "His banner over me was love," Cant. 2:4. The banner is an emblem of safety and protection. It is a sign of the presence of a host. Soldiers in an army encamp under their banner in security. So did the children of Israel in the wilderness. Every tribe kept their camps under their own standard. It is also a token of success and victory, Ps. 20:5. Christ has a banner for his saints, and that banner is love. All their protection comes from his love, and they want all the protection his love can give them. This safeguards them from hell, death, and all their enemies. Whatever presses on them must pass through the banner of the love of the Lord Jesus. They have, then, great

36

spiritual safety. This is another adornment of their communion with him.

(4.) **Comfort** – Support and consolation: Cant. 2:6, "His left hand is under my head, and his right hand embraces me." Here, Christ has the posture of a most tender friend towards one in sickness and sadness. The soul faints with love. There are spiritual longings for the enjoyment of his presence. And Christ comes in with his embraces. He nourishes and cherishes his church, Eph. 5:29; Isa. 63:9. The "hand under the head," is support, sustaining grace, in pressure and difficulties. The "hand that embraces," or the hand upon the heart, is joy and consolation. In both, Christ is rejoicing, as the "bridegroom rejoices over the bride," Isa. 62:5. To lie in the arms of Christ's love this way, under a perpetual influence of support and refreshment, is certainly to hold communion with him. And so, in verse 7, the spouse is most earnest to continue his fellowship, charging all to be still so that her Beloved will not be disturbed, or provoked to depart.

In brief, this whole book is filled with the description of the communion that exists between the Lord Christ and his saints. Therefore, it is unnecessary to take any more examples from it. I will only add one from Prov. 9:1-5, "Wisdom has built her house, she has hewn out her seven pillars; she has killed her beasts; she has mixed her wine; she has also furnished her table. She has sent forth her maidens: she cries out on the highest places of the city, 'Whoever is simple, let him turn in here.' As for the one who wants understanding, she says, 'Come, eat of my bread, and drink of the wine that I have mixed.'"

The Lord Christ, the eternal Wisdom of the Father, whom God makes wisdom to us, erects a spiritual house. In this house he makes provision for the entertainment of those guests whom he so freely invites. His church is the house that he has built on a perfect number of pillars, so that it might have a stable foundation. His slain beasts and mixed wine, with which his table is furnished, are those spiritually sumptuous things of the gospel that he has prepared for those who come by his invitation. Surely, to eat of this bread, and drink of this wine, which he has so graciously prepared, is to hold fellowship with him. In what other things is there nearer communion than in these?

I might further evince this truth by considering all the relationships which Christ and his saints have. These necessarily require a communion between them, if we assume they are faithful in those relationships. But this is something that will be spoken of in one signal instance later.

37

CHAPTER 2

WHAT WE HAVE IN UNIQUE FELLOWSHIP WITH THE LORD

CHRIST –

II. Having shown that the saints hold a unique fellowship with the Lord Jesus, it neatly follows that we show what it is they have in this unique communion with him. What they have is *grace*.

This is eminently ascribed to him everywhere. John 1:14, "He dwelt among us, full of grace and truth;" there is grace in the truth and substance of this communion. All that went before was only typical and representative. And in its truth and substance, grace comes only by Christ. "Grace and truth came by Jesus Christ," verse 17; "and of his fullness have all we received, and grace for grace," verse 16. That is, we have communion with him in grace. We receive from him all kinds of grace, and in that have we fellowship with him.

It is likewise in the apostolic benediction, in which the communication of spiritual blessings from the several persons of the godhead to the saints is so exactly distinguished. It is grace that is ascribed to our Lord Jesus Christ, 2Cor. 13:14, "The grace of the Lord Jesus Christ, and the love of God, and the communion of the Holy Spirit, be with you all."

In fact, Paul is so delighted with this that he makes it his motto, and the token by which he makes his epistles known, 2Thess. 3:17, 18, "The salutation of Paul with my own hand, which is the token in every epistle: so I write. The grace of our Lord Jesus Christ be with you all." He makes these two expressions equivalent: "Grace be with you," and, "The Lord Jesus be with you." Sometimes he makes the one the token in his epistles, sometimes the other, and sometimes he puts them both together. This is what we are specifically to see in the Lord Jesus. Grace is what we are to receive from him, gospel-grace, as revealed in the gospel. Christ is the headstone in the temple of God, to whom "Grace, grace," is to be cried, Zech. 4:7.

Grace is a word with various meanings. Its primary ones may be divided into three categories:

1. Grace of personal presence and attractiveness. So we say a person is "graceful and attractive" either for himself or because of his adornments. In Christ, this is the subject of nearly half the book of Canticles. It is also mentioned in Ps. 45:2, "You are fairer than the children of men; grace is poured into your lips." Under this category I also place that acceptance of grace which, in respect to us, I place in the third category. Those inconceivable gifts and fruits of the Spirit that

were bestowed on him, and produced in him, match his personal excellence, as will appear later.

2. Grace of free favor and acceptance. "By this grace we are saved." Grace is the free favor and gracious acceptance of God in Christ. It is used in this sense in the expression, "If I have found grace in your sight." It means being freely and favorably accepted. So he "gives grace" (that is, favor) "to the humble," James 4:6; Gen. 39:21, 41:37; Acts 7:10; 1Sam. 2:26; 2 Kings 25:27, etc.

3. Grace in the fruits of the Spirit. These sanctify and renew our nature, enabling us to do good, and preventing us from doing evil. Thus, the Lord tells Paul, "his grace was sufficient for him;" It refers to the assistance that he afforded him against temptation, Col. 3:16; 2Cor. 8:6, 7; Heb. 12:28.

These two latter categories, in respect to our receiving them from Christ, I call purchased grace, because he purchased them for us. Our communion with him in that purchase is termed a "fellowship in his sufferings, and the power of his resurrection," Phil. 3:10.

1. Let us begin with the first category, which I call personal grace. I will do two things: (1) Show what the personal grace of Christ is and what it consists of. And (2) Declare how the saints hold immediate communion with Christ in that personal grace.

(1.) In handling the first category, we are speaking of Christ as mediator. Therefore, by the "grace of his person," I do not mean his Deity apart from the office that he undertook for us as God and man. Nor do I mean the outward appearance of his human nature. I am not referring to him as exalted in glory, nor in his role on earth bearing our infirmities. His time on earth is only "to know Christ after the flesh," 2Cor. 5:16. Instead, I mean the graces of the person of Christ as he is vested with the office of mediator. I mean his spiritual eminence, attractiveness, and beauty, as he was appointed and anointed by the Father to the great work of bringing home all his elect to his heart. In this respect, the Scripture describes him as exceedingly excellent, attractive, and desirable. He is far above comparison with the best created good, or any other endearment that we can imagine.

Ps. 45:2, "You are fairer than the children of men: grace is poured into your lips" He is beyond comparison, more beautiful and gracious than any here below. The word *yafyafita* [OT:3302] is repeated to increase its significance, and to exalt its subject beyond all comparison. The Chaldee paraphrase of this passage is "*shofaracha malka Meshicha 'adif nivney nasha*" or "Your fairness, O king Messiah, is more excellent than the sons of men." "*Pulcher admodum prae filiis hominum;*" He is exceedingly desirable. His inward beauty and glory are expressed here by his outward shape,

39

form, and appearance. That is because outward beauty was so highly esteemed in those who ruled or governed. In Isa. 4:2, the prophet calls him "The branch of the Lord," and "The fruit of the earth," affirming that he will be "beautiful and glorious, excellent and attractive;" "for in him dwells all the fullness of the Godhead bodily," Col. 2:9.

In Cant. 5:9, the spouse is asked about this very thing. Concerning the personal excellence of the Lord Christ, her beloved, she is asked by the daughters of Jerusalem: "What has your Beloved more than another beloved, O you fairest among women?" She returns this answer in verse 10: "My Beloved is white and ruddy, the best among ten thousand." She describes his excellence to the end of the chapter, and there she concludes that "he is altogether lovely," verse 16. Particularly, he is affirmed here to be "white and ruddy," a mixture of colors that produces the most beautiful complexion.

[1.] He is white in the glory of his Deity, and ruddy in the preciousness of his humanity. "His teeth are white with milk, and his eyes are red with wine," Gen. 49:12. Whiteness (if I may say so) is the complexion of glory. In the appearance of the Most High, the "Ancient of days," in Dan. 7:9, it is said that, "His garment was white as snow, and the hair of his head was like pure wool." It is said of Christ in his transfiguration, when he had a mighty luster of the Deity on him, "His face shined like the sun, and his raiment was white as the light," Matt. 17:2. The other evangelist says it was, "White as snow, so that no cleaner on earth can whiten them more," Mark 9:3; Rev. 1:14. It was a divine, heavenly, surpassing glory that was upon him. Hence the angels and glorified saints who always behold him are said to be in white robes. They are fully translated into the image of his glory. His whiteness is the glory of his Deity. For this reason, the Chaldee paraphrase ascribes this whole passage to God. "They say to the house of Israel, 'Who is the God whom you will serve?' Then the congregation of Israel began to declare the praises of the Ruler of the world, and said, 'I will serve that God who is clothed in a garment white as snow, the splendor of the glory of whose countenance is like fire.'" Christ is also ruddy in the beauty of his humanity. Man was called Adam, from the red earth of which he was made. The word used here indicates he is the second Adam, partaker of flesh and blood, because the children also partook of flesh and blood, Heb. 2:14. The beauty and attractiveness of the Lord Jesus is in the union of both these in one person.

[2.] He is white in the beauty of his innocence and holiness, and ruddy in the blood of his sacrifice. Whiteness is the badge of innocence and holiness. It is said of the Nazarites, typical of their

40

holiness, "They were purer than snow, they were whiter than milk," Lam. 4:7. The prophet shows us that scarlet, red, and crimson are the colors of sin and guilt; whiteness is the color of innocence, Isa. 1:18. Our Beloved was "a Lamb without blemish and without spot," 1Pet. 1:19. "He did no sin, neither was guile found in his mouth," 1Pet. 2:22. He was "holy, harmless, undefiled, separate from sinners," Heb. 7:26. And yet the one who was so white in his innocence, was made ruddy in his own blood. That happened in two ways. Naturally, in the pouring out of his precious blood in that agony of his soul when thick drops of blood trickled to the ground, Luke 22:44. And it was done when the whips and thorns, nails and spears, poured it out abundantly: "There came forth blood and water," John 19:34. He was ruddy by being drenched in his own blood. He was ruddy morally, by the imputation of sin, whose color is red and crimson. "God made him to be sin for us, who knew no sin," 2Cor. 5:21. He who was white became ruddy for our sakes, pouring out his blood as a sacrifice for sin. This also renders him graceful. By his whiteness he fulfilled the law. By his redness he satisfied justice. "This is our Beloved, O you daughters of Jerusalem," Cant. 5:16.

[3.] He is white in love and mercy to his own. He is red with justice and revenge towards his enemies, Isa. 63:3; Rev. 19:13. This expresses his endearing excellence in the administration of his kingdom.

There are three things in general that this personal excellence and grace of the Lord Christ consists of: (1st.) His fitness to save, from the grace of his hypostatic union and its necessary effects. (2nd.) His fullness to save, from the grace of communion and its free consequences. (3rd.) His excellence to endear, from his complete suitability to all the wants of men's souls:

(1st.) His fitness to save. Christ is "hikanos," a fit Savior, suited to the work from his grace of union. The uniting of the natures of God and man in one person made him fit to be an ultimate Savior. He lays his hand upon God by partaking of God's nature, Zech. 13:7, and he lays his hand upon us, by partaking of our nature, Heb. 2:14, 16. And so he becomes an umpire between both. By this means, he closes the distance that sin created between God and us. We who were far off are made close in him (Eph. 2:13). On this account he had room enough in his breast to receive, and power enough in his spirit to bear, all the wrath that was prepared for us. Sin was infinite only in respect to the object, and punishment was infinite only in respect to the subject. This arises from his hypostatic union. Union is the conjunction of the two natures of God and man in one person, John 1:14; Isa. 9:6; Rom. 1:3, 9:5. The necessary consequences of this union are,

[1.] The human nature in the Son of God has no subsistence of its own, Luke 1:35; 1Tim. 3:16.

[2.] "Koinonia idiomaton," by which the properties and attributes of either nature, God or man, are interchangably spoken of using the name of Christ, Acts 20:28, 3:21.

[3.] His office as mediator is executed in his single person, but in respect to both his natures. Christ himself is "ho energon," the agent, as both God and man. He is the principium quo, or "energetikon." He is the principle that gives life and effectiveness to the whole work. Second, he is the principium quod. He is the operator, in which both natures are distinctly considered. Third, he is the "energeia," or "draskike tes fuseos kinesis." He is the effectual working of each nature in itself. And lastly, he is the "energema," or "apotelesma." He is the effect that is produced by all of these, and is related to all of them. This is the excellence I speak of in his personal union.

(2nd.) His fullness to save, from the grace of communion or the effects of his hypostatic union. These effects and consequences of his fullness are free. This fullness refers to all the equipping that he received from the Father, by the anointing of the Spirit, for the work of our salvation: "He is also able to completely save those who come to God by him," Heb. 7:25. All the fullness of the Spirit that was necessary for this purpose was communicated to him: "for it pleased the Father that in him all fullness should dwell," Col. 1:19. He did not receive "the Spirit by measure," John 3:34. From this fullness, he suitably supplies all those who are his, "grace for grace," John 1:16. Had it been given to him by measure, we would have exhausted it.

(3rd.) His excellence to endear, from his complete suitability to all the wants of the souls of men. There is no one who wants the things of God, that Christ cannot satisfy those wants. I am speaking of those who are given to him by his Father. Is he dead? No! Christ is life. Is he weak? No! Christ is the power and wisdom of God. Has he a sense of guilt? No! Christ is complete righteousness. He is "The Lord our Righteousness." Many poor creatures know their wants, but they do not know where to find their remedy. Indeed, whether it is life or light, power or joy, it is all wrapped up in him.

This will suffice for the present of the personal grace of the Lord Christ. He is fit to save, having pity and ability, tenderness and power, to carry on that work to completion. He has a fullness to save, speaking of redemption and sanctification, righteousness and the Spirit. And he is suitable to fulfill the wants of all our souls. By this he becomes exceedingly desirable and altogether lovely. And as to this, the saints have distinct fellowship with the Lord Christ. The manner of this fellowship will be declared in the ensuing chapter.

From this introduction to the description of the one with whom the saints have communion, some incentives may be proposed, and also some considerations that reveal the insufficiency of all other ways in which men engage their thoughts and desires. The daughters of Jerusalem, that is, ordinary professors of Christ, having heard the spouse describing her Beloved in Cant. 5:10-16, are instantly roused to seek him with her: "Where has your Beloved gone, that we may seek him with you?" Cant. 6:1. What Paul says of those who crucified him may be said of all those who reject him, or refuse communion with him: "Had they known him, they would not have crucified the Lord of glory." If men knew him, if they were acquainted with him in any way, they would not reject the Lord of glory. Christ calls them "simple ones," "fools," and "scorners" who despise his gracious invitation, Prov. 1:22. No one despises Christ except those who do not know him, whom the god of this world has blinded so they will not behold his glory.

Men naturally seek something to rest on, something with which to satiate and delight themselves, to hold communion with. There are two ways they pursue these things. Some set before themselves a goal. Perhaps it is pleasure, profit, or, in religion, acceptance by God. Others seek a casual distraction, pleasing themselves now with one thing, now with another, like those in Isa. 57:10. Because something comes in by the strength of their own hand, they will not give it up, even though they are weary of it. Perhaps you have been greedy pursuing some secular or religious goal. Or maybe you have been chasing meaningless distractions, wearying yourself on a long road to nowhere. Whatever condition you may be in, compare what you are aiming at, or what you are doing, with what you have already heard of Jesus Christ. If anything you have in mind is like him, or if anything you desire is equal to him, then reject him as unattractive. But if, indeed, all your ways are just vanity and frustration by comparison to him, then why you spend your "money for what is not bread, and your labor for what does not satisfy?" (Isa. 55:2).

Use 1. If you are still in the flower of your days, full of health and strength, and with all your vigor you pursue first one thing and then another, consider this: what are all your beloveds to this Beloved? What have you gotten by them? Show us the peace, quiet, and assurance of everlasting blessedness that they have given you. Their paths are crooked paths. Whoever walks in them will not know peace. Look, here is an object fit for your finest affections, one in whom you will find rest for your soul, one in whom there is nothing to grieve and trouble you to eternity. Behold, he stands at the door of your soul, and knocks. Do not reject him, for fear you may seek him and not find him! I beg you, study him a little. You do not love him because you do not know him. Why does one man spend his time in idleness and folly,

43

wasting precious time, perhaps in debauchery? Why does another associate himself with those who scoff at religion and the things of God? They do so only because they do not know our dear Lord Jesus. When he reveals himself to you, and tells you he is Jesus whom you have slighted and refused, it will break your heart, and make you mourn like a dove, that you neglected him! And if you never come to know him, it would be better if you had never been born. While it is called Today, do not harden your heart.

Use 2. Perhaps you are earnestly seeking righteousness, and you are a religious person. Consider this: Does Christ have his proper place in your heart? Is he your all? Does he dwell in your thoughts? Do you know him in his excellence and desirability? Do you count all things "loss and dung" compared to his exceeding excellence? Or do you prefer almost anything in the world to him?

44

CHAPTER 3

PERSONAL GRACE IN COMMUNION WITH THE LORD CHRIST –

(2.) The next thing to consider is the way we hold communion with the Lord Christ, in regard to that personal grace we spoke of. This is what the Scripture reveals to be a conjugal relationship. He is married to us, and we are married to him. This spiritual relationship is attended by suitable conjugal affections. And this is what gives us fellowship with him in his personal excellence.

The spouse expresses this in Cant. 2:16, "My Beloved is mine, and I am his." She is saying, "He is mine. I possess him. I have interest in him as my head and my husband; and I am his, possessed by him, owned by him, and given up to him. We are in a conjugal relationship."

In Isa. 54:5, "Your Maker is your husband; the LORD of hosts is his name; and your Redeemer the Holy One of Israel; he will be called the God of the whole earth." This is the reason why the church will not be ashamed or confounded in the midst of her troubles and trials. She is married to her Maker, and her Redeemer is her husband. In Isaiah 61:10, the prophet sets out the mutual glory of Christ and his church in their walk together. He says it is "as a bridegroom dresses himself with ornaments, and as a bride adorns herself with jewels." Such is their condition, because such is their relationship. He further expresses this in chap. 62:5, "As the bridegroom rejoices over the bride, so will your God rejoice over you." As it is with a couple on the day of their espousals, in the gladness of their hearts, so it is with Christ and his saints in this relationship. He is a husband to them, providing for them according to the estate into which he has taken them.

To this end we have his faithful engagement promise in Hos. 2:19, 20. "I will betroth you to me forever; yea, I will betroth you to me in righteousness, and in judgment, and in loving-kindness, and in mercies. I will even betroth you to me in faithfulness." This is the main design of the ministry of the gospel. It is to prevail with men to give themselves up to the Lord Christ as he reveals his kindness in this engagement. Hence, Paul tells the Corinthians that he "espoused them to one husband, that he might present them as a chaste virgin to Christ," 2Cor. 11:2. He prevailed with them for this purpose by preaching the gospel, so that they would give up themselves as a virgin to the one who betrothed them to himself as a husband.

This is a relationship in which the Lord Jesus exceedingly delights. He invites others to behold him in his glory. Cant. 3:14, "Go forth, O you daughters of Jerusalem, and behold King Solomon with the crown that his mother crowned him with on the day of his espousals, and in the day of the gladness of his heart." He calls the daughters of Jerusalem (i.e. all sorts of professors of Christ) to consider him as he betroths his church. When they do, he tells them that they will discover two things about him:

1. Honor. It is the day of his coronation, and his spouse is the crown with which he is crowned. As Christ is a diadem of beauty, and a crown of glory to Zion, Isa. 28:5, so Zion is also a diadem and a crown to him, Isa. 62:3. Christ makes this relationship with his saints his glory and his honor.

2. Delight. The day of his espousals, of taking poor sinful souls into his heart, is a day of gladness in his heart. John was only the friend of the Bridegroom. He stood and heard Christ's voice when he was taking his bride to himself; and yet he rejoiced greatly, John 3:29. How much more, then, is the joy and gladness of the Bridegroom himself! Zeph. 3:17, "He rejoices with joy, he joys with singing."

The gladness of Christ's heart, the joy of his soul, is to take poor sinners into this relationship with him. He rejoiced in thoughts of it from eternity, Prov. 8:31, and he always expresses the greatest willingness to undergo the hard task required to do that, Ps. 40:7, 8; Heb. 10:7. He was pained like a woman in childbirth until he accomplished it, Luke 12:50. Because he loved his church, he gave himself for it, Eph. 5:25. He despised the shame, and endured the cross, Heb. 12:2. He did this so that he might enjoy his bride, that he might be for her, and she for him, and not for another, Hos. 3:3. This is joy: when his mother crowns him. Believers are the mother and brother of this Solomon, Matt. 12:49-50. They crown him on the day of his espousals, giving themselves to him, and becoming his glory, 2Cor. 8:23.

He sets out his whole communion with his church under this frequent allusion to marriage. He takes the church to himself on the day of his marriage; the church is his bride, his wife, Rev. 19:7, 8. The entertainment he provides for his saints is a wedding supper, Matt. 22:3. The graces of his church are the adornments of his queen, Ps. 45:9-14. And the fellowship he has with his saints is the same as that between mutually beloved spouses in a conjugal relationship, Cant. 1. Hence Paul, in describing these two communal relationships, makes sudden and subtle transitions from the earthly to the spiritual in Eph. 5, from verse 22 to verse 32. He concludes by applying this relationship to Christ and the church.

The next inquiry is how we hold communion in these conjugal relationships and affections, and what they consist of. In this, there are some things common to Christ and the saints, and some things unique to each, as the nature of this relationship requires. These fall into two parts: *committing themselves to one another*, and *their consequential, conjugal affections for one another*.

[1.] There is a mutual commitment to one another.

This is the first act of communion under the personal grace of Christ. Christ makes the soul his, with all the love, care, and tenderness of a husband; and the soul gives itself wholly to the Lord Christ, to be his with all the loving, tender obedience required. In this we see the main part of the espousals between Christ and the saints. This is presented in a parable of himself and a harlot in Hos. 3:3. "You shall abide for me;" he says to her. "You shall *not* be for another, and I *will* be for you." "Poor harlot." The Lord Christ says in effect, "I have bought you for myself with the price of my own blood; and now, this is what we will consent to: *I will be for you, and you shall be for me*, and not for another.

[2] There is consequential affection for one another.

(1st). Christ gives himself to the soul, with all his excellence, righteousness, preciousness, graces, and eminence. He does so to be its Savior, head, and husband, and to dwell with it forever in this holy relationship. He looks upon the souls of his saints, likes them well, and considers them fair and beautiful, because he has made them so. Cant. 1:15, "Behold, you are fair, my companion; behold, you are fair; you have doves' eyes." Let others think what they please, Christ repeats that the souls of his saints are very beautiful, even perfect, through his own attractiveness that he puts upon them. Ezek. 16:14, "Behold, you are fair, you are fair." He remarks in particular that their spiritual light is excellent and glorious, like the eyes of a dove. It is tender, discerning, clear, and shining. Therefore, he adds a touching wish to enjoy his spouse. Cant. 2:14, "O my dove," he pleads, "that is in the clefts of the rock, in the secret places of the stairs, let me see your countenance, and let me hear your voice. For your voice is sweet, and your countenance is attractive;" He is telling her, "Do not hide yourself like one that flies to the clefts of the rocks. Do not be dejected, like one that hides behind the stairs, and is afraid to enter the company of someone who asks for her. Do not let your spirit be cast down at the weakness of your supplications. Let me hear your sighs and groans, your breathing and pantings to me. They are very sweet, very delightful. Your spiritual countenance, your appearance in heavenly things, is attractive and delightful to me." Nor does he leave her this way. In chap. 4:8 he presses her hard to come closer to him in this conjugal bond: "Come with me from Lebanon, my spouse... Look from the top of Amana, from the top of Shenir and Herman, from the lions' dens, from the mountains of the leopards." He is telling her, "Like the Israelites of old, you are wandering among lions and leopards, sins and troubles;

come away from there to me, and I will give you refreshment," Matt. 11:28.

At this invitation, the spouse boldly concludes in Cant. 7:10, that Christ desires her, that he does indeed love her, and that he aims to take her into this fellowship with him. So, in pursuing this union, Christ freely bestows himself upon the soul. Precious and excellent as he is, he becomes ours. He makes himself ours, along with all his graces. Hence, the spouse says, "'My Beloved is mine; in all that he is, he is mine." Because he is righteousness, he is "The LORD our Righteousness," Jer. 23:6. Because he is the wisdom of God, and the power of God, he is "made wisdom to us...," 1Cor. 1:30. Thus, "the branch of the LORD is beautiful and glorious, and the fruit of the earth is excellent and attractive for those of Israel who escape," Isa. 4:2. This is the first thing done on the part of Christ. He freely donates himself to be our Christ, our Beloved, for all the purposes of love, mercy, grace, and glory. To this end, his mediation is designed for a marriage covenant that is never to be broken. In summation, the Lord Jesus Christ is fitted and prepared to be a husband to his saints, his church. This is accomplished by his being equipped as mediator, and by his large purchase of grace and glory. He tenders himself to the saints in the promises of the gospel, and in all of his desirability. He convinces them of his good will towards them, and his all-sufficiency to supply their wants. Upon consenting to accept him, which is all he requires or expects from them, he engages himself to be theirs forever in a marriage covenant.

(2ndly) What is required on the part of the saints is their free, willing consent to receive, embrace, and submit to the Lord Jesus as their husband, Lord, and Savior. They are to abide with him, subject their souls to him, and be ruled by him forever. This commitment is either initial, solemn consent when they are first united to Christ, or it is consequential consent, reflected in renewed acts of consent all of their days. I speak of it especially in this ongoing sense that applies to communion, rather than a single event which primarily applies to union.

There are two things that complete this commitment of the soul:

(1.) Commitment means liking Christ for his excellence, grace, and suitability far above all other beloveds. It means preferring him in our judgment above all of them. In Cant. 5:9, the spouse is earnestly pressed by other professors of Christ, to give her thoughts concerning the excellence of her Beloved compared to other loves. She expressly answers that he is "the chief of ten thousand," 5:10, "altogether lovely," 5:16. He is infinitely beyond comparison with the choicest created good or affection imaginable. The soul views all that is in this world "the lust of the flesh, the lust of the eyes, and the pride of life" and sees that it is

48

all vanity. "The world passes away, and the lust of it," 1John 2:16, 17. These other loves are not to be compared to Christ in any way. The soul also views legal righteousness, blamelessness before men, living uprightly, and duties of conviction; it draws the same conclusion that Paul did in Phil. 3:8, "Doubtless, I count all these things loss for the excellence of the knowledge of Christ Jesus my Lord." The church does the same in Hos. 14:3. It rejects all appearing assistance, whether as good as Asshur or as promising as idols, so that God alone may be preferred. This is our introduction to conjugal communion with Jesus Christ in personal grace. It means constantly preferring him above all pretenders to our affections. It is counting everything loss and dung in comparison to him. Beloved peace, beloved natural relationships, beloved wisdom and learning, beloved righteousness, and beloved duties are all considered loss when compared with Christ.

(2.) Commitment means accepting Christ, by an act of the will, as our only husband, Lord, and Savior. This is called "receiving" Christ, John 1:12. It is not only the solemn act by which we first close with him, but the constant frame of mind to abide with him, and own him as our husband, Lord and Savior. We consent to take Christ on his own terms, and to be saved by him in his own way. We say, "Lord, I would have taken you and salvation in my own way, so that I might have attained it in part by my own endeavors and works of the law. I am now willing to receive you and be saved by you in *your* way, which is merely by grace. Though I would have walked according to my own mind, I now give myself up to be entirely ruled by your Spirit. In you have I righteousness and strength. In you I am justified. And in you I glory." Then we are carrying on communion with Christ in the grace of his person. This is receiving the Lord Jesus in his attractiveness and eminence. Believers should exercise their hearts in this commitment abundantly. This is having choice communion with the Son Jesus Christ. Let us receive him in all his excellence as he bestows himself on us. We should be frequent in our thoughts of faith, comparing him with our other beloveds, with sin, the world, and legal righteousness. We should prefer him above all of those things, counting them loss and dung by comparison. We should be persuaded of his sincerity, of his willingness to give himself up for us, and of all that he is as our mediator. Let us give our hearts to him. Let us tell him that we will be for him, and not for another. Let him know it from us. He delights to hear it. In fact, he says, "Sweet is our voice, and our countenance is attractive" (Cant. 2:14). We will not fail to receive sweet refreshment from him.

I will now turn aside to a fuller description of some of the personal excellences of the Lord Christ, which endear the hearts of his saints to him. These strengthen our hearts in committing ourselves to the Lord Christ as our husband, and they make way for stirring up those consequential conjugal affections that were mentioned earlier.

1. He is exceedingly excellent and desirable in his Deity and glory. He is "Jehovah our Righteousness," Jer. 23:6. It is the reason for Zion's rejoicing at his coming to her, "Behold your God!" Isa. 40:9. "We have seen his glory," says the apostle. What glory is that? "The glory of the only-begotten Son of God," John 1:14. The best of the saints have been afraid and amazed at the beauty of an angel. The stoutest sinners have trembled at the glory of one of these creatures that present only the back parts of their glory. Yet angels themselves cover their faces at the presence of our Beloved. They are conscious of their utter disability to bear the rays of his glory, Isa. 6:2; John 12:39-41. He is "the fellow of the Lord of hosts," Zech. 13:7. Though he once appeared in the form of a servant, yet "he thought it not robbery to be equal with God," Phil. 2:6. In the glory of this majesty, he dwells in inaccessible light. We "cannot find out the extent of the Almighty by searching: it is as high as heaven; what can we do? It is deeper than hell; what can we know? The measure of it is longer than the earth, and broader than the sea," Job 11:79. We may all say to one another, "Surely we are more brutish than any man, and do not have the understanding of a man. We neither learned wisdom, nor did we have the knowledge of the holy. Who has ascended up into heaven, or descended? Who has gathered the wind in his fists? Who has bound the waters in a garment? Who has established all the ends of the earth? What is his name, and what is his Son's name, if you can tell," Prov. 30:2-4.

If anyone should ask, as did those in the Canticles, what is in the Lord Jesus, our beloved, more than in other beloveds, that makes him so desirable, and amiable, and worthy of acceptance? What is he more than others? Then I will ask in return, "What is a king more than a beggar?" He is much more in every way; and yet there is nothing more. The king and beggar were born alike, and must die alike; after that is the judgment. "What is an angel more than a worm?" A worm is a creature, and an angel is a creature; God has made the one to creep in the earth, and the other to dwell in heaven. There is still a difference in extent between them. They may agree in some things, but compared to the infinite they are nothing. And what are all the nothings of the world to the God who is infinitely blessed forevermore? Will the dust in the balance, or the drop in the bucket, be placed in the scale against Christ? This is the one whom the sinners in Zion are afraid of, and who cry, "Who among us will dwell with the devouring fire, who among us will dwell with everlasting burnings?" I might give you a glimpse of his excellence in many of those properties and attributes by which he reveals himself to the faith of poor sinners. But it would be like someone who goes into a garden where there are innumerable flowers

50

in great variety. He cannot take in all he sees, except one crop here and another there. I will try to open a door and give an inlet to the infinite excellence of the graces of the Lord Jesus as he is, "God blessed forevermore." I will present the reader with one or two examples, leaving him to gather whatever else he pleases for his own use.

So then, observe the endless, bottomless, boundless grace and compassion that is in the one who is our husband, as he is the God of Zion. All the grace that can possibly dwell at once in a created nature cannot serve our need. We are too indigent to be suited with such a supply. There was a fullness of grace in the human nature of Christ. He did not receive "the Spirit by measure," John 3:34. It was a fullness like that of the light in the sun, or of the water in the sea as far as its sufficiency. It was a fullness incomparably above the measure of angels. Yet it was not properly an infinite fullness. It was a created, and therefore a limited fullness. If this grace could be separated from the Deity, then surely so many thirsty, guilty souls who drink deep and large draughts of grace and mercy from him every day, would drain him to the very bottom. It would be no supply at all, except in a moral way. But when the conduit of his humanity is inseparably united to the infinite, inexhaustible fountain of the Deity, who can look into its depths? If there is grace enough for sinners in an all-sufficient God, then it is in Christ. Indeed, there cannot be enough in anyone else. The Lord gives this reason for the peace and confidence of sinners in Isa. 54:4-5, "You shall not be ashamed, neither be you confounded; for you shall not be put to shame." But how will this be? So much sin, and not ashamed! So much guilt, and not confounded! "Your Maker," he says, "is your husband; the LORD of hosts is his name; and your Redeemer the Holy One of Israel; he will be called the God of the whole earth." This is the basis of all peace, confidence, and consolation. This is the grace and mercy of our Maker, the God of the whole earth. Kindness and power are so tempered in him that he makes us, and he mars us he is our God and our *Goel* [OT:1350], our Redeemer. "Look to me," he says, "and you will be saved; for I am God, and none else," Isa. 45:22, "Surely, one will say, 'In the LORD I have righteousness'" verse 24.

It is on this ground that all the world should prepare to drink free grace, mercy, and pardon, drawing water continually from the wells of salvation. They should be prepared to draw from one single promise, which is an angel standing by crying, "Drink, O my friends. Drink abundantly. Take enough grace and pardon to suffice for the world of sin which is in every one of you." They would not be able to deplete the grace of the promise one hair's breadth. There is enough for millions of worlds, if they existed, because it flows from an infinite, bottomless fountain. "Fear not, O worm Jacob: I am God, and not man." This is the basis of sinners' consolation. This is that "head of gold" mentioned in

51

Cant. 5:11, that most precious fountain of grace and mercy. This infinite grace, as to its spring and fountain, will answer all objections that might hinder us from drawing close to communion with him, and from freely embracing him. Will it not suit us in all our distress? What is our finite guilt before it? Show me the sinner that can spread his iniquities to the same dimensions of this grace. Here is mercy enough for the greatest, the oldest, and the stubbornest transgressor. "Why will you die, O house of Israel?" Beware those who would rob you of the Deity of Christ. If grace for me was limited to what can be stored in a mere man, then I would rejoice to be under rocks and mountains (Rev. 6:16).

Hence, consider his eternal, free, unchangeable love. If the love of Christ for us were the love of a mere man, however excellent, innocent, and glorious, then it must have a beginning and an ending, and perhaps it would be fruitless. The love of Christ in his human nature towards his own is exceeding, intense, tender, precious, compassionate, abundantly heightened by a sense of our miseries, the feeling of our wants, and the experience of our temptations. It all flows from that rich stock of grace, pity, and compassion, which was bestowed on him on purpose, for our good and our supply. Yet this love, as such, cannot be infinite or eternal, nor from itself can it be absolutely unchangeable. If it were it no more than this, though it is not to be paralleled or fathomed, our Savior could not say, "As the Father has loved me, so have I loved you," John 15:9. His love could not be compared with the divine love of the Father in those properties of eternity, fruitfulness, and unchangeableness, which are the chief anchors of the soul. Instead, his love is:

(1.) Eternal: "Come near to me and hear this. I have not spoken in secret from the beginning; from that time, there am I: and now the Lord GOD, and his Spirit, has sent me," Isa. 48:16. He is himself "yesterday, today, and forever," Heb. 13:8; and so is his love. It is the love of the one who is "Alpha and Omega, the first and the last, the beginning and the ending, which is, was, and is to come," Rev. 1:11.

(2.) Unchangeable. Our love is a reflection of ourselves as we are, and so are all our affections. The love of Christ is also a reflection of himself. We love someone one day, and hate him the next. He changes, and we also change. Today he is our right hand, our right eye; the next day we say, "Cut him off, pluck him out." But Jesus Christ is still the same, and so is his love. "In the beginning he laid the foundation of the earth, and the heavens are the works of his hands; they will perish, but he remains, they all will wax old like a garment; and he will fold them up like a garment. They will be changed, but he is the same, and his years do not fail," Heb. 1:10-12. He is the LORD, and he changes not. Therefore we are not consumed.

Whom he loves, he loves to the end. His love never had a beginning, and it will never have an ending.

(3.) Fruitful. It is fruitful in all its gracious issues and effects. A man may love another like he loves his own soul, yet perhaps that love cannot help the other. He may pity him in prison, but not relieve him; he may bemoan him in misery, but not help him; he may suffer with him in trouble, but not ease him. We cannot love grace into a child, nor can we love mercy into a friend. We cannot love them into heaven, even though it may be the great desire of our soul. It was love that made Abraham cry, "O that Ishmael might live before you!" but it may not be. But the love of Christ, being the love of God, is effectual and fruitful in producing all the good things that he wills for his beloved. He loves life, grace, and holiness into us; he loves us into covenant, and he loves us into heaven. Love in him is willing good to someone. And whatever good Christ wills for someone by his love, his willingness effects that good.

These three qualifications make the love of Christ exceedingly eminent, and they make him exceedingly desirable. How many millions of sins has this love overcome in every one of the elect, each one enough to condemn them all! What mountains of unbelief has it removed! Look at the life of any one saint, consider the frame of his heart, see the many stains and spots, the defilements and infirmities that contaminate it, and tell me whether the love that bears with all this is not to be admired. And is his love not the same towards thousands every day? What streams of grace, purging, pardoning, quickening, assisting, flow from it every day! This is our Beloved, O you daughters of Jerusalem.

2. He is desirable and worthy of our acceptance as considered in his humanity. I will only note two things in this: (1.) His freedom from sin; (2.) His fullness of grace; in both of these, the Scripture portrays Christ as exceedingly lovely and amiable.

(1.) Christ was free from sin. He is the Lamb of God, without spot, and without blemish, the male of the flock to be offered to God. God's curse falls on all other offerings, and on those who offer them, Mal. 1:14. The purity of the snow is not to be compared with the whiteness of this lily, of this rose of Sharon, even from the womb: "For such a high priest was fit for us, who is holy, harmless, undefiled, and separate from sinners," Heb. 7:26. Sanctified people, whose stains are washed away in any measure, are exceedingly fair in the eye of Christ himself. "You are all fair my love," he says, "you have no spot in you" Cant. 4:7. How fair, then, is the one who never had the least spot or stain!

It is true that Adam had this spotless purity at his creation; so had the angels. But they came immediately from the hand of God, without any intervening cause of sin. Jesus Christ is a plant and root out of dry ground, a blossom from the stem of Jesse, a bud from the loins of sinful man. He was born of a sinner after there had been no innocent flesh in the world for four thousand years. Everyone on the roll of his genealogy was infected with it. To have a flower of wonderful rarity grow in paradise, in a garden of God's own planting, and not be sullied in the least, is not so strange. But, as the psalmist says, to hear of such a flower growing in a wood, to find it in a forest, to have a spotless bud bloom in the wilderness of corrupted nature, is a thing which even angels desire to look into (1Pet. 1:12). This whole nature was not only defiled, but accursed; it was not only unclean, but guilty, guilty of Adam's transgression in whom we have all sinned. That the human nature of Christ should be derived from this heritage and yet be free from guilt, free from pollution, is to be adored.

Objection. But you will say, "How can this be? Who can bring a clean thing from an unclean thing? How could Christ take our nature, and yet not its defilements and guilt? If Levi paid tithes in the loins of Abraham, how is it that Christ did not sin in the loins of Adam?"

Answer. There are two things in original sin:

[1.] There is the guilt of the first sin, which is imputed to us. We all sinned in him. "Eph hoi pantes hemarton," Rom. 5:12, whether we render it relatively "in whom," or illatively, "being all have sinned." It is all one. That one sin is the sin of us all. We were all in covenant with him. He was not only a natural head to us, but also a federal head. As Christ is to believers, Rom. 5:17; 1Cor. 15:22, so Adam was to all of us; his transgression of that covenant is reckoned to us.

[2.] There is the derivation of a polluted and corrupted nature from him: "Who can bring a clean thing out of an unclean thing?" "What is born of the flesh is flesh" and nothing else. Our wisdom and our mind are also corrupted, because a polluted fountain will have polluted streams. The first person had a corrupted nature, and that nature corrupts all succeeding generations.

Christ was free from both of these marks of original sin:

1st. He was never federally in Adam, and thus he was not liable to the imputation of Adam's sin. It is true that sin was imputed to him when he was made sin. Thereby he took away the sin of the world, John 1:29. But it was imputed to him in the covenant of the Mediator, through his voluntary acceptance, not in the covenant of Adam by legal imputation. Had sin been reckoned to him as a descendant from Adam, he would not have been a fit high priest to offer sacrifices for us. He would not be "separate from

54

sinners," Heb. 7:26. If Adam had stood in his innocence, Christ would not have been incarnate to be a mediator for sinners. Therefore, the need for his incarnation, morally, did not take place until after the fall. Though Christ was in Adam in a natural sense from his first creation, in respect to the purpose of God (Luke 3:23, 38), he was not in Adam in a legal sense until after the fall. So, as to himself, Christ had no more to do with the first sin of Adam, than he did with the personal sin of anyone else whose punishment he voluntarily took upon himself. In the same way, we are not liable for the guilt of those who followed Adam, even though naturally we were no less in them than we were in him. Therefore, all the days of his flesh, Christ served the Father in a covenant of works. And in these works he was accepted by God, having done nothing to annul that covenant. This does not in the least take away from his perfection.

2nd. The pollution of our nature was prevented in Christ from the instant of conception. "The Holy Spirit will come upon you, and the power of the Highest will overshadow you, therefore also that holy thing that will be born of you will be called the Son of God," Luke 1:35. He was "made of a woman," Gal. 4:4. But that portion of which was made was sanctified by the Holy Spirit, so that what was born would be a holy thing. The union of soul and body is how a man assumes his whole nature. In that union he is polluted by sin, being a son of Adam. Not only was this prevented by the sanctification of the Holy Spirit, but the Spirit accompanied the very separation of his bodily substance in the womb to that sacred purpose for which it was set apart. Thus, on all accounts, he is "holy, harmless, undefiled." Add to this that he "did no sin, neither was guile found in his mouth," 1Pet. 2:22; he "fulfilled all righteousness," Matt. 3:15; because of his perfect obedience, his Father was always "well pleased" with him, verse 17; he charges his angels with folly, and being unclean in his sight. Take all of this into account; and his excellence and desirability in this regard lies before us. Such he was, and such he is. And yet, for our sakes, he was content not only to be considered a transgressor by the vilest of men, but to undergo from God the punishment that was due to the vilest of sinners.

(2.) The fullness of grace in Christ's human nature presents the amiableness and desirability of it. If I were to consider his perfection in this part of his excellence, it would all fit the purpose at hand. What he had from the womb, Luke 1:35, what grew and improved in their exercise in the days of his flesh, Luke 2:52, and the complement of them all in glory, affirm his desirability. I am only taking a view of these things in transit. Two things lie in open sight to all that

55

consider them: all *kinds* of grace, and all *degrees* of grace, were in Christ. Both make up that fullness that was in him. It is created grace that I mean here, and therefore I speak of its kinds. It is grace that is inherent in a created nature, not an infinite nature; and therefore I speak of its degrees.

This is the Beloved of our souls: "holy, harmless, undefiled," and "full of grace and truth." He is full to,

• be sufficient for every purpose of grace;
• emulate, as an example of obedience to men and angels;
• provide certainty of uninterrupted communion with God;
• afford readiness in giving supply to others;
• suit him to all the occasions and necessities of the souls of men;
• obtain a glory not unbecoming a subsistence in the person of the Son of God;
• promise a perfect victory over all temptations in trials;
• render an exact correspondence to the whole law, every righteous and holy law of God;
• exhaust the utmost capacity of a limited, created, finite nature;
• reveal the greatest beauty and glory of a living temple of God;
• warrant the full pleasure and delight of his Father;
• establish an everlasting monument to the glory of God, who has given such inconceivable excellence to the Son of man

And this is the second thing to consider in endearing our souls to our Beloved.

3. Consider that he is all this in one person. We have not been speaking of two persons, God and man, but one person who is both God and man. The Word that was with God in the beginning, and was God, John 1:1, is also made flesh, verse 14. This was not done by converting himself into flesh, or by appearing in the outward shape and likeness of flesh. It was done by taking that holy thing that was born of the virgin, Luke 1:35, into a personal union with himself. So the "mighty God" is a "child given to us," Isa. 9:6. That holy thing born of the virgin is called "The Son of God," Luke 1:35. What made Christ Jesus a man was the union of soul and body, the subsistence of both united in the person of the Son of God. As to the proof for this, I have spoken of it elsewhere at large. I propose it only in general now to show the amiableness of Christ on its account. From this union arise the grace, peace, life, and security of the church, and of all believers. This may be clearly evinced by a few considerations:

(1.) By this union he was fit to suffer, and able to bear what was due to us. And he did so in that very act in which the "Son of man gave his life as a ransom for many," Matt. 20:28. "God redeemed his church with his own blood," Acts 20:28. In this was the "love of God seen, that he gave his life for us," 1John 3:16. On this account, there was room enough in his breast to receive the points of all the swords that were sharpened by the law against us. And there was strength enough in his shoulders to bear the burden of the curse that was due to us. From this he was so willing to undertake the work of our redemption, Heb. 10:7, 8, "Lo, I come to do your will, O God," because he knew his ability to go through with it. Had he not been man, he could not have suffered. Had he not been God, his suffering could not have benefited either himself or us, because he could not have satisfied the infinite need. The suffering of a mere man could not bear any portion of what was infinite. The great and righteous God gathered together all the sins that had been committed by his elect from the foundation of the world, and he searched the hearts of all that were to come to the end of the world. He took them all, from the sin of their nature to the least deviation from the rectitude of his most holy law, the highest provocation of their regenerate and unregenerate conditions. What if he had laid all of these on a mere holy, innocent creature? Oh, how would they have overwhelmed him, and buried him, forever out of the presence of God's love! Therefore, the apostle premises the purging of our sin with this glorious description of him: "He has spoken to us by his Son, whom he has appointed heir of all things, by whom he also made the worlds; who being the brightness of his glory, and the express image of his person, and upholding all things by the word of his power," has "purged our sins," Heb. 1:2, 3. It was him that purged our sins, who is the Son and heir of all things, and by whom the world was made. He was the brightness of his Father's glory, and the express image of his person. He did it, and he alone was able to do it. For this work, "God was manifested in the flesh," 1Tim. 3:16. The sword awoke against the companion of the Lord of hosts, Zech. 13:7. By the wounds of that great shepherd, the sheep are healed, 1Pet. 2:24, 25.

(2.) Hence, Christ becomes an endless, bottomless fountain of grace to all those who believe. The fullness that it pleased the Father to commit to Christ, to be the great treasury and storehouse of the church, did not, and does not, lie in his human nature itself. It lies in the person of the mediator, God and man. Consider what his communication of grace consists of, and this will be evident. The foundation is laid in his satisfaction, merit, and purchase; these are the morally procuring cause of all the grace that we receive from Christ. Hence, all grace becomes his; all the things of the new covenant, the promises of God, all the mercy, love, grace, and glory that was promised, became his. It is not as though they were all actually invested in or resided in his human nature, and were communicated to us by some portion of what inhered in that nature. But they are morally his, by a compact, to be bestowed by him as he thinks good, and as he is mediator, both God and man. He is the only begotten Son made flesh, John 1:14, "from whose fullness we receive, grace for grace." The real communication of grace happens when Christ sends the Holy Spirit to regenerate us. The Spirit creates daily supplies in our hearts of all the habitual grace that we partake of. Being both God and man, Christ in his role as mediator sends the Holy Spirit, as declared at large in John chapters 14-16. This, then, is what I mean by the fullness of grace that is in Christ, and from which we have both our beginning and all our supplies. This makes Christ, as the Alpha and Omega of his church, the beginner and finisher of our faith. He is excellent and desirable to our souls. Upon paying the great price of his blood, and gaining our full acquittal based on his satisfaction, all grace becomes his, in a moral sense. It is at his disposal. He bestows it on, or works it in, the hearts of his people by the Holy Spirit. And he does so according to his infinite wisdom and our need. Considering this, how glorious he is! What we deem most excellent is what best suits our needs when we are lacking. What is excellent is what gives bread to the hungry, water to the thirsty, and mercy to the perishing. All our relief is thus found in our Beloved. In him is the life of our souls, the joy of our hearts, our relief against sin, and our deliverance from the wrath to come.

(3.) Thus Christ is fitted to be a mediator, a days-man, an umpire between God and us. He is one with God, one with us, and one in himself, in the unity of one person. His ability and universal fitness for his office of mediator are regularly demonstrated. In this office he is "Christ, the power of God, and the wisdom of God." In this office shines the infinitely glorious wisdom of God, which we may better admire than express. What person who is acquainted at all with these things does not fall down with reverence and astonishment? How glorious is the Beloved of our souls! What is there that does not encourage us to take up our rest and peace in his heart? Unless we are so obstructed by unbelief that no consideration can relieve or refresh the heart, it is impossible not to be endeared to Christ by this. We should dwell on thoughts of it. This is the hidden mystery. It is great without controversy, and admirable to eternity. What poor, low, perishing things we contemplate! If we gained no advantage by this astonishing dispensation, its excellence, glory, beauty, and depths would still deserve the flower of our inquiries, the vigor of our spirits, and the substance of our time. But when our life, peace, joy, inheritance, eternity -when our all -lies in this very thing, will not thoughts of it always dwell in our hearts? Will they not always refresh and delight our souls?

(4.) Christ is excellent and glorious in the fact that he is exalted, and invested with all authority. When Jacob heard of the exaltation of his son Joseph in Egypt, and saw the chariots that Joseph sent for him, his spirit fainted and recovered again. This was because of his abundant joy and other overwhelming affections. Is our Beloved lost, who came to earth for our sakes, who was poor and persecuted, reviled, and killed? No! He was dead, but he is now alive, and he lives forever. He has the keys of hell and death. Our Beloved has been made a lord and ruler, Acts 2:36. He is made a king. God sets his king on his holy hill of Zion, Ps. 2:6. He is crowned with honor and dignity after he has been "made a little lower than the angels for the suffering of death," Heb. 2:7-9. And what is he made king of? "All things are put in subjection under his feet," verse 8. And what power does our Beloved have over them? "All power in heaven and earth," Matt. 28:18. As for men, he has been given power "over all flesh," John 17:2. And in what glory does he exercise this power? He gives eternal life to his elect; ruling them in the power of God, Micah 5:4, until he brings them to himself. For his enemies, his arrows are sharp in their hearts, Ps. 45:5. He dips his vesture in their blood. Oh, how glorious he is in his authority over his enemies! In this world he terrifies, frightens, awes, convinces, and bruises their hearts and consciences. He fills them with fear, terror, and disquiet, until they yield him feigned obedience. Sometimes, with outward judgments, he bruises, breaks, and turns the wheel upon them. He stains all his vesture with their blood, and fills the earth with their caresses. At the last, he will gather them all together – beast, false prophet, nations, etc. – and cast them into the lake that burns with fire and brimstone.

In his authority, he is gloriously exalted above angels, good and bad, Eph. 1:20-22, "far above all principality, and power, and might, and dominion, and every name that is named, not only in this world, but also in what is to come." They are all under his feet; they are at his command and absolute disposal. He is at the right hand of God, the highest exaltation possible. Having received a "name above every name..." he is in full possession of a kingdom over the whole creation, Phil. 2:9. Thus he is glorious in,

• his throne which is at "the right hand of the majesty on high;"

• his commission, which is being granted "all power in heaven and earth;"

• his name, which is a name above every name, "Lord of lords, and King of kings;"

• his scepter, "a scepter of righteousness is the scepter of his kingdom;"

• his attendants, "his chariots are twenty thousand, even

thousands of angels," among them he rides on the heavens, and sends out the voice of his strength, attended with ten thousand times ten thousand of his holy ones;

• his subjects, all creatures in heaven and in earth, nothing is left that is not put in subjection to him;

• his way of rule, and the administration of his kingdom, full of sweetness, efficacy, power, serenity, holiness, righteousness, and grace, in and towards his elect, full of terror, vengeance, and certain destruction towards the rebellious angels and men;

• the issue of his kingdom, when every knee will bow before him, and all will stand before his judgment-seat.

And what a small portion of his glory we have pointed to! This is the beloved of the church. He is its head, and its husband. This is the one with whom we have communion. But I will treat the whole exaltation of Jesus Christ at large elsewhere.

Having specified these general motives for communion with Christ, taken from his excellence and perfection, I will reflect on the description of him that is given by the spouse in Cant. 5:10-16,

"My Beloved is white and ruddy, the best among ten thousand. His head is like most fine gold, his locks are bushy, and black as a raven. His eyes are like the eyes of doves by rivers of water, washed with milk, and fitly set. His cheeks are like a bed of spices, like sweet flowers. His lips are like lilies, dripping sweet-smelling myrrh. His hands are like gold rings, set with beryl. His belly is like bright ivory overlaid with sapphires. His legs are like pillars of marble, set upon sockets of fine gold. His countenance is like Lebanon, as excellent as the cedars. His mouth is most sweet. He is altogether lovely. This is my Beloved, and this is my friend, O daughters of Jerusalem."

The general description given of him in verse 10 has been considered before. The ensuing particulars are examples to prove the assertion that he is "the best among ten thousand."

The spouse begins with his head and face, verses 11-13. She speaks in general to its substance. It is "fine gold." Then she speaks in particular to its adornments, "his locks are bushy, and black as a raven."

1. "His head is as the most one gold," or, "His head gold, solid gold;" some translate it, "made of pure gold;" others say, "*chrusion kefale*" [NT:5553,2776 *top gold*]; the LXX retain part of both Hebrew words, "*ketem paz*," rendering them "*massa auri*" [OT:3800,6337 *heavy gold*].

Two things are eminent in gold: splendor (glory), and duration. This is how the spouse speaks of the head of Christ. His head is his government, authority, and kingdom. Hence it is said, "A crown of pure gold was on his head," Ps. 21:3. His head is said to be gold because of the crown of gold that adorns it. The monarchy in Daniel was most eminent for its glory and duration, and so it is termed a "head of gold," Dan. 2:38. And these two things are eminent in the kingdom and authority of Christ:

(1.) It is a glorious kingdom. Christ is full of glory and majesty, and in his majesty he rides "prosperously," Ps. 45:3, 4. "His glory is great in the salvation of God: honor and majesty are laid upon him: he is made blessed forever and ever," Ps. 21:5, 6. I might insist that nothing renders a kingdom or government glorious except that it is of Christ in all its excellence. It is a heavenly, spiritual, universal, and shaken kingdom; all of which render it glorious.

(2.) It is durable, firm solid gold. "His throne is forever and ever," Ps. 45:6; "of the increase of his government there will be no end, upon the throne of David, and upon his kingdom, to order it, and to establish it with judgment and with justice from henceforth even forever," Isa. 9:7. "His kingdom is an everlasting kingdom," Dan. 7:27, "a kingdom that will never be destroyed," chap. 2:44; for he must reign until all his enemies are subdued. This is the head of gold: the splendor and eternity of his government.

And if you take the head in a natural sense, either it refers to the glory of his Deity, or the fullness and excellence of his wisdom (which the head is the seat of). The allegory is not to be limited as long as we keep to the analogy of faith.

2. For the adornments of his head, his locks are said to be "bushy," or curled. They are "black as a raven." This is added to illustrate the blackness without any allusion to the nature of the raven. Take the head spoken of in a political sense: his locks of hair are said to be curled, as if entangled, but really falling in perfect order and beauty, like bushy locks. These are his thoughts, counsels, and ways in administering his kingdom. They are black or dark because of their depth and unsearchableness, just as God is said to dwell in thick darkness. They are curled or bushy because of their exact interweavings, speaking of his infinite wisdom. His thoughts are many as the hairs of the head, seemingly perplexed and entangled, but really set in an attractive order, just like curled bushy hair. It is deep and unsearchable, dreadful to his enemies, but full of beauty and attractiveness to his beloved. Such are the thoughts of his heart, and the counsels of his wisdom, in reference to the administrations of his kingdom. They are dark, perplexed, and involved to a carnal eye. They are deep, manifold, ordered, attractive, and desirable in themselves, and to his saints.

In a natural sense, black and curled locks denote attractiveness,

61

and vigor of youth. In the execution of his counsels, and in all his ways, the strength and power of Christ appears glorious and lovely.

The next thing described is his eyes. Verse 12, "His eyes are as the eyes of doves by rivers of water, washed with milk, and fitly set." The reason for this allusion is obvious: doves are tender birds, not birds of prey. Of all other birds, they have the brightest, shining, and piercing eye. Their delight in streams of water is known. Being washed in milk, or clear, white, crystal water, adds to their beauty. And their eyes here are said to be "fitly set." That is, they are in due proportion of beauty and luster, as a precious stone in the fullness of a ring, as the word signifies.

Eyes are for sight, discerning, knowledge, and acquaintance with the things that are seen; the knowledge, understanding, and discerning Spirit of Christ Jesus are intended here. In the allusion, four things are ascribed to the eyes: 1. Tenderness; 2. Purity; 3. Discerning; and, 4. Glory.

1. Tenderness the tenderness and compassion of Christ towards his church is intended here. He looks on it with the eyes of galley doves; he looks with tenderness and careful compassion; he looks without anger, fury, or thoughts of revenge. This is how the eye interpreted in Deut. 11:12, "The eyes of the LORD your God are upon that land." Why? "It is a land that the LORD your God cares for." And he cares for it in mercy. So are the eyes of Christ on us, the eyes of one who cares for us in tenderness, who lays out his wisdom, knowledge, and understanding with tender love, on our behalf. He is the foundation-stone of the church on which "are seven eyes," Zech. 3:9. In these eyes are perfection of wisdom, knowledge, care, and kindness to guide him.

2. Purity as pure as washed doves' eyes. This may be taken either subjectively, for the excellence and immixed cleanness and purity of his sight and knowledge in himself, or it can be taken objectively, for delighting to behold purity in others. "He is of purer eyes than to behold iniquity," Hab. 1:13. "He has no pleasure in wickedness; the foolish will not stand in his sight," Ps. 5:4, 5. The righteous soul of Lot was distressed by seeing the filthy deeds of wicked men (2Pet. 2:8). And he had eyes of flesh in which there was a mixture of impurity. How much more do the pure eyes of our dear Lord Jesus abominate all the filthiness of sinners! But in this lies the excellence of his love for us. He carefully takes away our filth and stains so that he may delight in us. Seeing that we are so defiled, and that it could not be done another way, he removes it by his own blood. "Even as Christ also loved the church, and gave himself for it, that he might sanctify and cleanse it, with the washing of water by the word, that he might present it to himself a glorious church, not having spot, or wrinkle, or any such

62

thing; but that it should be holy, and without blemish" Eph. 5:25-27. The purpose of this undertaking is so that the church may be gloriously presented to himself, because he is of purer eyes than to behold it with joy and delight in any other condition. He does not leave his spouse until he can say of her, "You are all fair, my love; there is no spot in you," Cant. 4:7. Partly, he takes away our spots and stains by the "renewing of the Holy Spirit." And wholly, he adorns us with his own righteousness.

3. Discerning. He sees as doves see: quickly, clearly, thoroughly, and to the bottom of what he looks upon. Hence, in another place it is said that his "eyes are like a flame of fire," Rev. 1:14. Why? So that the churches might know that he is the one who "searches the reins and hearts," Rev. 2:23. He has discerning eyes. Nothing is hidden from him. All things are open and naked before the one with whom we have to deal. It is said of him, while he was in this world, that "Jesus knew all men, and did not need the testimony of men, for he knew what was in a man," John 2:24, 25. His piercing eyes look through all the thick coverings of hypocrites, and their show of pretence. He sees the inside of all; and what men are inside, they are that to him. He does not see as we see. Instead, he ponders the hidden man of the heart. No humble, broken, and contrite soul will lose one sigh or groan in pursuit of him, or in communion with him. No pant of love or desire is hidden from him. He sees what is kept in secret. No performance of the most glorious hypocrite will prevail with him. His eyes look through all, and the filth of their hearts lies naked before him.

4. Beauty as well as glory is intended here. Everything of Christ is beautiful, for he is "altogether lovely," verse 16. But he is most glorious in his sight and wisdom. He is the wisdom of God's eternal wisdom itself; his understanding is infinite. Our knowledge is spotted and stained! Even when it is perfect, it will still be finite and limited. His is without a spot of darkness, and without the foil of limitation.

Thus, he is beautiful and glorious. His "head is of gold, his eyes are doves' eyes, washed in milk, and fitly set."

The next thing insisted on is his cheeks. Verse 13, "His cheeks are like a bed of spices; like sweet flowers," or "towers of perfumes" [marginal reading], or well-grown flowers. There are three things evidently pointed at in these words:

    1.   A sweet savor, as from spices, flowers, or towers of perfume;

    2.   Beauty and order, like spices set in rows or beds, as the words imply;

    3.   Eminence in that characteristic, such as sweet, well grown, or great flowers.

63

These things are in the cheeks of Christ. The Chaldee paraphrase, which applies this whole song to God's dealings with the people of the Jews, makes these cheeks with the lines that are drawn in them to be the two tablets of stone. But that allusion is strained, as are most conjectures of that scholiast.

The cheeks of a man are the seat of his attractiveness and manlike courage. The attractiveness of Christ is from his fullness of grace in himself for us. His manly courage respects the administration of his rule and government from his fullness of authority. This attractiveness and courage are called the husband's cheeks by his spouse. She describes him as a beautiful, desirable person, to show that spiritually he is so. And to his cheeks she ascribes,

1. A sweet savor, order, and eminence. God is said to smell a sweet savor from the grace and obedience of his servants. In Gen. 8:21, the LORD smelled a savor of rest from the sacrifice of Noah. In the same way, the saints smell a sweet savor from God's grace laid up in Christ, Cant. 1:3. It is what they rest in, delight in, and are refreshed with. The smell of aromatic spices and flowers pleases the natural sense, refreshes the spirits, and delights the person. Likewise, the graces of Christ please the saints' spiritual sense, refresh their drooping spirits, and give delight to their souls. If Christ is close to them, they smell his raiment, as Isaac smelled the raiment of Jacob. They say, "It is like the smell of a field that the LORD has blessed," Gen. 27:27; and their souls are refreshed with it.

2. Order and beauty are like spices set in a garden bed. So are the graces of Christ. When spices are set in order, anyone may recognize what is useful, and gather it accordingly. Complementing one another makes them beautiful. So too are the graces of Christ. In the gospel they are presented distinctly and in order, so that sinners may view them by faith, and take from him according to their need. They are ordered for the use of saints in the promises of the gospel. There is light, and life, and power in him, and there is all consolation in him a constellation of graces, shining with glory and beauty. Believers take a view of them all, see their glory and excellence, but fix especially on what is most useful to them in their present condition. One may take light and joy, while another takes life and power. By faith and prayer, they take and gather these things in this bed of spices. No one who comes to Christ goes away unrefreshed. What may they not take, and what may they not gather? What is it that the poor soul wants? Behold, it is provided here, and laid out in order in the promises of the gospel. These promises are like the beds in which these spices are planted for our use. Thus, the covenant is said to be "ordered in all things," 2Sam. 23:5.

3. Eminence. His cheeks are "a tower of perfumes" held up, made

conspicuous, visible, and eminent. So it is with the graces of Christ when they are held out and lifted up in the preaching of the gospel. They are a tower of perfumes, a sweet savor to God and man.

The next clause of that verse is, "His lips are like lilies, dropping sweet-smelling myrrh." Two natural perfections are alluded to here: First, the glory of color in the lilies, and second, the sweetness of savor in the myrrh. The glory and beauty of the lilies in those countries was such that our Savior tells us, "Solomon, in all his glory, was not arrayed like one of them," Matt. 6:29. The savor of myrrh was such that when the Scripture presents things of an excellent savor, it compares them to the sweetness of myrrh (Ps. 45:8). The sweet and holy ointment was chiefly made from it, Exod. 30:23-25. Mention is frequently made of it in other places for the same purpose. It is said of Christ that "grace was poured into his lips," Ps. 45:2. Men wondered or were amazed by the words of grace that proceeded out of his mouth "tois logois tes charitos," [Luke 4:22]. So what is meant by the lips of Christ dropping sweet-smelling myrrh, is the savor, excellence, and usefulness of the word of Christ. In this he is excellent and glorious indeed. The glory, beauty, and usefulness of his word surpasses the excellence of those natural things that are most precious in their own way. Hence, those who preach his word to save the souls of men, are said to be a "sweet savor to God," 2Cor. 2:15, and the savor of the knowledge of God is said to be manifested by them, verse 14. I could insist on several properties of myrrh, to which the word of Christ is compared here: its bitterness in taste, its ability to preserve from spoiling, its use in perfumes and unctions; but I only insist on generalities. What the Holy Spirit means is that the word of Christ is sweet, savory, and precious to believers. They see him as excellent, desirable, and beautiful in the precepts, promises, exhortations, and bitter threats of his word.

The spouse adds that, "His hands are as gold rings set with beryl," verse 14. The word "beryl," in the original, is "Tarshish," which the Septuagint has retained. It does not restrict it to any particular precious stone; some say onyx; others say chrysolite. It is any precious stone shining with a sea-green color, for the word also signifies the sea. Gold rings set with precious, glittering stones, are both valuable and desirable for profit and adornment. So are the hands of Christ. That is, all the works of his hands the effects, by the cause. All of his works are glorious. They are all fruits of his wisdom, love, and bounty.

"And his belly is as bright ivory, overlaid with sapphires." The smoothness and brightness of ivory, the preciousness and heavenly color of the sapphires, give luster to the excellence of Christ. This is what is compared to his belly, or rather his bowels (which includes the heart). It is the inward bowels, and not the outward bulk that is signified. It is unnecessary to show that affections are what is meant by "bowels" in the Scripture, whether ascribed to God or man. The tender love, and the unspeakable affections and kindness of Christ to his church and his people, is thus represented. What a beautiful sight it is to the eye, to see pure polished ivory set up and down with heaps of precious sapphires! How much more glorious are the tender affections, mercies, and compassion of the Lord Jesus to believers!

Verse 15. The strength of his kingdom, the faithfulness and stability of his promises, his height and glory in his dominion, the sweetness and excellence of communion with him, is represented in these words: "His legs are like pillars of marble set upon sockets of fine gold; his countenance is like Lebanon, as excellent as its cedars: his mouth is most sweet."

When the spouse has gone this far in describing him, she concludes with this general assertion: "He is wholly desirable, altogether to be desired or beloved." She could have said, "I have considered some things of greatest value, price, usefulness, beauty, and glory here below, and compared some of the excellences of my Beloved to them. I can go no higher. I find nothing better or more desirable to compare with him, or to represent his loveliness and desirability. All of this comes short of his perfection, beauty, and attractiveness. 'He is all wholly to be desired, to be beloved.'"

• He is lovely in his person, in the glorious all-sufficiency of his Deity, in the gracious purity and holiness of his humanity, in his authority and majesty, and in his love and power.

• He is lovely in his birth and incarnation. When he was rich, he became poor for our sakes, taking on flesh and blood because we partook of the same. He was made of a woman, so that he might be made under the law for us, and for our sakes.

• He is lovely in the whole course of his life. He exercised more than angelic holiness and obedience in the depth of poverty and persecution. For doing good, he received evil. For giving blessings, he was cursed, reviled, and reproached all his days.

• He is lovely in his death, and in that he was most lovely to sinners. He was never more glorious and desirable than when he came broken and dead from the cross. For then he had carried all our sins into a land of forgetfulness; then he had restored peace and reconciled us; then he had procured life and immortality for us.

• He is lovely in his whole undertaking, in his life, death, resurrection, and ascension. He was a mediator between God and us to recover the glory of God's justice, and to save our souls. We, who were set at such an infinite distance from God by sin, were brought near to God to enjoy him.

• He is lovely in the glory and majesty with which he is crowned.

Now he has sat down at the right hand of the Majesty on high. There, although he is terrible to his enemies, he is full of mercy, love, and compassion towards his beloved ones.

• He is lovely in all those supplies of grace and consolation, in all the dispensations of his Holy Spirit, of which his saints partake.

• He is lovely in all the tender care, power, and wisdom that he exercises to protect, safe-guard, and deliver his church and his people in the midst of all the opposition and persecution to which they are exposed.

• He is lovely in all his ordinances, and the whole of that spiritually glorious worship which he has appointed to his people, and by which they draw close and have communion with him and his Father.

• He is lovely and glorious in the vengeance he takes, and will finally execute, upon the stubborn enemies of himself and his people.

• He is lovely in the pardon that he has purchased and dispenses, in the reconciliation that he has established, in the grace he communicates, in the consolation he administers, in the peace and joy he gives his saints, and in his assured preservation of them to glory.

What will I say? There is no end of his excellence and desirability. "He is altogether lovely. This is our beloved, and this is our friend, O daughters of Jerusalem."

A second consideration of the excellence of Christ will endear the hearts of those who stand with him in this conjugal relationship. It arises from what is the great darling of men who misapprehend it. In its true conception, it is the great aim of the saints. And this is wisdom and knowledge. Let it be made clear that all true and solid knowledge is only found in, and attained from, the Lord Jesus Christ. The hearts of men must be engaged to him if they are to be true to themselves and their most predominate principles. This is the great design of all men, once they are freed from their professed slavery to the world, and the pursuit of sensual, licentious courses. It is so that they may be wise. The ways that men generally use to pursue that end will be considered later. The purpose of this digression is to show that all wisdom is laid up in Christ, and that it is to be obtained from him alone. This is to the glory and honor of our dear Lord Jesus Christ, and to establish our hearts in communion with him.

In 1Cor. 1:24, the Holy Spirit tells us that "Christ is the power of God, and the wisdom of God." This is not referring to the essential Wisdom of God that results from being the eternal Son of the Father. For that reason he is called "Wisdom" in the Proverbs, chap. 8:22-23. Instead, it refers to the wisdom of God that results from his being crucified, verse 23. As he is crucified, so he is the wisdom of God. That is, all the wisdom that God has presented to discover and manifest himself, and to save sinners, the wisdom that makes foolish all the wisdom of the world, is in Christ crucified. It is held out in him, and by him; and it can be obtained only from him. And thereby we see the glory of God in him, 2Cor. 3:18. For he is not only said to be "the wisdom of God," but he is also "made wisdom to us," 1Cor. 1:30. He is made wisdom to us not by creation, but by ordination and appointment. He not only teaches us wisdom as the great prophet of his church, but we become acquainted with the wisdom of God by knowing Christ. This is our wisdom. However promised, wisdom can only be obtained this way. The sum of what is contended for is asserted in Col. 2:3, "In him are hidden all the treasures of wisdom and knowledge."

There are two things that might seem to be colored with wisdom: civil wisdom or prudence in managing our affairs, and our ability in learning and literature. But God rejects both of these as having no use at all to the end of true wisdom. In the world, there is what is called "understanding," but it comes to nothing. There is what is called "wisdom," but it becomes folly. "God brings to nothing the understanding of the prudent, and makes foolish this wisdom of the world," 1Cor. 1:19-20. If there is neither wisdom nor knowledge without the knowledge of God (Jer. 8:9), then it is all contained in the Lord Jesus Christ: "No man has seen God at any time; the only begotten Son, who is in the heart of the Father, has revealed him." God is not seen at any other time, John 1:18, nor is he known by any other means, than by the revelation of the Son. The Son manifests God from his own heart, and therefore it is said that he is "the true Light, which lights every man that comes into the world," verse 9. He is the true Light, which he has in himself. No one has any light except from him. All who come to him have it. All who do not come to him remain in darkness. More will be said of this human wisdom later.

FIRST, all true wisdom and knowledge are summed up in these three areas:

I. The knowledge of God, his nature, and his properties;

II. The knowledge of ourselves in reference to God's will concerning us; and

III. The skill to walk in communion with God:

I. The knowledge of the works of God, and the chief end of all, necessarily accompany all three.

1. In these three is summed up all true wisdom and knowledge; and,

2. None of them has any purpose, is obtained or manifested, except in and by the Lord Christ.

1. By the work of creation, and by creation itself, God revealed many of his properties to his creatures who are capable of his knowledge. His power, goodness, wisdom, and all-sufficiency are thereby known. The apostle asserts this in Rom. 1:19-21. He calls it "*to gnoston tou Theou*," that is, his eternal power and Godhead (verse 20). In verse 21, he asserts that knowing God comes by the creation. Yet, there are some properties of God that all the works of creation cannot reveal or make known, such as his patience, long-suffering, and forbearance. All things being made good, there was no place to exercise or manifest any of these properties. The whole fabric of heaven and earth alone, as first created, will not reveal such things as patience and forbearance in God. Yet, they are eminent properties of his nature. God himself proclaims this in Exod. 34:6-7: "The LORD, the LORD God, merciful and gracious, longsuffering, and abounding in goodness and truth, keeping mercy for thousands, forgiving iniquity and transgression and sin, by no means clearing the guilty, visiting the iniquity of the fathers upon the children and the children's children to the third and the fourth generation."

Therefore, the Lord goes further. He also reveals these properties by the works of his providence, in preserving and ruling the world that he made. By cursing the earth, and filling all the elements with signs of his anger and indignation, he has "revealed from heaven his wrath against all ungodliness and unrighteousness of men," Rom. 1:18. By not immediately destroying all things, he has manifested his patience and forbearance to all. Paul tells us in Acts 14:16-17 that, "He suffered all nations to walk in their own ways; yet he sent a witness to his doing good; he gave rain from heaven and fruitful seasons, filling their hearts with food and gladness." In Psalm 104, the psalmist gives us a large account of God's goodness and wisdom. By these ways he gave witness to his own goodness and patience. And so it is said, "He endures with much long-suffering..." Rom. 9:22. But now we are at a standstill. By all this, we have only an obscure glimpse of God, seeing not so much as his back parts. Moses did not see that until he was put into the rock; and that rock was Christ. We cannot even glimpse some of the most eminent and glorious properties of God apart from the Lord Christ. We see them only by and in him. Some we have no light of except *in* him, and all the rest we have no true light except *by* him:

(1.) Of the first sort are love and pardoning mercy. We cannot even imagine these in our heart except by Christ:

[1.] Love; I mean love to sinners. Without this, man is the most miserable of all creatures. We cannot have the least glimpse of it but in Christ. The Holy Spirit says in 1Jn. 4:8, 16 that "God is love." That is, he is not only of a loving and tender nature, but he is one who will exercise himself in a dispensation of his eternal love towards us. He is one who has purposes of love for us from of old, and will fulfill them all towards us in due season. But how is this demonstrated? How may we become acquainted with it? He tells us in verse 9, "In this was manifested the love of God, because God sent his only begotten Son into the world, that we might live through him." This is the only revelation that God has made of any such a property in his nature, or of any thought that he would exercise it towards sinners. It is revealed in the fact that he has sent Jesus Christ into the world that we might live by him. Where now is the wise, the scribe, the disputer of this world, with all their wisdom? Their voice must be that of the hypocrites in Zion, Isa. 33:14-15. Wisdom that cannot teach me that God is love will always pass for folly. Let men point to the sun, moon, and stars, or to showers of rain and fruitful seasons, and tell what they learn of this love by them. Men should not think themselves wiser or better than those who went before them, who, to a man, got nothing by these things, but were left without excuse.

[2.] Pardoning mercy, or grace. Without this, even God's love would be fruitless. The only discovery of this grace that a sinful man can make may be seen in the father of us all. When Adam sinned, he had no reserve for mercy, but hid himself instead, Gen. 3:8. He did it *"leruach hayom,"* [OT:7307, 3117] when the wind blew a little at the presence of God. He did it foolishly, thinking to "hide himself among trees!" Ps. 139:7, 8. "The law was given by Moses, but grace and truth came by Jesus Christ," John 1:17. Pardoning mercy comes by Christ alone. It is that pardoning mercy which is manifested in the gospel, and in which God will be glorified to all eternity, Eph. 1:6. I do not mean general mercy, which is that wish for acceptance or "pathos" that some put their hopes in. If we ascribe such a feeling to God, it would be the greatest dishonor that can be done to him. Not one ray of pardoning mercy shines outside of Christ. It is completely treasured in him, and revealed by him. Pardoning mercy is God's free, gracious acceptance of a sinner upon satisfaction of God's justice in the blood of Jesus. We cannot discover it without this satisfaction of justice, consistent with the glory of God. It is a mercy of inconceivable condescension in forgiveness, tempered with exact justice and severity. In Rom. 3:25, God is said "to set forth Christ to be a propitiation through faith in his blood, to declare his righteousness in the remission of sins." His righteousness is also manifested in the business of forgiveness of sins. Therefore, it is said to be wholly in Christ, Eph 1:7. He alone purchases this gospel grace and pardoning mercy, and it is revealed in him alone. The main purpose of all typical institutions was to manifest that remission and forgiveness is wholly wrapped up in the Lord Christ. Apart from him there is not the least conjecture that we can make of it, nor can we taste the least morsel of it. If God had not sent the Lord Christ, all the angels in heaven and all the men on earth could not have imagined anything like this grace of pardoning mercy in the nature of God. The apostle asserts that the full manifestation and exercise of this mercy is in Christ alone. "After that, the kindness and love of God our Savior towards man appeared," Tit. 3:4-5. That is, it appeared in sending Christ, and in the declaration of him in the gospel. Then this pardoning mercy and our salvation apart from works were discovered.

These are of the properties of God by which he will be known. They cannot be glimpsed except by and in Christ. Whoever knows him without these properties does not know him at all. They know an idol, not the only true God. "He that has not the Son, has not the Father," 1John 2:23. Not to have God as a Father is not to have him at all. And he is known as a Father only as he is love, and full of pardoning mercy in Christ. The Holy Spirit tells us how this knowledge is to be had in 1John 5:20. "The Son of God has come and has given us an understanding, that we may know the one who is true." By him alone we gain the understanding necessary to know the one who is true. Now, Christ reveals these properties of God in his doctrine, in the revelation that he makes of God and his will as the great prophet of the church, John 17:6. Through this doctrine, the knowledge of these properties is exposed to all. It is done with evidence far surpassing what the creation can reveal of his eternal power and Godhead. But the life of this knowledge lies in being acquainted with the person of Jesus Christ in whom the express image and beams of his Father's glory shine forth, Heb. 1:3.

(2.) There are other properties of God that can be discovered apart from Christ, but they are clearly, eminently, and savingly discovered only in Jesus Christ. For example,

[1.] His vindictive justice in punishing sin;

[2.] His patience, forbearance, and long-suffering towards sinners;

[3.] His wisdom in managing things for his own glory;

[4.] His all-sufficiency in himself and to others.

All of these, though they may have inferior manifestations outside of Christ, clearly shine only in him. Thus it may be wise to be acquainted with them.

[1.] His vindictive justice - God has manifested his indignation and anger against sin in many ways. Men cannot help but know that it is "the judgment of God, that those who commit such things are worthy of death," Rom. 1:32. In the law he has threatened to kindle a fire in his anger that will burn to the very heart of hell. And even in many providential dispensations, "his wrath is revealed from heaven against all the ungodliness of men," Rom. 1:18. Men must confess that he is a God of judgment. The angels were cast from heaven for their sin, shut up under chains of everlasting darkness to the great judgment day. Sodom and Gomorrah were overthrown and burned to ashes so they might be "examples to those who would thereafter live in ungodliness," 2Pet. 2:6. Someone who only considers these things will discover much of God's vindictive justice, and his anger against sin. But this shines far more clearly into us in the Lord Christ:

1st. In Christ, God has manifested the naturalness of this righteousness to him. It was impossible to divert his vindictive justice from sinners without interposing a propitiation. Those who claim that the necessity of satisfaction rests merely on the free act and will of God, leave no just and indispensable foundation for the death of Christ. They assume it might have been otherwise. God did not spare his only Son, but made him an offering for sin. He would accept no atonement other than his Son's blood. Plainly, he has manifested that his holiness and righteousness require him to render indignation, wrath, tribulation, and anguish in return for sin. Knowing how natural this vindictive justice is, and how necessary it is to execute it in response to sin, is the only true and useful knowledge of it. Looking at it as something that God may or may not do, does not make his justice a property of his nature, but a free act of his will. And a will to punish where one may do otherwise without injustice, is ill will rather than Justice.

2dly. This justice is far more gloriously manifested in the penalty inflicted on Christ for sin than it would be otherwise. The following will give some insight into this thing. See a world that was made good and beautiful, wrapped in wrath and curses, and clothed with thorns and briers. See the whole beautiful creation made subject to vanity, and given up to the bondage of corruption. Hear it groan in pain under that burden. Consider legions of angels, most glorious and immortal creatures, cast down into hell, bound with chains of darkness, and reserved for a more dreadful judgment for one sin. View the ocean of blood spilt to eternity on this account. But what is all this when it is compared to that view of it seen with a spiritual eye in the Lord Christ? All these things are worms, and of no value in comparison to him. See the one who is the wisdom of God, and the power of God, always beloved of the Father. See him, then fear, and tremble, and bow, and sweat, and pray, and die. See him lifted up on the cross, the earth trembling under him, as if unable to bear his weight. See the heavens

72

darkened over him, as if shut against his cry, with him hanging between both as if refused by both. And all of this is because our sins were laid on him. Of all things, this most abundantly manifests the severity of God's vindictive justice. It is to be learned here, or nowhere.

[2.] His patience, forbearance, and long-suffering towards sinners - There are many glimpses of the patience of God shining out in the works of his providence. But all of them are far beneath the discovery of it that we have in Christ, especially in these three things:

1st. The manner of its discovery. It is evident to all that ordinarily God does not immediately punish men upon their offenses. It may be learned from his constant way in governing the world. Despite all provocations, he still does good to men. He causes his sun to shine upon them, sending them rain and fruitful seasons, filling their hearts with food and gladness. Hence, it was easy to conclude that there is an abundance of goodness and forbearance in him. But all this is still very much in darkness, because it is only the outworking of men's experience from their observations. The management of God's patience has proved a snare almost universally to those towards whom it has been exercised, Eccles. 8:11. It has also been a temptation to those who have observed it, Job 21:7; Ps. 73:2-4, etc.; Jer. 12:1; Hab. 1:13. The discovery of God's patience in Christ is of another nature completely. In him the very nature of God is discovered to be love and kindness. He has promised, sworn, and solemnly engaged himself by covenant, to exercise this patience towards sinners. So that we will not hesitate about what God's purpose is in this, there is a stable foundation in the reconciliation and atonement that is made in the blood of Christ.

Whatever discovery could be made of the patience and forbearance of God, if it was not also revealed that the other properties of God fully applied to us, such as his justice and revenge for sin, then there could be little consolation from the former. Though God may teach men his goodness and forbearance by sending rain and fruitful seasons, yet at the same time he reveals "his wrath from heaven against the ungodliness of men," Rom. 1:18. They can only tremble at these dispensations, not knowing which to expect. Yet this is the best that men can have or attain apart from Christ. Men might satiate themselves with the good things that were administered in this patience. Yet they were not delivered from their bondage to death, and the darkness that attends it. The law reveals no patience or forbearance in God. Instead, as to the issue of transgressions, it speaks of nothing but sword and fire. But

73

now with the revelation that we have in Christ, we also discover the satisfaction of God's justice and wrath against sin. We need not fear his justice interfering with the works of his patience, which are so sweet to us. Hence, "God is reconciling the world to himself in Christ," 2Cor. 5:19. He is manifesting himself in Christ as one who has no more to do to glorify himself than to forbear, reconcile, and pardon sin in him.

2dly. In the nature of it. Without Christ, what is revealed of that forbearance? Merely delaying the punishment for the offense, and continuing with temporal mercies. Men are prone to abuse such things. They may perish with their hearts full of them to eternity. What lies hidden in Christ, and what he reveals, is full of love, sweetness, tenderness, kindness, and grace. It is the Lord's waiting to be gracious to sinners, waiting for an advantage to show love and kindness, and to endear us to him. "Therefore the LORD will wait, that he may be gracious to you; and therefore he will be exalted, that he may have mercy upon you," Isa. 30:18. No revelation of God is sweeter than this. When we are experientially convinced that God has from time to time overlooked many iniquities, we are astonished. We admire that he did not take advantage of these provocations to cast us out of his presence. We find that, with infinite wisdom and long-suffering, God has arranged all his dispensations to recover us from the power of the devil, to rebuke and chasten our spirit for our sins, and to endear us to him. There is nothing sweeter to the soul than this. Therefore, the apostle says in Rom. 3:25 that everything comes "through the forbearance of God." God makes way for complete forgiveness of sins through his forbearance, which the law does not.

3dly. They differ in their ends and aims. What is the aim and design of God in his forbearance that is manifested and discovered outside of Christ? The apostle tells us in Rom. 9:22, "What if God, willing to show his wrath, and to make his power known, endured with much long-suffering the vessels of wrath fitted for destruction?" It was to leave them without excuse, so that his power and wrath against sin might be manifested in their destruction. Therefore he calls it "suffering them to walk in their own ways," Acts 14:16. Elsewhere, as in Ps. 81:12, he presents this as a most dreadful judgment, "I gave them up to their own hearts' lusts, and they walked in their own counsels." This is as dreadful a condition as a creature can fall into in this world. In Acts 17:30, he calls it a "winking at the sins of their ignorance," as if taking no care nor thought of them in their dark condition. This is how it appears in its antithesis. "But *now* he commands all men everywhere to repent." Before Christ, he did not notice them enough to command

74

them to repent, at least not by any clear revelation of his mind and will. And therefore the apostle exhorts them in Rom. 2:4, "Do you despise the riches of his goodness, forbearance, and long suffering, not knowing that God's goodness leads you to repentance?" This is spoken to the Jews, who had advantages over others to understand these things. They could learn the natural tendency of God's goodness and forbearance in Christ to lead us to repentance. Otherwise, in general he intimates that by sheer reason, men ought to make another use of his forbearance than they usually do. In verse 5, he charges them with ignoring it: "But after your hardness and impenitent heart..." At best, then, by reason of their own incorrigible stubbornness, God's patience with men who are outside of Christ proves to be like the waters of the river Phasis. They are sweet at the top and bitter at the bottom. Men swim for a while in the sweet and good things of this life, Luke 16:20. Then, being filled with them, they sink to the depths of all bitterness.

But now, evidently and directly, the purpose of that patience and forbearance of God is exercised in Christ and discovered in him. It is saving and bringing into God those towards whom he is pleased to exercise them. Therefore, Peter tells us in 2Pet. 3:9, that God is "long-suffering towards us, not willing that any should perish, but that all should come to repentance." For its purpose is to accomplish his will concerning our repentance and salvation. Its nature and purpose are well expressed in Isa. 54:9. "This is like the waters of Noah to me: for as I have sworn that the waters of Noah should no more go over the earth, so have I sworn that I would not be wrath." It is God's taking a course, in his infinite wisdom and goodness, to ensure that we will not be destroyed despite our sins. And therefore, in Rom. 15:5, these two things are laid together in God, and come together from him. He is "the God of patience and consolation." His patience is a matter of the greatest consolation. This is another property of God that may appear in other things, yet its treasures are hidden in Christ. No one learns any spiritual advantage from it that does not learn it in Christ.

[3.] His infinite wisdom in managing things for his own glory, and the good of those towards whom he has thoughts of love. The Lord has laid out and manifested infinite wisdom in his works of creation, his providence, and the governing of his world. In wisdom he has made all his creatures. "How manifold are his works! In wisdom he has made them all; the earth is full of his riches," Ps. 104:24. So in his providence, in his support and guidance of all things, he has arranged them for his own glory and their appointed ends. All these things "come forth from the LORD of hosts, who is wonderful in counsel, and excellent in working,"

75

Isa. 28:29. His law is also to be forever admired for the excellence of the wisdom it contains, Deut. 4:7, 8. Yet there is something that Paul is astonished at, and in which God will forever be exalted. He calls it "The depth of the riches of the wisdom and knowledge of God," Rom. 11:33. And this is hidden in and revealed only by Christ.

Christ is said to be "the wisdom of God," and he is "made wisdom to us." So the design of God, which is carried along in Christ and revealed in the gospel, is called "the wisdom of God." It is a "mystery; even the hidden wisdom which God ordained before the world; which none of the princes of this world knew," 1Cor. 2:7, 8. In Eph. 3:10, it is called, "The manifold wisdom of God." Paul tells us that principalities and powers, the angels themselves, could not discover the depth and riches of this wisdom, or become acquainted with it in the least, until God actually uncovered it by gathering a church of sinners. Hence, Peter informs us that those who are so well acquainted with all the works of God, still bow down and earnestly desire to look into these things, 1Pet. 1:12. It takes much wisdom to create an extraordinary work, fabric, or building. But if someone defaces it to give it more beauty and glory than ever, this is excellent wisdom indeed. In the beginning, God made all things good, glorious, and beautiful. When these things were innocent and beautiful, clearly marked with God's wisdom and goodness, they were very glorious. This was especially true of man, who was made for his special glory. All this beauty was defaced by sin. The whole creation was rolled up in darkness, wrath, curses, and confusion. The great praise of God was buried in heaps of it. Man, especially, was lost. He came short of the glory of God for which he was created, Rom. 3:23.

Here, the depth of the riches of the wisdom and knowledge of God opens itself. A design in Christ shines out from God's heart, lodged there from eternity. It is to restore things to a state exceedingly advantageous to his glory. It is infinitely above what appeared at first, and it will put sinners into an inconceivably better condition than they were in before the entrance of sin. God now appears glorious. He is known to be a God who pardons iniquity and sin, and advances the riches of his grace. This was his design, Eph. 1:6. In setting forth his Son for a propitiation, he has infinitely vindicated his justice in the eyes of men, angels, and devils. It is also to our advantage. We are more fully established in his favor, and we are carried on towards a greater glory than formerly revealed. Thus Paul tells us, "Without controversy, great is the mystery of godliness," 1Tim. 3:16. We receive "grace for grace," for the grace lost in Adam, we receive better grace in Christ.

Confessedly, this is a depth of wisdom indeed. The love of Christ to his church, and his union with it to carry on this business, "is a great mystery," Eph. 5:32.

So, then, the great and unspeakable riches of the wisdom of God are hidden in Christ:

- in pardoning sin,
- saving sinners,
- satisfying justice,
- fulfilling the law,
- repairing his own honor, and
- providing us a greater weight of glory;

All of this was designed while it was still impossible for angels or men to imagine how to repair the glory of God, or deliver one sinning creature from everlasting ruin. Hence it is said that at the last day God "will be glorified in his saints, and admired in all those who believe," 2Thess. 1:10. It will be an admirable thing, and God will be forever glorious in bringing believers to himself. Saving sinners through believing will be found a far more admirable work than creating the world out of nothing.

[4.] His all-sufficiency in himself and for others is the last category that I will name.

God's all-sufficiency in himself is his absolute and universal perfection. This means nothing is wanting in him, and he wants nothing outside himself. His fullness cannot be increased or decreased. He is also all-sufficient for others. This is his power to communicate himself and his goodness to them in a way that satisfies and fulfills whatever is good and desirable to them. To communicate his goodness, God abundantly manifested its outward effect in the creation. He made all things good and perfect. But giving himself as an all-sufficient God who is to be enjoyed by his creatures, and to offer all that is in him to satiate and bless them, are things discovered by and in Christ alone. In Christ he is a Father. In Christ he is a God in covenant. In this covenant he has promised to lay himself out for them. In Christ he has promised to give himself to their everlasting fruitfulness. He is their exceedingly great reward.

And so I have insisted on the second sort of properties in God. Although we have an obscure glimpse of them in other things, clear knowledge and acquaintance with them can only be had in the Lord Christ. What remains is to briefly declare that none of the properties of God can be known savingly and consolingly except in Christ. Consequently, all the wisdom of the knowledge of God is hidden in Christ alone, and it is to be obtained from him alone.

2. There is no saving or consoling knowledge of any property of God, except what is found in Christ Jesus alone. It is laid up in him and manifested by him. Some observe the justice of God, and know that this is his righteousness. They know that those who sin "are worthy of death," Rom. 1:32. But the only purpose of his justice is to make them cry, "Who among us will dwell with the devouring fire?" Isa. 33:14. Others fix their eyes upon his patience, goodness, mercy, and forbearance. Yet it does not lead them to repentance at all. Instead, "they despise the riches of his goodness, and after their hardness and impenitent hearts they store up wrath for themselves against the day of wrath," Rom. 2:4, 5. Others, by God's works of creation and providence, come to know "his eternal power and Godhead; but they do not glorify him as God, nor are they thankful. They become vain in their imagination, and their foolish hearts are darkened," Rom. 1:20. Whatever men discover of truth outside of Christ, they "hold it captive under unrighteousness," Rom. 1:18. Hence, Jude tells us in verse 10 that "what they know naturally corrupts them like brute beasts."

To have a saving knowledge of the properties of God that consoles us, three things are required:

(1.) That God has manifested the glory of them all in a way that does us good.

(2.) That he yet exercises and displays them to the utmost in our behalf.

(3.) That being manifested and exercised this way, they are fit and powerful to bring us to enjoy him forever. That is our blessedness.

Now, all three of these lie hidden in Christ. We cannot glimpse them at all outside of him.

(1.) We are to accept that God has actually manifested the glory of all his attributes in a way that does us good. God is infinitely righteous, just, and holy. He is unchangeably true and faithful. What good will it do our souls to know these things if we do not know how he preserves the glory of his justice and faithfulness apart from threats of our ruin and destruction? What comfort will it bring us? How will it endear our hearts to God? Is it only righteous for him to repay our iniquities with tribulation? What benefit of this consideration did Adam have in the garden? (Gen. 3). What sweetness and encouragement is there in knowing that God is patient and full of forbearance if the glory of these things is exalted only by his tolerating vessels of wrath that are fitted for destruction? What will it avail us to hear God proclaim "The LORD, The LORD God, merciful and gracious, abundant in goodness and truth," if we only consider that he will "by no means clear the guilty." Does our iniquity

78

preclude the exercise of all his other properties towards us? Under such a naked consideration of the properties of God, his justice will make men fly and hide, Gen. 3; Isa. 2:21, 33:15-16. His patience will render them obdurate, Eccles. 8:11. His holiness will completely deter them from thoughts of approaching him, John 24:19. What relief do we have from thoughts of his immensity and omnipresence if all we want to do is fly from him? (Ps. 139:11, 12). What relief is there if we have no pledge of his gracious presence with us?

What brings salvation is when we see that God has glorified all his properties in a way that does us good. He has done this in Jesus Christ. In Christ, God made his justice glorious. He did so by laying all our iniquities on Christ, causing him to bear them all as the scapegoat in the wilderness. He did not spare him but gave him up to death for us all. Thus he exalted his justice and indignation against sin in a way that frees us from its condemnation, Rom. 3:25, 8:33, 34. In Christ, God has made his truth and his and his faithfulness glorious by exactly accomplishing all of his absolute threats and promises. "In the day you eat of it you shall die the death" Gen. 2:17. This is followed with a curse. "Cursed is every one that does not continue..." Deut. 27:26, Gal. 3:10. That fountain-head and combination from which all others flow is accomplished and fulfilled in Christ. The truth of God contained in them is laid down in a way that does us good. Christ, by the grace of God, tasted death for us, Heb. 2:9. He delivered us when we were subject to death, verse 15. He fulfilled the curse by being made a curse for us, Gal. 3:13. So that in his very threats, God's truth is made glorious in a way that is for our good. And as for his promises, "They are all 'yes', and in him they are 'Amen', to the glory of God by us," 2Cor. 1:20. His mercy, his goodness, and the riches of his grace are made eminently glorious in Christ, and they are advanced for our good! God has set him forth to declare his own righteousness for the forgiveness of sin. In Christ, he has made way to exalt the glory of his pardoning mercy towards sinners forever. The great design of the gospel is to manifest this, as Paul admirably sets it out in Eph. 1:5-8. In the gospel, our souls must either become acquainted with these attributes of God, or forever live in darkness.

This is a saving knowledge. And it is full of consolation when we can see all the properties of God made glorious and exalted in a way that does us good. This wisdom is hidden only in Jesus Christ. Hence, when he desired his Father to glorify his name (Jn. 12:28), that is, to glorify God's nature, properties, and will in the work of redemption that he had in hand, Christ was instantly answered from heaven: "I have both glorified it, and will glorify it again." God gives his name its utmost glory in Christ.

(2.) The second requirement is knowing that God will yet exercise and lay out those properties of his to the utmost in our behalf. He has made them all glorious in a way that may tend to our good, yet it does not absolutely follow that he will *use* them for our good; for we see innumerable persons perishing forever despite manifesting himself in Christ. For that reason, God has committed all his properties into the hand of Christ to be managed in our behalf and for our good. He is "the power of God, and the wisdom of God" (1Cor. 1:24). He is "the LORD our Righteousness" (Jer. 23:6). And he is "made wisdom to us of God, and righteousness, sanctification, and redemption" (1Cor. 1:30). Having glorified his Father in all his attributes, Christ now has the *exercise* of these attributes committed to him, so that he might be the captain of salvation to those who believe. If there is anything that will do us good in the righteousness, goodness, love, mercy, and all-sufficiency of God, then the Lord Jesus is fully interested in dispensing it in our behalf. Hence God is said to be "reconciling the world to himself" in Christ, 2Cor. 5:18. Whatever is in God, he lays it out to reconcile the world in and by the Lord Christ. And thus Christ becomes "the LORD our Righteousness," Jer. 23:5-6; Isa. 45:24, 25.

(3.) The only requirement remaining is that these attributes of God, so manifested and exercised, are powerful and able to bring us to the everlasting enjoyment of God. To show this, the Lord wraps up the whole covenant of grace in one promise: "I will be your God." In the covenant, God becomes our God and we are his people. Thereby all his attributes are also ours. We are tempted to doubt when we see the inconceivable difficulty in this, and what unimaginable obstacles lie against us. We fear that there may not be enough to deliver and save us. But God says in Gen. 17:1, "I am." He is saying, "I am God Almighty" (all-sufficient). "I am wholly able to perform all my undertakings and to be your exceedingly great reward. I can remove all difficulties, answer all objections, pardon all sins, and conquer all opposition. I am God all-sufficient." Now, you know in whom this covenant and all its promises are ratified, and in whose blood it is confirmed. It is in the Lord Christ alone. Only in Christ is God an all-sufficient God to anyone, and an exceedingly great reward. Hence, Christ himself is said to "save to the uttermost those who come to God by him," Heb. 7.

I say that these three things are required to be known if we are to have a saving acquaintance with any of the properties of God, and to have any consolation from such knowledge. All of these are hidden only in Christ, and such knowledge is to be obtained from him alone.

This, then, is the first part of our first demonstration. All true and sound wisdom and knowledge is laid up in the Lord Christ, and is to be obtained from him alone. Because our wisdom consists mainly in the knowledge of God, his nature, and his properties, it lies wholly hidden in Christ and cannot possibly be obtained except by him.

II. The knowledge of ourselves in reference to God's will concerning us.

This SECOND part of our wisdom consists in three things that our Savior sends his Spirit to convince the world of: "sin, righteousness, and judgment," John 16:8. To know ourselves in reference to these three things is a main part of true and sound wisdom. They all concern the supernatural and immortal end to which we are appointed. None of these can be attained except in Christ.

1. Concerning sin. There is a sense and knowledge of sin left in the consciences of all men by nature. They know in themselves what is good and evil in many things, and whether to approve or disapprove of what they do in reference to a judgment to come, Rom. 2:14, 15. But this knowledge is obscure. It relates mostly to greater sins. In sum, it is what the apostle gives us in Rom. 1:32. "They know the judgment of God, that those who do such things are worthy of death." This is one of the common presumptions and notions received by mankind. It is "righteous with God, that those who do such things are worthy of death." And if it is true that no nation is so barbarous or rude as not to retain some sense of a Deity, then it is also true that no nation is without a sense of sin, and God's displeasure for it. For this is the very first concept of God in the world: that he is the rewarder of good and evil. From this arose all the sacrifices, purgings, and expiations that were generally spread over the face of the earth. But this knowledge of sin and its effects was very dark.

The law gives a further knowledge of sin. It is the law which was "added because of transgressions." Doctrinally, this revives all that sense of good and evil that was first implanted in man. It is a glass into which whoever is able to look spiritually may see sin in all its ugliness and deformity. The truth is, the law wonderfully uncovers sin on every account. Look at the law in its purity, holiness, compass, and perfection. Look at its manner of delivery with its dread, terror, thunder, earthquakes, and fire. Look at its sanctions in death, curse, and wrath. The law sees our pollution, guilt, and exceeding sinfulness. Yet all this is insufficient to give us a true and thorough conviction of sin. The glass is clear, but we do not have the eyes to look into it. The rule is straight but we cannot apply it. And therefore Christ sends his Spirit to convince the world of sin, John 16:8. Though for some purposes the Spirit makes use of the law, his unique work is conviction. Conviction alone gives a useful knowledge of sin. The discovery of sin may also be said to be by Christ, and to be part of the wisdom that is hidden in him. But there is a twofold regard (besides this one) in which this wisdom appears to be hidden in him. *First*, some concerns of sin are more clearly demonstrated in the Lord Christ's being made sin for us than in any other way. *Secondly*, there is no knowledge of sin that gives a spiritual and saving improvement except in him.

For the first, there are four things in sin that clearly shine out in the cross of Christ:

      (1.) The desert of sin.
      (2.) Man's impotency because of sin.
      (3.) The death of sin.
      (4.) A new outcome for sin.

      (1.) The desert of sin clearly shines in the cross of Christ for two reasons: [1.] Because of the person suffering for it, and [2.] Because of the penalty he underwent.

      [1.] The person suffering for it. The Scripture often presents this very emphatically, and places great weight on it: "For God so loved the world, that he gave his only begotten Son," John 3:16. It was his only Son that God sent into the world to suffer for sin. "He spared not his own Son, but delivered him up for us all," Rom. 8:32. To see a slave beaten and corrected argues that a fault was committed, but perhaps not a very great one. The correction of a son argues a great provocation. That of an only son implies the greatest imaginable provocation. Sin was never seen more abominably sinful and full of provocation than when its burden was upon the shoulders of the Son of God. God made his Son sin for us. He is the Son of his love, his only begotten son who was full of grace and truth. He did this to manifest his indignation against it, and to show how utterly impossible it is for him to let the least sin go unpunished. He lays hand on his son, and does not spare him. The father imputed our sin to the dear Son of his heart upon his own voluntary assumption of it. He said to his Father, "Lo, I come to do your will," (Heb. 10:9) and all our iniquities were laid on him (Isa. 53:6). He will not spare him any of sin's deserts that are due. It is most clear from the blood of the cross of Christ that the demerit of sin makes it altogether impossible for God to pass by anyone to let it go unpunished. If he did it for anyone, he would have done it for his only Son. But he did not spare him.

      Moreover, God does not delight in or desire the blood, tears, cries, and inexpressible torments and sufferings of the Son of his love. He does not delight in the anguish of anyone. "He does not willingly afflict nor grieve the children of men," (Lam. 3:33) much less the Son of his heart. He only required that his law be fulfilled, his justice be satisfied, and his wrath be atoned for. Nothing less than all this would bring it about. If the debt of sin might have been compounded at a cheaper rate, it would never have required the price of the blood of Christ. Here then, take a view of the desert of sin. It is far more evident in this than in all the threats and curses of the law. You may respond, "When found in a poor worm like me, I thought sin was worthy of death; but I never imagined it would have this effect when charged on the Son of God."

[2.] Further, consider what he suffered. Being so excellent as he was, perhaps it was only a light affliction and trial that he underwent, especially considering the strength that he had to bear it. Yet, it made this "fellow of the LORD of hosts," this "lion of the tribe of Judah," this "mighty one," "the wisdom and power of God," tremble, sweat, cry, pray, and wrestle with strong supplications. Some of the Catholic devotionists tell us that one drop of the blood of Christ was enough to redeem the entire world, but they err. They do not know the desert of sin, or the severity of the justice of God. If one drop less than was shed, or one pang less than was laid on would have done it, then those other drops would not have been shed, nor those other pangs been laid on. God did not cruciate the dearly beloved of his soul for nothing. But there is more than all this:

It pleased God to bruise him, to put him to grief, to make his soul an offering for sin, and to pour out his life to the point of death. He hid himself from him. He was far from the voice of his cry until Christ cried out, "My God, my God, why have you forsaken me?" God made him sin and a curse for us. He executed the sentence of the law on him. He brought him into such an agony that Christ sweated thick drops of blood. He was grievously troubled and his soul was heavy unto death. The one who was the power of God and the wisdom of God stooped under the burden of our sin until the whole frame of nature seemed astonished at it. Now this clearly presents the desert of sin, and reveals God's indignation against it. Would you, then, see the true demerit of sin? Take the measure of it from the mediation of Christ, especially his cross. It brought the one who was the Son of God, equal to God, whom God blessed forever, into the form of a servant who had nowhere to lay his head. All his life it pursued him with afflictions and persecutions. And lastly, it brought him under the rod of God that bruised him, broke him, and slew the Lord of life. Hence there is deep humiliation for it, because of the one whom we have pierced. And this is the first spiritual view of sin that we have in Christ.

(2.) The wisdom of understanding our impotency is wrapped up in him because of sin. By our impotency, I understand two things:

[1.] Our disability to make any atonement for sin with God.

[2.] Our disability to answer his mind and will with the obedience that he requires.

[1.] For the first, atonement is only discovered in Christ. The sons of men have made many inquiries into an alternative atonement. They have tried many ways to accomplish it without him. After this fruitless search they ask, "Will any type of sacrifices atone for my sin? Even though appointed by God, such as burnt offerings and year-old calves? Even though very costly, such as thousands of rams and ten thousand rivers of oil? Even though dreadful and tremendous, those doing violence to nature, such as giving my children to the fire?" (Mic. 6:6-7). Will any of these things make an atonement? David emphatically determines this business in Ps. 49:7-8. "None of them" (of the best or richest of men) "can by any means redeem his brother, nor give to God a ransom for him; for the redemption of their soul is precious, and it ceases forever." It cannot be done. No atonement can be made. Yet men still attempt it. For that reason they heaped up sacrifices, some costly, some bloody and inhuman. The Jews, to this day, think that God was atoned for sin by the sacrifices of bulls, goats, and the like. And the Socinians acknowledge no atonement other than men's repentance and new obedience. In the cross of Christ, the mouths of all are stopped as to this thing. For,

1st. God has revealed there that no sacrifices for sin, even though appointed by him, could ever make those who offered them perfect, Heb. 10:11. Those sacrifices could never take away sin. Those services that they performed could never make them perfect in their conscience, Heb. 9:9, as the apostle proves in chap. 10:1. And therefore, the Lord rejects all sacrifices and offerings whatever that are made for any such purpose, verses 6-8. In their stead, Christ says, "Lo, I come." By him we are "justified from all things from which we could not be justified by the law," Acts 13:39. God, in Christ, has condemned all sacrifices as wholly insufficient to make an atonement for sin. The event of the cross has manifested how great a thing it was to instruct the sons of men in this wisdom.

2dly. He has also written "vanity" on all other endeavors that have been undertaken for that purpose. By setting forth his only Son "to be a propitiation," he leaves no doubt on the spirits of men that they could make no atonement by themselves, Rom. 3:24-26. For "if righteousness were by the law, then Christ died in vain." To what purpose would he be made a propitiation if we were not weak and without strength to accomplish it ourselves? This is what the apostle argues in Rom. 5:6. When we had no power, then by his death Christ made an atonement for us (5:8-9).

This wisdom is also hidden in Christ. Men may see consequences for their sin that fill them with dread and astonishment, such as those in Isa. 33:14. But such a sight and view

84

of sin that might lead them to any comfortable settlement about it, will only be discovered in this treasury of heaven: the Lord Jesus.

[2.] Our disability to answer the mind and will of God with all or any of the obedience that he requires, is only to be discovered in Christ. This, indeed, is a thing that many will not be acquainted with to this day. It is no easy task to teach a man that he cannot do what he ought to do, and for which he condemns himself if he does not do it. Man rises up with all his power to plead against a conviction of impotency, not to mention the proud conceits and expressions of the philosophers. How many who would be called Christians still creep by degrees in their persuasion that they have the power to fulfill the law! And where would men get this knowledge that we do not have this power? Nature will not teach that. It is proud and conceited. And it is one part of its pride, weakness, and corruption, not to know it at all. The law will not teach it. For though it will show us what we have done amiss, it will not reveal to us that we cannot do better. In fact, by requiring exact obedience of us, it takes for granted that such power exists in us. It takes no notice that we have lost it, and it is unconcerned to say otherwise. This, then, also lies hidden in the Lord Jesus. Rom. 8:2-4, "The law of the Spirit of life in Christ Jesus has made me free from the law of sin and death. For what the law could not do, in that it was weak through the flesh, God sending his own Son in the likeness of sinful flesh, and for sin, condemned sin in the flesh; that the righteousness of the law might be fulfilled in us." The law cannot produce righteousness, nor obedience. It is weak to any such purpose, because of the flesh and the corruption that has come upon us.

These two things are done in and by Christ: First, sin is condemned as to its guilt, and we are set free from that guilt. The righteousness of the law, by Christ's obedience, is fulfilled in us who could never do it ourselves. And, secondly, the obedience that is required of us is worked in us by his Spirit. The perfect obedience that we have in Christ is imputed to us, and the sincere obedience that we have from his Spirit is bestowed on us. This is the most excellent glass in which we see our impotency. For why do we need his perfect obedience to be made ours, unless we do not have and cannot attain perfect obedience ourselves? Why do we need his Spirit of life to quicken us, unless we are dead in trespasses and sins?

(3.) The death of sin is discovered in the cross of Christ. Sin is dying in us to some extent while we are still alive. This is a third concern about sin that it is wise to be acquainted with, and this wisdom is hidden only in Christ. Sin is dying in two ways: it is dying in its exercise in our mortal members, and it is dying in its root, principle, and power in our souls. The first way may be seen in part outside of

85

Christ. Christless men may have the outward exercise of sin dying in them just like those who are in Christ. Men's bodies may be unable to serve their lusts, or practicing such lusts may no longer interest them. Sin is never more alive than when it is dying in this way. But there is another way of dying. And this is in the root and principle of it. It is the daily decaying of its strength, power, and life; and this is to be had in Christ alone. Sin is not apt to die or decay on its own. Instead, it is apt to gain ground, strength, and life in us to eternity. We may prevent all its actual eruptions, and yet its original enmity against God will still grow. In believers, it is dying and decaying until it is utterly abolished. The opening of this treasury of wisdom is found in Rom. 6:3-6, etc. "Do you not know that as many of us as were baptized into Jesus Christ were baptized into his death? Therefore we are buried with him by baptism into death. Just as Christ was raised from the dead by the glory of the Father, even so we also should walk in newness of life. For if we have been planted together in the likeness of his death, we will also be in the likeness of his resurrection, knowing this: that our old man is crucified with him so that the body of sin might be destroyed, and so that we should not serve sin any longer." This is the design of the apostle in the beginning of that chapter. He not only manifests where the principle and motivation of our mortification and the death of sin come from (the death and blood of Christ), but also the way sin continues and dies in us (the way that Christ died for sin). He was crucified for us, and thereby sin was crucified in us. He died for us, and the body of sin is destroyed so that we should not serve sin. As he was raised from the dead so that death would not have dominion over him, so we are also raised from sin so that it should not have dominion over us. This wisdom is hidden only in Christ. Moses at his dying day had all his strength and vigor. So do sin and the law to all those who are out of Jesus: at their dying day, sin has not decayed in any way. Now, knowing this is the best part of our wisdom, next to receiving the righteousness that was prepared for us. This is wisdom indeed: to be truly acquainted with the principle of the dying of sin, to feel virtue and power flowing from the cross of Christ for that purpose, and to find sin crucified in us as Christ was crucified for us. This wisdom is found in Christ alone.

(4.) Sin is appointed and ordained for a glorious purpose that others are unacquainted with, and it is discovered in Christ. Sin in its own nature tends to dishonor God, to debase his majesty, and to ruin the creature in whom it is found. Hell itself is only filling wretched creatures with the fruit of their own devices. The combinations and threats of God in the law manifest one other purpose for sin, which is to demonstrate the vindictive justice of God by measuring out a fit recompense. But here the law and the light stop, revealing no other use

86

or purpose for sin at all. In the Lord Jesus there is another and more glorious end that is manifested. It is the praise of God's glorious grace in the pardon and forgiveness of sin. God provided in Christ that the thing which tended toward his dishonor would be managed to his infinite glory. Of all the things that he desires to exalt, it is that he may be known and believed to be a "God pardoning iniquity, transgression and sin" (Ex. 34:7; Mic. 7:18). To return, then, to this part of our demonstration:

Much of our wisdom consists in the knowledge of ourselves, in reference to our eternal condition. In this depraved condition of nature, there is nothing we are more concerned with than sin. Without knowledge of that, we do not know ourselves. "Fools mock at sin." (Prov. 14:9). A true saving knowledge of sin can be obtained only in the Lord Christ. In him we may see the desert of our iniquities, and their pollution. These could not be borne or expiated except by his blood. There is no wholesome view of these things except in Christ. In him and in his cross we discover our universal impotency to either atone God's justice, or to live up to his will. The death of sin is procured by, and discovered in, the death of Christ. So is the manifestation of the riches of God's grace in pardoning it. A real and experimental acquaintance with all of this is our wisdom; and it is more valuable than all the wisdom of the world.

2. Concerning righteousness. Righteousness is the second thing of which the Spirit of Christ convinces the world. It is the main thing that it is our wisdom to be acquainted with. All men are persuaded that God is a most righteous God. That is the natural concept of God that Abraham insisted on in Gen. 18:25, "Will not the Judge of all the earth do right?" They "know that this is the judgment of God, that those who commit such things are worthy of death," Rom. 1:32. They know that "it is a righteous thing with him to recompense tribulation to offenders," 2Thess. 1:6. He is "a God of purer eyes than to behold evil," Hab. 1:13. And therefore, "the ungodly cannot stand in judgment," Ps. 1:5. Hence, the great inquiry of everyone who is the least convinced of immortality and the judgment to come, concerns the righteousness with which to appear in the presence of this righteous God. They are more or less solicitous about this all their days. And so, as the apostle says in Heb. 2:15, "through the fear of death they are subject to bondage all their life." They are perplexed about the issue of their righteousness for fear it will end in their death and destruction.

(1.) Naturally, what first presents itself to men involved in this inquiry is the law. It provides them direction and assistance. It assuredly promises them a righteousness that will withstand the trial of God, provided they follow its direction. The law has many reasonable pleas to persuade people to embrace it for their

87

righteousness before God. It was given out from God himself for that purpose. It contains the whole obedience that God requires of any of the sons of men. It has the promise of life annexed to it: "Do this, and live." "The doers of the law are justified;" and, "If you will enter into life, keep the commandments." Most certainly it must be wholly fulfilled if we think to stand with boldness before God. This being some part of the law's plea, no man seeks after righteousness that does not at one time or another attend to it, and attempt to follow its direction. Many who will not admit to it do so every day. They labor to correct their lives, amend their ways, perform the duties required, and pursue a righteousness according to the prescript of the law. Many men continue for a long time in this course of action with much perplexity. They sometimes hope, but more often fear. They are sometimes ready to quit, other times vowing to continue. Their consciences are in no way satisfied, nor do they attain any measure of righteousness all their days. After they have strained and wearied themselves, perhaps for a long season, they come with fear, trembling, and disappointment to the same conclusion as the apostle. "By the works of the law no flesh is justified." And with dread they cry that if God were to mark what is done amiss, there is no standing before him. The apostle testifies to the fact that they have this issue in Rom. 9:31, 32. "Israel, who followed after the law of righteousness, has not attained to the law of righteousness. Why is this? Because they did not seek it by faith, but by the works of the law." It was not solely for want of effort that they were disappointed, for they earnestly followed after the law of righteousness. It was from the nature of the thing itself. It would not bear it. Righteousness was not to be obtained that way. "For," says the apostle, "if those who are of the law are heirs, then faith is made void, and the promise is made of no effect; because the law works wrath," Rom. 4:14, 15. The law itself cannot give life, Gal. 3:21. "If there had been a law given which could have given life, then truly righteousness would have been by the law." In the next verse, he gives the reason why it could not give life. It is because "the Scripture concludes all under sin." That is, it is very true, and the Scripture affirms it, that all men are sinners; and the law speaks not one word to sinners other than death and destruction. Therefore, the apostle tells us plainly that God himself found fault with this way of attaining righteousness, Heb. 8:7, 8. He complains of it; that is, he declares it insufficient for that end and purpose.

Now, there are two considerations that reveal to men the vanity and hopelessness of seeking righteousness by the law:

[1.] They have already sinned: "For all have sinned, and come short of the glory of God," Rom. 3:23. They understand that although they could fulfill the whole law for the time to come, there is a score, a reckoning, already upon them, that they do not know how to answer for. They may consult their guide, the law itself, as to how to be eased of the account that is past. But it has no word of direction or consolation. Instead, it bids them prepare to die. The sentence has been issued, and there is no escaping it.

[2.] If all former debts were blotted out, they are still unable to fulfill the law for the future. They can as well move the earth with a finger, as answer the law's requirement of perfection.

Therefore, they conclude that this labor is lost. "By the works of the law no flesh will be justified."

(2.) Secondly, being disappointed by the severity and inexorableness of the law, men generally resort to some other way to satisfy the necessary righteousness. For the most part, this is done by fixing on some way of atonement to satisfy God, and then making up the difference with hopes of mercy. Set aside the ways of atonement and expiation which the Gentiles depended on, and the many inventions of the Papists, such as indulgences and purgatory. It is normal for all persons convinced of their sin to search for this righteousness, partly by trying to make satisfaction for what is past, and partly by hoping for general mercy. This is what the apostle calls seeking righteousness "as it were, by the works of the law," Rom. 9:32. It is not done directly, "but as it were" by the works of the law, substituting one thing for another. And he tells us the result of this business in chap. 10:3. "Being ignorant of God's righteousness, and going about to establish their own righteousness, they have not submitted themselves to the righteousness of God." By this personal righteousness they were enemies to the righteousness of God. The ground for establishing their own righteousness was that they were ignorant of the righteousness of God. Had they known the righteousness of God, and what exact conformity to his will he requires, they would never have undertaken such a fruitless enterprise "as it were by the works of the law." Yet many will stick to this approach for a long time. Something they do, something they hope for; some old faults they will buy off with new obedience. And this pacifies their consciences for a season. But when the Spirit comes to convince them of righteousness, this will not hold. Therefore,

(3.) They see themselves as needing two qualifications –

[1.] As sinners, they are liable to the law of God, and they are under its curse. Seeking to appear in the presence of God would be in vain unless *the law can be satisfied*. Then nothing from their sin will ever be laid to their charge.

[2.] As creatures, they were made for a supernatural and eternal end. Therefore, they are bound to answer the whole mind and will of God in *the obedience required* at their hands.

89

It has been revealed to them that both these qualifications are beyond the scope of their own endeavors and the assistance that they formerly rested on. If their eternal condition is of any concern to them, then it is their wisdom to discover a righteousness that may completely fulfill both of these qualifications.

Now, both of these are to be had only in the Lord Christ, who is our righteousness. This wisdom and all its treasures are hidden in him.

1st. He expiates former iniquities. He makes satisfaction for sin, and he procures its remission. Rom. 3:24, 25, "Being justified freely by his grace, through the redemption that is in Christ Jesus: whom God has set forth to be a propitiation through faith in his blood, to declare his righteousness for the remission of sins that are past, through the forbearance of God." "All we like sheep have gone astray," Isa. 53:6. "Through his blood we have redemption, the forgiveness of sins," Eph. 1:7. "God spared not his own Son, but delivered him up for us all," Rom. 8:32. This alone is our righteousness. It removes the whole guilt of sin by which we come short of the glory of God. It is on this account that we are assured that none will ever lay anything to our charge or condemn us, Rom. 8:33, 34. There is "no condemnation to those who are in Christ Jesus," 8:1. We are purged by the sacrifice of Christ so as to have "no more conscience of sin," Heb. 10:2. That is, nothing troubles the conscience about it. This wisdom is hidden only in the Lord Jesus. Atonement is discovered in him alone. Give me the wisdom that will cut all scores concerning sin, and let the world take what remains. But,

2nd. Something more required. It is not enough that we are not guilty; we must also be actually righteous. Not only is all sin to be answered for, but all righteousness is to be fulfilled. By taking away the guilt of sin we are considered innocent, but something more is required to consider us obedient. Nothing teaches me that an innocent person will go to heaven (be rewarded), if he is not obedient. Adam was innocent at his first creation, but he was to "do this," to "keep the commandments," before he entered into "life." He had no title to life merely by his innocence. This, moreover, is required: that the whole law be fulfilled and all of the obedience be performed that God requires at our hand. This is the soul's second inquiry, and it finds a resolution only in the Lord Christ: "For if, when we were enemies, we were reconciled to God by the death of his Son, much more, being reconciled, we will be saved by his life," Rom 5:10. His death reconciled us, and then we are saved by his life. The actual obedience, which he yielded to the whole law of God, is that righteousness by which we are saved. If that is so, then we are found in him, not holding our own righteousness which is of the law, but the righteousness which is of God by faith, Phil. 3:9. I will handle this at large later.

90

I suppose it is not a difficult task to persuade men who are convinced of immortality and the judgment to come, that the main part of their wisdom lies in this: to find a righteousness that will accompany them forever, and withstand the severe trial of God himself. Now, all the wisdom of the world is folly in discovering this thing. The utmost that man's wisdom can do is to find the most wretched, burdensome, and vexing ways of perishing eternally. All the treasures of this wisdom are hidden in Christ. He "of God is made to us wisdom and righteousness," 1Cor. 1:30.

3. Concerning Judgment. We come to the last thing, which I will only touch on, and that is judgment. The true wisdom of this is also hidden in the Lord Christ. In particular, I mean the judgment that is to come. So at present I take the word in that context (John 16:8). I will not speak about what concern this is to us to know. It is about that principle which influences the sons of men and distinguishes them from the beasts that perish. I will not insist on the obscure intimations it has through the present proceedings of Providence in governing the world. Nor will I speak of that greater light it shines in the threats and promises of the law. The wisdom of judgment is hidden in the Lord Jesus in two regards:

(1.) As to the truth of it.

(2.) As to the manner of it:

(1.) The truth of this judgment is confirmed in and by him in two ways: [1.] By his death. [2.] By his resurrection:

[1.] *By his death.* In the death of Christ, God has given an abundant assurance of a righteous and universal judgment to come. He has done so by punishing and condemning sin in the flesh of his own Son, in the sight of men, angels, and devils. On what conceivable grounds could he be induced to lay such a load on his Son, except that he will certainly reckon one day with the sons of men for all their works and ways before him? The death of Christ is a most solemn exemplar of the last judgment. Those who believe him to be the Son of God will not deny a judgment to come.

[2.] *By his resurrection.* Acts 17:31: God has given faith and assurance of this thing to all by raising Christ from the dead. He has appointed him to be the judge of all, in whom and by whom he will judge the world in righteousness.

(2.) And, as to the manner of judgment, it will be by the one who has loved us and given himself for us. He is himself the righteousness that he requires of our hands. And on the other side, it will be by the one who has been reviled, despised, and condemned by the men of the world in his person, grace, ways, worship, and servants. This holds out unspeakable consolation on

91

the one hand, and terror on the other, so that the wisdom of this is also hidden in Christ.

And this concludes the second part of our first demonstration. Thus, the knowledge of ourselves, in reference to our supernatural end, is no small portion of our wisdom. The things of the greatest concern in this are sin, righteousness, and judgment. What was proved is that the wisdom of all of these is hidden in the Lord Jesus alone.

III. The THIRD part of our wisdom is to walk with God.

Six things are required to walk with another:

1. Agreement. 2. Acquaintance. 3. A way. 4. Strength. 5. Confidence. 6. A mutual end. All of these and their wisdom are hidden in the Lord Jesus.

1. Agreement. The prophet tells us that two cannot walk together unless they are agreed, Amos 3:3. Until agreement is made, there is no communion, no walking together. God and man by nature (or while man is in the state of nature) are at the greatest enmity. He declares nothing to us but wrath, Rom. 1:18. We are said to be children of wrath. That is, we are born unattracted to walking with God, Eph. 2:3. While we remain in that condition, "the wrath of God abides on us," John 3:36. The only revelation that God makes of himself to us is that he is inexpressibly provoked, and therefore he is preparing against the day of wrath, and the revelation of his righteous judgment. The day of meeting between him and sinners is called "The day of wrath," Rom. 2:5, 6. We do not come short in our enmity against him. In fact, we began it first and we continue in it longest. To express this enmity, the apostle tells us that our very minds, the best part of us, are "enmity against God," Rom. 8:7, 8. We are not, will not, and cannot be subject to him because our enmity manifests itself by universal rebellion against him. Whatever we do that seems otherwise is either hypocrisy or flattery. Indeed, it is a part of this enmity to lessen it. In this state, the wisdom of walking with God must be most remote from the soul. He is a "light, and in him is no darkness at all." We are darkness, and in us there is no light at all. He is life, a "living God." We are dead, dead sinners, dead in trespasses and sin. He is "holiness" and glorious in it. We are wholly defiled, an abominable thing. He is "love." We are full of hatred, both hating and being hated. Surely this is no foundation for agreement, or upon that foundation, of walking together. Nothing can be more remote than this frame from such a condition. The foundation of this, then, is laid in Christ, hidden in Christ. "He," says the apostle, "is our peace; he has made peace" for us, Eph. 2:14-15. He slew the enmity in his own body on the cross, verse 16.

(1.) He takes the cause of the enmity that was between God and us out of the way. That cause is sin and the curse of the law. He makes an end of sin by making atonement for iniquity, Dan. 9:24. And he blots out the hand-writing of ordinances, Col. 2:14. He redeems us from the curse by "being made a curse for us," Gal. 3:13.

(2.) He destroys the one who would continue the enmity, and make the breach wider, Heb. 2:14. "Through death he destroyed the one who had the power of death, that is, the devil;" and Col. 2:15, he "spoiled principalities and powers."

(3.) He made "reconciliation for the sins of the people," Heb. 2:17. By his blood he made an atonement with God, to turn away the wrath which was due to us, thus making peace. Hereupon God is said to be "in Christ, reconciling the world to himself," 2Cor. 5:19. And being reconciled himself, verse 18, he lays down the enmity on his part and proceeds to what remains, to slay the enmity on our part, so that we may also be reconciled.

(4.) And also, Rom. 5:11, "By our Lord Jesus Christ we receive the atonement." We accept the peace made and tendered, laying down our enmity to God. And thus we confirm an agreement between us in his blood, so that "through him we have access to the Father," Eph. 2:18.

Now, the whole wisdom of this agreement, without which there is no walking with God, is hidden in Christ. Outside of him, God is a consuming fire and we are like dry stubble. Yet we set ourselves in battle array against that fire. If we are brought together, we will be consumed. So approaching God outside of Christ is to our detriment. In Christ's blood alone we have this agreement. And let us not think that we have taken any step in the paths of God with him, or that any duty is accepted, or that all is not eternally lost, if we have not done it on the account of Christ.

2. Acquaintance. Two may meet together in the same path and have no quarrel between them, no enmity. If they are strangers, they may pass by without the least communion together. It does not suffice that the enmity between God and us is taken away. We must also have an acquaintance with him. Our not knowing him is a great cause and a great part of our enmity. Our understanding is "darkened," and we are "alienated from the life of God...," Eph. 4:18. This acquaintance, then, must also be added if we are ever to walk with God, which is our wisdom. And this wisdom is also hidden in the Lord Christ, and comes from him. It is true that there are a number of other means, such as his word and his works, that God has given to men to disclose himself and give them some acquaintance. As the apostle says in Acts 17:27, he did this so that "they should seek the Lord, if haply they might find him." Yet, the knowledge of God that we have by his works is weak and imperfect. And what we have by the letter of the word does not save us without additional help, because of our blindness. For even if they were as bright as the sun in the firmament, if we have no eyes in our heads, what can it avail us? No saving acquaintance with God that might direct us to walk with him can be obtained this way. This also is hidden in the Lord Jesus, and comes forth from him. "He has given us an understanding, that we should know him that is true," 1John 5:20. No other light that we may have will do it without his giving us understanding. He is the true Light which lights every one that is enlightened, John 1:9. He opens our understanding that we may understand the Scriptures, Luke 24:45. None has known God at any time, "except that he has revealed him," John 1:18. God dwells in that "light which no man can approach," 1Tim. 6:16. None has ever had any such acquaintance with him so as to have seen him except by the revelation of Jesus Christ. Hence he tells the Pharisees that, notwithstanding all their great knowledge which they pretend, they had "neither heard the voice of God at any time, nor seen his shape," John 5:37. They had no manner of spiritual acquaintance with God. Instead, to them he was like a man whom they had never heard nor seen. Acquaintance with God means knowing his love, and that he is full of kindness, patience, grace, and pardoning mercy. On that knowledge of him alone can we walk with him. Such knowledge can only be had in Christ. This, then, is also hidden in him.

3. **A way in which we must walk with God**. At the beginning, God assigned us a path to walk in with him in a covenant of works, which was the path of innocence and exact holiness. Because of sin, this path is so filled with thorns and briers, so stopped up by curses and wrath, that no flesh living can take one step in that path. If we ever think to hold communion with God, a new way for us to walk in must be found. And this also depends on the former account: it is hidden in Christ. Except by and in Christ, the world cannot discover a path in which a man may walk one step with God. Therefore, the Holy Spirit tells us that, for that purpose, Christ has consecrated, dedicated, and set apart "a new and living way" into the holiest of all, Heb. 10:20. It is a new one, for the first, old one was useless. It is a living one, for the other is dead. Therefore, he says in verse 22, "Let us draw near." Having a way to walk in, let us draw near. And this way that he has prepared for us is none other than himself, John 14:6. In answer to those who would go to the Father and hold communion with him, he tells them, "I am the way; and no man comes to the Father but by me." He is the medium of all communication between God and us. In him we meet; in him we walk. All influences of love, kindness, and mercy from God to us are through him. All our returns of love, delight, faith, and obedience to God are all through him. He is that "one way" that God so often promises his people. And it is a glorious way, Isa. 35:8, a high way, a way of holiness, a way in which none can err once they

enter it, as further presented in Isa. 42:16. All other ways, all other paths but this, go down to the chambers of death. They all lead to a walk that is contrary to God.

4. Strength. But suppose all this is done, that an agreement is made, an acquaintance given, and a way provided. Yet if we have no strength to walk in that way, what will all this avail us? This, then, must also be added. Of ourselves we have no strength, Rom. 5:6. We are poor weaklings, not able to go a step in the ways of God. When we are set in the way, we either throw ourselves down, or temptations cast us down, and we make no progress. The Lord Jesus tells us plainly that, "without him we can do nothing," John 15:5, nothing that will be the least acceptable to God. Nor can all the creatures in heaven and earth give us the least assistance. Contending to do it in our own power comes to nothing. This part of the wisdom is also hidden in Christ. All strength to walk with God comes from him. "I can do all things through Christ, who strengthens me," says St. Paul, Phil. 4:13. He denies that of ourselves we have any sufficiency, 2Cor. 3:5. We can do nothing in ourselves, being such weaklings, but we can do all things in Jesus Christ as giants. And therefore, in him we are "more than conquerors" against all opposition in our way, Rom. 8:37. That is because "from his fullness we receive grace for grace," John 1:16. From him have we the Spirit of life and power whereby he bears us on eagles' wings, swiftly and safely in the paths of walking with God. Any step we take, that is in any way by strength that is not immediately from Christ, is one step towards hell. He takes us by the arm first and teaches us to go, until he leads us on to perfection. He has milk and strong meat to feed us. He strengthens us with all might, and he is with us in running the race that is set before us.

5. Confidence. Where will we take this confidence from to walk with our God who is "a consuming fire?" Heb. 12:29. Was there not such a dread upon his people of old that it was taken for granted among them that, if they saw God at any time, it was not to be endured and they must die? Can any, without extreme horror, think of that dreadful appearance that he made to them on Mount Sinai? Moses himself, who was their mediator, said, "I exceedingly fear and quake," Heb. 12:21. All the people said, "Do not let God speak with us lest we die!" Exod. 20:19. Though men understand the goodness and kindness of God, upon discovering any part of his glory, they tremble and are filled with dread and astonishment! Has it not been so with the "choicest of his saints?" Hab. 3:16; Isa. 6:5; Job 42:5-6. From where, then, should we assume this boldness to walk with God? The apostle informs us of its source in Heb. 10:19. It is "by the blood of Jesus." And so, in Eph. 3:12, "In him we have boldness, and access with confidence." We are not standing far off, like the people at the giving of the law, but drawing close to God with boldness. We can do so on this account: the dread and terror of God entered by sin. Adam did not have the least thought of hiding himself until he had sinned. The guilt of sin is on the conscience; and it is left in the hearts of all that God is a most righteous revenger of sin. This fills men with dread and horror at an apprehension of his presence, fearing that he has come to recall their sins. But now this conscience of sin has been taken away by the sacrifice and atonement that the Lord Jesus has made. That is, the dread of revenge from God because of the guilt of sin has been taken away. He has removed the slaying sword of the law, and that gives us great boldness with God. He is now no longer revealed to us as a revenging Judge, but as a tender, merciful, and reconciled Father. Moreover, although by nature there is a spirit of bondage on us that fills us with innumerable tormenting fears, he takes it away. He gives us "the Spirit of adoption, whereby we cry Abba, Father," and behave ourselves with confidence and gracious boldness, like children. For "where the Spirit of the Lord is, there is liberty," 2Cor. 3:17. There is freedom from all that dread and terror which the administration of the law brought with it. Just as there is no sin that God will more severely revenge than any boldness that a man takes with him outside of Christ; so there is no grace more acceptable to him than that boldness which he is pleased to afford us in the blood of Jesus.

6. Mutual end. There is only one more thing to add, and it is that two cannot walk together unless they have the same design in hand, aiming at the same end. In a word, this is also given to us in the Lord Jesus. The end of God is the advancement of his own glory. No one can aim at this end except in the Lord Jesus. The sum of all this is that the whole wisdom of our walking with God is hidden in Christ, and it is to be obtained from him alone.

And so have I brought my FIRST demonstration of what I intended to a close. I have manifested that all true wisdom and knowledge is laid up in, and laid out by, the Lord Jesus. And this is done by an induction of the particular areas in which our wisdom consists. I have one more demonstration to add, and I will be brief.

SECONDLY, the truth that all true wisdom is hidden in Christ will be further manifested by considering the insufficiency and vanity of anything else that may lay claim or pretend to a title of wisdom.

There are two things in the world that pass for wisdom:

1. Learning or literature, which is skill and knowledge in the arts, sciences, tongues, and knowledge of things that are past.

2. Prudence and skill in managing ourselves in reference to others, that is, in civil affairs for the public good. This is primarily the fairest flower within the border of nature's garden.

Concerning both of these, I will briefly show,

(1.) That they are utterly insufficient to encompass and obtain the ends to which they are designed.

(2.) That both of them in conjunction, with their utmost improvement, cannot obtain the true general end of wisdom.

Both of these considerations will set the crown in this issue on the head of Jesus Christ:

(1) FIRST, as to their utter insufficiency.

1. Learning itself, if it were all in one man, is not able to encompass the particular end to which it is designed. "Vanity and vexation" are written upon its forehead (Ecc. 1:14; 2:26).

The particular end of literature is none other than to remove some part of the curse that has come upon us by sin. Learning is the product of the soul's struggling with the curse of sin. Adam, at his first creation, was completely furnished with all that knowledge, apart from things not yet existing, such as what we now call tongues. There was no restraint, much less darkness, on his understanding that would make him sweat for a way to improve it. Take his knowledge of nature. It is manifest from his suitably naming all the creatures, and the approval given in Scripture of his nomination of things, that he was clearly acquainted with their natures. Hence Plato could observe that the one who first imposed names on things was most wise; in fact, he had more than human wisdom. Let the wisest man living, or even a collection of the wisest men in the world, demonstrate their skill and learning by giving names to all living creatures suitable to their natures and expressive of their qualities. They would quickly realize the loss they have incurred by sin. Adam was made perfect. The whole purpose of ruling the creatures and living to God, for which Adam was made, required knowledge of the nature of the one and the will of the other. All of this was lost by sin. The multiplication of tongues was imposed as a curse for a later rebellion. The whole design of learning is to disentangle the soul from this issue of sin. Ignorance, darkness, and blindness have come upon the understanding. Acquaintance with the works of God, spiritual and natural, has been lost. Alienation of communication has resulted from the multiplication of tongues. Unruly passions and affections, and innumerable darkening prejudices, have also come upon us. The aim and tendency of literature is to remove this confusion and corruption. It is to disentangle the mind in its competence, to recover an acquaintance with the works of God, and to reduce the effects of the curse of the division of tongues on the soul. Ignoring the "vanity and vexation of spirit," and the innumerable evils that attend this, in itself it is insufficient to attain its end. To this purpose I desire to observe two things:

(1.) The knowledge to be recovered was given to man for his

walk with God, and that was the supernatural end to which he was appointed. After he was furnished with all his endowments, the law of life and death was given to man so that he might know why he received them. Therefore, all knowledge in him was spiritualized and sanctified. In respect to its principle and end, even the knowledge that he had by nature was spiritual.

(2.) The loss of that knowledge is part of the curse that was inflicted on us for sin. Whatever we come short in from the state of the first man in innocence, whether it is in the loss of good or the addition of evil, it is all from the curse for sin. The blindness, ignorance, darkness, and deadness that are ascribed to us in the state of nature, are also part of the curse.

On these two considerations, it is most apparent that learning in itself cannot attain the end it aims at. For,

[1.] The light by which it is discovered is little, weak, obscure, imperfect, uncertain, and conjectural. Knowledge is not in the least measure spiritualized by this light, or brought into that order of living to God, and with God, in which it first lay. This is wholly beyond its reach. As to this end, the apostle assures us that the most men come to is darkness and folly, Rom. 1:21, 22. Who is not familiar with the profound inquiries, subtle arguments, acute insights, and admirable discoveries of Socrates, Plato, Aristotle, and others? What did they attain by all their studies and endeavors to help them walk with God? "*Emorantesan*," [NT:3471] says the apostle, "They became fools." The one who, by general consent, bears the crown of wisdom from them all, and with whom to have lived was counted an inestimable happiness, died like a fool, sacrificing a cock to AEsculapius. Another tells us that Jesus Christ alone is "the true Light" that lights us, John 1:9. None has any true light that is not immediately from him. After all the learning of men, if they have nothing else, they are still natural men. They do not perceive the things of God. Their light is still only darkness, and how great is that darkness! It is the Lord Jesus alone who is anointed to open the eyes of the blind. Men cannot spiritualize a notion, or make it glorifying to God. After all their endeavors, they are still blind and dark. They are darkness itself, knowing nothing as they should. I know how men of such lofty attainments are apt to say, "Are we blind also?" with great contempt for others. But God has blasted all their pride: "Where," he asks, "is the wise? Where is the scribe...," 1Cor. 1:20. I will not add what Paul has cautioned, seeming to condemn philosophy as fitted to spoil souls, or what Tertullian and other ancients have spoken of it. I am very confident that it was the abuse, and not the true use and advantage of it, that they opposed. But,

[2.] Because the darkness and ignorance that learning strives to remove has come upon us as a curse, learning is unable to remove it. Someone who has attained the greatest height of literature, if he does not have Christ, is as much under the curse of blindness, ignorance, stupidity, and dullness, as the poorest, silliest soul in the world. The curse is only removed in Christ who was made a curse for us. Everything that is penal is taken away only by the one on whom all our sins were placed for punishment. The more abilities the mind is furnished with, the more it embraces the curse, and the more it strengthens itself to act out its enmity against God. All that it receives only helps it to set up high thoughts and imaginations against the Lord Christ. So this knowledge comes short of what it is designed to attain, and therefore it cannot be the solid wisdom we are inquiring after.

There are a number of other things by which it would be easy to blur the face of this wisdom, such as its intricacy, difficulty, uncertainty, and unsatisfactoriness. It betrays its followers into accepting what they most profess to avoid, which is blindness and folly. I hope I will not need to add anything to clear myself for not giving due esteem and respect to literature. My intent is only to cast it down at the feet of Jesus Christ, and to set the crown upon his head.

2. Nor can the second part of the choicest wisdom outside of Christ attain the unique end to which it is appointed; and that is prudence in the management of civil affairs. No perishing thing is more glorious or useful for the common good of human kind. Now, the immediate end of this prudence is to keep the rational world in bounds and order, to draw circles around the sons of men, and to keep them from passing their allotted bounds and limits which might lead to their mutual disturbance and destruction. All kinds of trouble and disturbance arise from lack of regulation: one man breaks in on the rights, uses, interests, and relations of another, thus setting the world at variance. The purpose of all earthly wisdom is to cause all things to move in their proper sphere, just as the celestial orbs, despite their diverse and various motions, keep their own allotments within the compass of their assigned lines.

Now, it will be a very easy task to demonstrate that civil prudence is unable to attain this end. The present condition of affairs throughout the world, and those of former ages, will abundantly testify to this. But I will further reveal the vanity of it for this end in a few observations.

(1.) Through the righteous judgment of God lopping off the top flowers of the pride of men, it frequently comes to pass that those who are furnished with the greatest abilities of civil administration use it for purposes directly contrary end to their natural aim. From whom do we get, for the most part, all the commotions in the world, the breaking up of bounds, and setting the whole frame of nature on fire? Is it not from men such as these? Were men not so wise, perhaps the world would be quieter; the end of wisdom is to keep it quiet. This seems to be a curse that God has spread on the wisdom of the world.

(2.) God has leavened the wisdom and counsel of the wisest of the sons of men with folly and madness. This makes a constant path towards the advancement of his own glory. In the depth of their policy, men advise things as unsuitable to attain their ends as anything that might proceed out of the mouth of a child or a fool. They ensure their own disappointment and ruin better than anything that could be invented against them. "He destroys the wisdom of the wise, and brings to nothing the understanding of the prudent," 1Cor. 1:19. He largely describes this in Isa. 19:11-14. Drunkenness and staggering is the outcome of all their wisdom; and so the Lord gives them the spirit of giddiness. See also Job 5:12-14. They meet in the day-time when all things seem clear about them. One wonders how they could miss their way. Then God makes it darkness to such as these, Ps. 33:10. Hence God, as it were, sets them at work, and then undertakes their disappointment. Isa. 8:9, 10: "Go about your counsels," says the Lord, "and I will ensure that it comes to nothing." And Ps. 2:1-4, when men are deep at their plots and contrivances, God is said to hold them in derision, to laugh at them in scorn, seeing the poor worms industriously working out their own ruin. Never has this been clearer than in the days in which we live. Scarcely any wise men have been brought to destruction except by their own evident folly. Nor has the wisest counsel of most of them been one jot better than madness.

(3.) This wisdom, which should tend toward universal quietness, has almost constantly given universal disquiet to those in whom it has been most eminent. "In much wisdom is much grief," Eccles. 1:18. And in the issue of it, some have done away with themselves, such as Ahithophel; and many have been violently dispatched by others. There is indeed no end to the folly of this wisdom. The great men of the world destroy its reputation; really it is found in few of them. Events that are ascribed to their care, vigilance, and foresight are ordinary for the most part. These men do not contribute the least mite to their outcome. Inferior men, who have learned to adore what is above them, reverence the meetings and conferences of those in greatness and esteem. The weakness and folly of those who are revered is little known. Where this wisdom has been most eminent, it has dwelt so close to the borders of atheism, and been attended with such falseness and injustice, that it has made its possessors wicked and infamous.

I will not need to give any more instances to manifest the insufficiency of this wisdom to attain its unique and immediate end. The vanity of anything is that it comes short of the mark it aims at. It is far from being true and solid wisdom. On its forehead you may read "Disappointment."

This is the first reason why true wisdom cannot consist in either of these things, because they come short even of the particular and immediate ends they aim at.

(2) SECONDLY, both of these in conjunction, even with their utmost improvement, are not able to reach the true general end of wisdom. This assertion is also easy to demonstrate. But it is so professedly done by the one who had the largest portion of both of them of any of the sons of men (Solomon in his Preacher), that I will not insist on it any further.

Let me draw to a close. If true and solid wisdom is not to be found in these, if the pearl is not hidden in this field, and if these two are but vanity and disappointment, then it serves no purpose to seek true wisdom in anything else on earth. Therefore, with one accord, let us set the crown of this wisdom on the head of the Lord Jesus.

Let the reader review the tendency of this whole digression. Its aim is to draw our hearts to the more cheerful entertainment of, and delight in, the Lord Jesus. If all wisdom is laid up in him, and can only to be attained by having an interest in him, and if all things beside him and without him that lay claim to being wisdom are folly and vanity, then let those who would be wise learn where to rest their souls.

CHAPTER 4.

CONSEQUENTIAL AFFECTIONS FROM COMMUNION WITH CHRIST

The communion having begun between Christ and the soul, it is carried on by consequential affections, affections suiting such a relationship. Christ, having given himself to the soul, loves the soul; and the soul, having given itself to Christ, loves him also. Christ loves his own. He "loves them to the end," John 13:1; and the saints love Christ. They "love the Lord Jesus Christ in sincerity," Eph. 6:24.

Now the love of Christ, with which he follows his saints, consists in these four things:

    I. Delight.

    II. Valuation.

    III. Pity or compassion.

    IV. Bounty.

The love of the saints to Christ comes under these four things: Delight; Valuation; Chastity; and Duty. Two of these are of the same kind, and two of them are distinct. That is what is required in this relationship in which all things do not stand on equal terms.

I. The first thing on the part of Christ is *Delight*.

Delight is the flowing of love and joy, the rest and complacence of the mind in a suitable, desirable good that is enjoyed. Christ delights exceedingly in his saints: "As the bridegroom rejoices over the bride, so will your God rejoice over you," Isa. 62:5. Hence, he calls the day of his espousals, the day of the "gladness of his heart," Cant. 3:11. It is known that usually this is the most unmixed delight that the sons of men are made partakers of in their pilgrimage. The delight of the bridegroom in the day of his espousals is the greatest height that an expression of delight can be carried to. In Christ, this corresponds to the relationship that he takes us into. His heart is glad in us, without sorrow. And every day while we live is his wedding-day. It is said of him, Zeph. 3:17, "The Lord your God in the midst of you" (that is, dwelling among us and taking our nature, John 1:14) "is mighty. He will save. He will rejoice over you with joy. He will rest in his love. He will joy over you with singing." This is a full description of delight in all its parts, joy and exultation, rest and complacence. "I rejoiced," says he, "in the habitable parts of the earth, and my delights were with the sons of men," Prov. 8:31. The thoughts of communion with the saints were the joy of his heart from eternity.

A compact and agreement existed between his Father and him to have him divide a portion with the strong and save a remnant for his inheritance. His soul rejoiced in thoughts of the pleasure and delight he would take in them, when he would actually bring them into communion with himself. Therefore, in the preceding verse (8:30) it is said he was as "'amon." We say, "As one brought up with him," "*alumnus*;" the LXX render it "*harmodzousa*," and the Latin, with most other translations, "*cuncta componens*," or "*disponens*." The word, taken actively, signifies one whom another takes into his care to bring up, and has things disposed of for his advantage. This is how Christ took us then into his care, and rejoiced in thoughts of the execution of his trust. Concerning them he says, "Here will I dwell, and here will I make my habitation forever." He has chosen them for his temple and his dwelling-place, because he delights in them. This makes him take them so close to himself in every relationship. As he is God, they are his temple. As he is a king, they are his subjects; he is the king of saints. As he is a head, they are his body; he is the head of the church. As he is a first-born, he makes them his brethren; "he is not ashamed to call them brethren," Heb. 2:11.

I choose this one instance to prove this: Christ reveals his secrets, his mind, to his saints, and he enables them to reveal the secrets of their hearts to him. This is an evident demonstration of great delight. It was Samson's carnal delight in Delilah that prevailed with him to reveal to her what was of greatest concern to him. He would not hide his mind from her, even though it cost him his life. It is only a heart friend to whom we will open our heart. Nor is there, possibly, greater evidence of delight in close communion than this: we will reveal our heart to the one we take into society; we will not entertain him with things that are common and vulgarly known. And therefore have I chosen this instance, from among a thousand that might be given, of this delight of Christ in his saints.

He communicates his mind to his saints, and to them only. He communicates the counsel of his love, the thoughts and purposes of his heart for our eternal good. He communicates the ways of his grace, the workings of his Spirit, the rule of his scepter, and the obedience of his gospel. All spiritual revelation is by Christ. He is "the true Light that lights every man that comes into the world," John 1:9. He is the "Day-spring," the "Day-star," and the "Sun"; it is impossible for any light to exist but by him. It is from him that "the secret of the Lord is with those who fear him, and he shows them his covenant," Ps. 25:14. As he expresses it at large in John 15:14-15, "You are my friends, if you do what I command you. Henceforth I do not call you servants; for the servant does not know what his lord does: but I have called you friends; for all things that I have heard from my Father I have made known to you." He makes them his friends, and uses them as friends, as heart friends, in whom he is delighted. He makes known his entire mind to them, everything that his Father has committed to him to reveal as Mediator, Acts 20:24. And the apostle declares how this is done, 1Cor. 2:10, 11, "God has revealed these things to us by his Spirit; for we have received him, that we might know the things that are freely given us of God." He sends us his Spirit as he promised, to make known his mind to his saints, and to lead them into all truth. And from this the apostle concludes, "We have known the mind of Christ," verse 16; "for he uses us as friends, and declares it to us," John 1:18. There is nothing in the heart of Christ that concerns his friends, that he does not reveal to them. All his love, his good-will, the secrets of his covenant, the paths of obedience, and the mystery of faith, is told to them.

And all this is spoken in opposition to unbelievers, with whom he has no communion. These know nothing of the mind of Christ that they ought to know: "The natural man does not receive the things that are of God," 1Cor. 2:14. There is a wide difference between understanding the doctrine of the Scripture in the letter of it, and truly knowing the mind of Christ. We have this understanding by special unction from Christ, 1John 2:27, "We have an unction from the Holy One, and we know all things," 1John 2:20.

In this communion, the things that Christ reveals to those in whom he delights are under two headings:

1. Himself
2. His kingdom.

1. Himself. John 14:21, "He that loves me will be loved of my Father; and I will love him, and will manifest myself to him." He is saying, "I will manifest myself in all my graces, desirability, and loveliness; he will know me as I am, and such I will be to him: a Savior, Redeemer, the chief of ten thousand." He will be acquainted with the true worth and value of the pearl of price. Should others look at him as having neither form nor attractiveness, and being in no way desirable, he will manifest himself and his excellence to those in whom he is delighted. They will see him as altogether lovely. He will veil himself to all the world, but the saints will behold his beauty and his glory with open face. They will be translated into the image of that same glory, as by the Spirit of the Lord, 2Cor. 3:18.

2. His kingdom. They will be acquainted with the government of his Spirit in their hearts. They will also be acquainted with his rule and the administration of authority in his word and among his churches.

(1.) Thus, he manifests his delight in his saints. He communicates his secrets to them. He lets them know his person, his excellence, his grace, his love, his kingdom, his will, the riches of his goodness, and the bowels of his mercy. He does so more and more, while the world will not see or know any such thing.

(2.) He enables his saints to communicate their mind and reveal their souls to him, so that they may walk together as intimate friends. Christ knows the minds of all. He knows what is in man, and does not need any man to testify of him, John 2:25. He searches the hearts and tries the reins of all, Rev. 2:23. But all do not know how to communicate their mind to Christ. It will not comfort a man that Christ knows his mind; for he knows everyone's mind, whether they want him to or not. But it is consoling that a man can make his heart known to Christ. Hence the prayers of the saints are incense, aromatic. While those of others are like howling, cutting off a dog's neck, or offering swine's blood. They are an abomination to the Lord. Now, three things are required to enable a man to communicate his heart to the Lord Jesus:

[1.] *Assistance for the work*, for we cannot do it ourselves. And the saints have this assistance by the Spirit of Jesus. "Likewise the Spirit also helps our infirmities: for we know not what we should pray for as we ought; but the Spirit itself makes intercession for us with groanings that cannot be uttered. And he that searches the heart knows the mind of the Spirit, because he makes intercession for the saints according to the will of God," Rom. 8:26, 27. All attempts to have communion with God without the supplies of the Spirit, without his effectual working in our hearts, are of no value or purpose. This opening of our hearts to the Lord Jesus is what he exceedingly delights in. And from this comes that affectionate call of his to us, to encounter him in this way. Cant. 2:14, "O my dove, who is in the secret places of the stairs, let me see your countenance, let me hear your voice; for sweet is your voice, and your countenance is attractive." When the soul for some reason is driven to hide itself, neglected, in the most unlikely place, then he calls for this communication of the soul by prayer to him. In return, he gives the assistance of the Spirit of supplication.

[2.] *A way by which to approach* God with our desires. He has also provided this for us. John 14:5, 6, "Thomas says to Jesus, Lord, we know not where you go; and how can we know the way? Jesus says to him, I am the way; no man comes to the Father, but by me." The way we had to go to God at our creation is quite closed by sin. The sword of the law, enflamed by sin, turns every way to block all passages to communion with God (Gen. 3:24). Jesus Christ has "consecrated a new and living way" (for the saints) "through the veil, that is to say, his flesh," Heb. 10:20. He has consecrated and set it apart for believers, and for them alone. Others pretend to go to God with their prayers, but they do not come close to him. How can they possibly come to the end when they do not go in the way? Christ is the only way to the throne of grace; none comes to God but by him. "By him we have an access in one Spirit to the Father," Eph. 2:18. The saints have these two things, then, to open their hearts at the throne of grace. They have assistance and a way. The assistance of the Spirit (without which they are nothing), and the way of Christ's mediation (without which God is not to be approached).

[3.] *Boldness to go to God.* The voice of sinners in themselves, if acquainted with the terror of the Lord, asks, "Who among us will dwell with the devouring fire? Who among us will dwell with everlasting burnings?" Isa. 33:14. And no wonder! Shame and trembling before God are the proper consequences of sin. God will revenge that carnal, atheistic boldness which sinners outside of Christ use towards him. But now we have "boldness to enter into the holiest by the blood of Jesus, by a new and living way that he has consecrated for us through the veil, that is to say, his flesh: and having a high priest over the house of God, we may draw near with a true heart, in full assurance of faith," Heb. 10:19, 20. The truth is, such is the glory and terror of the Lord, and such is the infinite perfection of his holiness, that upon clearly seeing it, the soul concludes that it cannot serve him itself. There is no advantage in drawing close to him, except to add to the fierceness of our destruction. It is in Christ alone, because of his offering and intercession, that we have any boldness to approach to him.

The Lord Christ has provided these three advantages to the saints, in communicating their minds to him, because he delights in them. And because this is of great importance, I will give an example so that you may see the difference between spiritually revealing our minds to Christ in this acceptable manner, and praying only when convicted of sin, which others practice. The example I will give is from the assistance we have by the Spirit.

1st. The Spirit of Christ reveals our own wants to us, so that we may reveal them to him: "We do not know what we should pray for as we ought," Rom. 8:26. No teachings inferior to those of the Spirit of God are able to acquaint the soul with its own wants, burdens, and temptations. It is a heavenly discovery to know them. The prayer of someone who has this assistance is more than half made before he begins to pray. His conscience is affected by what he has to do. His mind and spirit contend within him, especially where he finds himself most straitened. He brings his burden on his shoulders, and unloads it on the Lord Christ. He finds where he is dead, dull, cold, unbelieving, and tempted beyond his strength, where the light of God's countenance is wanting. He does not do this because of some troubling conviction, but because of a holy sense and weariness of sin. And the soul has a sense of all these by the Spirit, an inexpressible sense and experience. Without this, prayer is not prayer. Men's voices may be heard, but they do not speak from their hearts. The *sense* of want is the *spring* of desire. Without this sense, given by the Holy Spirit, there is neither desire nor prayer.

2dly. The expressions and words of such wanting people may come far short of the laboring of their hearts. Therefore, in and after their supplications "the Spirit makes intercession with sighs and groans that cannot be uttered." Other's words may go far beyond their hearts. It would be well if their spirits matched their expressions. Someone who has this assistance of the Spirit can provide no clothing broad enough to cover the desires of his heart. And so, in his best and most fervent supplications, he is doubly dissatisfied with them: 1. They are not a righteousness he can rest on; if God marked what was amiss in them, they could not withstand the trial. 2. His heart is not poured out in them; they were not delivered in proportion to the holy desires and labors they expressed, even though in Christ he may be greatly refreshed by them. The more he speaks, the more he finds he has left unspoken.

3dly. The intercession of the saints, thus assisted, is according to the mind of God. That is, the saints are guided by the Spirit to make requests for those things which it is God's will for them to desire, which he knows are good for them, and which are useful and suited to them in their current condition. There are many ways by which we may know when we make our supplications according to the will of God. I will give an example of one. It is when we ask according to the promise. When our prayers are regulated by the promise, we make them according to the will of God. So David prayed in Ps. 119:49, "Remember the word on which you have caused me to hope." He prays, and regulates his desire by the word of promise in which he trusted. But men may ask for what is in the promise, and yet not have their prayers regulated by it. They may pray for what is in the promise, but not as it is in the promise. So James says, some "ask and receive not, because they ask amiss, so that they may spend it on their lusts," chap. 4:3. Although we may request the things that God would have us request, if we do not request them in the way and for the purpose he desires, then we ask amiss.

Two things are required to pray for the things in the promise, as they are in the promise:

(1st.) We must look at them as promised in Christ. That is, the only reason we have to hope for attaining the things we ask for, is the mediation and purchase of Christ in whom all the promises are found. This is what it means to ask the Father in Christ's name. God is the father, the fountain of what we ask for, and Christ is the procurer.

(2dly.) We must ask for them for the purpose of the promise, not to spend on our lusts. When we ask pardon for sin, while secretly intending in our hearts to continue in sin, we are asking for the choicest mercy of the covenant only to spend it on our lusts. The apostle tells us the purpose of the promise in 2Cor. 7:1, "Having these promises, let us cleanse ourselves from all pollution of the flesh and spirit, perfecting holiness in the fear of God." When we ask what is in the promise, as it is in the promise, for this purpose of the promise, then our supplications are according to the will of God.

This is the first conjugal affection that Christ exercises towards believers. He delights in them, which is evident from the example given. In return, to carry on the communion between them, the saints delight in Christ. He is their joy, their crown, their rejoicing, their life, food, health, strength, desire, righteousness, salvation, and blessedness. Without him they have nothing; in him they will find all things. Gal. 6:14, "God forbid that I should glory, save in the cross of our Lord Jesus Christ." From the foundation of the world, he has been the hope, expectation, desire, and delight of all believers. The promise of Christ was all that God needed to give Adam to relieve and comfort him in his inexpressible distress, Gen. 3:15. Eve perhaps thought that the promised seed was her first-born when she said, "I have gotten a man from the LORD" and this was the basis of her joy, Gen. 4:1. Noah was given to Lamech as a type of Christ and means of salvation, for which Lamech cries out, "This same one will comfort us concerning our work and the toil of our hands, because of the ground that the LORD cursed," Gen. 5:29. He was rejoicing in the one who would take away the curse by being made a curse for us. When Abraham was in the height of his glory, returning from the conquest of the kings of the east, God appears to him with a glorious promise. Gen. 15:1, "Fear not, Abram: I am your shield, and your exceeding great reward." What could his soul desire more than that? Alas! He cries what Reuben later cries upon the loss of Joseph, "The child is not, and where will I go?" Verse 2, "Lord God, what will you give me, seeing I go childless?" "You have promised that in my seed all the earth will be blessed. If I do not have that seed, Ah! What good will all other things do me?" For this reason it is said that he "rejoiced to see the day of Christ; he saw it, and was glad," John 8:56. The thought of the coming of Christ, which he looked on at the distance of two thousand years, was the joy and delight of his heart. In blessing his sons, Jacob lifted up his spirit when he came to Judah in whom he considered the Shiloh to come, Gen. 49:8, 9. A little afterward, wearied by the forethought and consideration of his posterity's distress, he turns to the great delight of his soul for relief: "I have waited for your Salvation, O God." He waited for the *one* who was to be the salvation of his people. Such examples are endless. Old Simeon sums up the whole of it: Christ is God's salvation, and Israel's glory, Luke 2:30, 31. Whatever was called the glory of old, was either Christ himself or a type of him. The glory of man is their delight. Hence, in Haggai 2:7 he is called "The Desire of all nations." They desire and long after the one whom their soul loves and delights in. The saints' delight in him is made his eminent description. Mal. 3:1: "The Lord whom you seek will suddenly come to his temple, the messenger of the covenant in whom you delight." "He whom you seek, in whom you delight," is the description of Christ. He is their delight and the person they desire.

In the pattern of communion with Jesus Christ described in the Canticles, this delight is insisted on abundantly. The spouse tells us that she sits down under his shadow with great delight, Cant. 2:3. And she manifests that this delight is vigorous and active in several ways. We should labor to find our hearts likewise delighted in him:

1. She took great care to keep his company and society once she obtained it. Cant. 2:7, "I charge you, O you daughters of Jerusalem, by the roes and by the hinds of the field, do not stir nor awake my love till he pleases." Having obtained sweet communion with Christ, as described in the preceding verses, here she expresses her delight in that communion and her desire to continue it. Therefore, following on the former allusion, she speaks as one would to her companion, someone at rest with the one she loved. "I charge you by all that is dear to you, by the things you most delight in, things that are most lovely among the creatures, all the pleasant and desirable things that you can think of, that you do not disturb him." Her entire aim and desire is that nothing of sin or provocation may happen to cause Christ to depart from her. She wants nothing to remove him from that arrangement in which he seemed to take rest in her: "O do not stir my love until he pleases!" that is, never. Love itself, in the abstract, is represented here by "*ha'ahavah*," [OT:160]. That word is often used to express a "pathos," or earnest affection. Once a believer's soul has obtained sweet and real communion with Christ, it looks around, watching out for any temptation, any way by which sin might approach to disturb his enjoyment of his dear Lord and Savior, his rest and his desire. It charges itself not to omit anything, or do anything, that may interrupt the communion that has been obtained! Temptations commonly enter through delightful diversions from actual communion with Christ. They tend to disturb that rest and contentment which Christ takes in

us. Therefore, our strong and active desire is that our companions do not divert us by their proposals or allurements into any frame that Christ cannot delight or rest in. A believer who has Christ in his arms is like someone who has found great spoils, or a pearl of great price. He looks around in every direction, fearing anything that may deprive him of it. Riches make men watchful. Sensing the actual possession of Christ, in whom all the riches and treasure of God are found, will make men look around to ensure keeping him. The line of choicest communion is the line of greatest spiritual desire: carelessness in the pretended enjoyment of Christ, is manifest evidence of a false heart.

2. The spouse manifests her delight in him by her utmost impatience at his absence. She desires still nearer communion with him. Chap. 8:6, "Set me as a seal upon your heart, as a seal upon your arm: for love is as strong as death; jealousy is as cruel as the grave, its coals are coals of fire with a most vehement flame." The allusion is doubtless from the high priest of the Jews, in his spiritual representation of the church before God. He had a breastplate which he is said to wear on his heart, Ex. 28:29. In it, the names of the children of Israel were engraved in the manner of seals or signets. He wore them for a memorial before the Lord. He had the same on his shoulders or arms, Ex. 28:11-12. Both represented the priesthood of Christ who bears the names of all who belong to him before his Father in the "holy of holies," Heb. 9:24. The seal on the heart is near. It is inward, tender love and care, which makes an impression and an image on the heart of the thing that is so loved. The spouse is saying "Set me as a seal upon your heart. Let me be constantly fixed in your most tender and affectionate love. Let me always have a place in your heart. Let me have an engraving, a mighty impression of love upon your heart that will never be obliterated." The soul is never satisfied with thoughts of Christ's love for it. Its language is, "O that it were more, that it were more! That I were as a seal on his heart!" The soul knows on serious thoughts that the love of Christ is inconceivable, and cannot be increased. But it would devise a way to work up itself to understanding it. And therefore she adds here, "Set me as a seal upon your arm." The heart is the fountain, but it is closed and hidden. The arm is for manifesting and exercising power. Says the spouse, "Let your love be manifested to me in your tender and powerful persuasion of me." Two things are evident in this request. First, Christ's continuing mindfulness of the soul: its condition is still in his eye, and engraved on his arm, Isa. 49:15, 16. He exalts his power to preserve it, which is suitable to the love his heart has for it. Second, Christ's manifestation of his hidden love and care for the soul: it is being made visible on his arm, or becoming evident by its fruit. This is what she wants to be assured of. Without this sense of assurance, no rest can be obtained.

The reason she gives for her earnest supplication, is what principally evinces her delight in him: "Love is strong as death, jealousy is cruel as the grave," or "hard as hell" Cant. 8:6; [OT:7186 *hard*; 7585 *sheol*]. This is the intent of the loftily presented metaphors in this and the following verses: "I am not able to bear the expressions of my love to you, unless I may always have society and fellowship with you. There is no satisfying my love without it. It is like the grave that still says *give*, give. Death is not satisfied without its prey. If it does not have its whole desire, it has nothing at all. Nor can it be withstood in its appointed season; no ransom will be accepted. That is how my love is. If I do not have you wholly, then I have nothing. Nor can the entire world bribe or divert my love. It can no more be turned aside than death can in its time. Also, I am not able to bear my jealous thoughts: I fear you do not love me, that you have forsaken me, because I know I do not deserve to be loved. These thoughts are hard as hell; they give my soul no rest. If I do not find myself on your heart and arm, then I am like someone who lies down on a bed of coals" [OT:7565 "a live coal"]. This argues a holy greediness of delight.

3. She further manifests this delight by her anxiety, concern, and agitation at his loss and withdrawal. We bewail the loss of someone we delight in, but easily bear the absence of someone whose presence does not delight. Her state is revealed in Cant. 3:1-3, "Twisting on my bed, I sought the one whom my soul loves. I sought him, but did not find him. I will rise now, and go about the city. In the streets and the broadways I will seek the one whom my soul loves. I sought him, but did not find him. The watchmen that go about the city found me. I said to them, 'Have you seen the one my soul loves?'" With the soul, it is night during times of darkness, trouble, or affliction. Whenever Christ is absent, it is night for a believer. Christ is the sun. If his light goes down for them, if his beams are eclipsed, if in his light they see no light, then it is all darkness for them. Whether the coming night of trouble made her discover Christ's absence, or the absence of Christ made it night for her, is not expressed here. I rather think the latter, because, setting that aside, all things seem to be well with her. The absence of Christ will indeed make it night, dark as darkness itself, even in the midst of all other glowing consolations. But is the spouse content with this dispensation? She is upon her bed, that is, a bed of ease (as this book uses the phrase). But in the absence of Christ, a believer finds no peace, no opportunity for ease and rest. Though he is on his bed, having nothing to disquiet him, he does not rest if Christ, who is his rest, is not there. She "sought him." Seeking Christ by night on the bed means alone, in immediate inquest, and in the dark. This has two parts: searching our own souls for the cause of his absence; and secondly, searching the promises for his presence.

111

(1.) The soul longs to have Christ warming, cherishing, and reviving it with love, being close to it, supping with it, always filling its thoughts with himself, dropping myrrh and sweet tastes of love into it. When, on the contrary, other thoughts crowd in and trouble the heart, and Christ is not close when the soul seeks him, it quickly inquires into the cause of all this. It calls itself to account for what it has done, and how it has behaved, to cause Christ to withdraw himself. Here it accomplishes a diligent search. It considers the love, tenderness, and kindness of the Lord Jesus, and what delight he takes in abiding with his saints. And so his departure is not without cause and provocation. "How," it asks, "have I demeaned myself, that I have lost my Beloved? Where have I been wandering after other lovers?" And when the miscarriage is found out, the soul abounds in revenge and indignation.

(2.) Having driven this to some point, the soul then applies itself to the promises of the covenant in which Christ is most graciously exhibited. It considers one and then ponders another to find a taste of him. It considers diligently whether it can see the delightful countenance and favor of Christ in them or not. But now, as it often happens, the soul may find nothing but the carcass, the bare letter in the promise. If the soul comes to this discovery, as it might come to the empty grave of Christ, it may be said "He is risen, he is not here." The soul is amazed and does not know what to do. It is like a man who has a jewel of great price with no occasion to use it. He lays it aside in what he supposes is a safe place. In agony and extreme want he may seek his jewel. If he does not find it in the place he expected, he will be filled with amazement. He does not know what to do. So it is with this pearl of the gospel. After a man has sold all that he has for it, and enjoyed it for a season, to have it missing in a time of need must necessarily perplex him. So it was with the spouse here. "I sought him," she says, "but I did not find him." This is a thing that sometimes happens to us in our communion with Christ.

But what does she now do? Does she give up and search no more? No! She says, verse 2, "'I will arise;' I will not give over. I must have Christ or die. I will now arise," (or, 'let me arise,') "and go about this business."

[1.] She resolves to pursue another course than her previous one, a more vigorous inquest: "I will arise and make use of means other than those of private prayer, meditation, self-searching, and inquiring into the promises," This course carries two things with it,

1st. *Resolution*, and a zealous, violent throwing off of the frame in which she lost her love. "'I will arise;' I will not rest in this frame. I am lost if I do." So, sometimes God calls his church to arise and shake itself out of the dust. Do not abide in that condition.

2dly. *Diligence.* "I will now take another course; I will leave no way unattempted, no means untried, by which I may possibly recover communion with my Beloved."

This is the condition of a soul that does not find the wanted presence of Christ in its private and more retired inquiries. It is dull in prayer, wandering in meditations, rare in thoughts of him. "I will not bear this frame: I will, in his strength, vigorously pursue whatever way God has appointed until this frame is altered and I find my Beloved."

[2.] Then there is the path she puts herself on as she goes about the city. Not to strain the allegory too far, the city intended here is the city of God, the church. Passing through the broad and narrow streets is the diligent inquiry that the spouse makes in all the paths and ordinances that are given to the church. This is the next thing the soul addresses itself to in the absence of Christ: when it does not find him in any private endeavors, it vigorously applies to the ordinances of public worship. It looks after Christ in prayer, preaching, and administration of the seals. Indeed, the great inquiry believers make in every ordinance is in pursuit of Christ. The more they find of him, the more sweetness and refreshment they have, and no more. Especially when deserted, they are motivated to inquire after him. They listen to every word, every prayer, to find if anything of Christ appears in them: any light, life, or love from him. "Oh, that Christ would meet me at length in this or that sermon, and restore my poor heart to some sight of his love, to some taste of his kindness!" The anxiety of a believer is inexpressible when he does not find Christ's former presence, whether for grace or consolation. The frame of such a heart is couched in the redoubling of the expression, "I sought him, I sought him" (Cant. 3:1). It presents an inconceivable passion, and a suitably industrious desire. Being disappointed at home in her search, the spouse proceeds into the city.

Yet notice this also: "She sought him, but did not find him." It sometimes happens that nothing will help. "They will seek him, and not find him" (Prov. 1:28). They will not come close to him. Those who enjoy anything of the presence of Christ should take heed what they do. If they provoke Christ to depart, if they lose him, it may cost them many a bitter inquiry before they find him again. They may pray and meditate and search the promises in private. They may heed all ordinances in public with earnestness and diligence. It is a sad condition when a soul does all this just to get one glimpse of the face of Jesus Christ, and it is all in vain.

What now follows this set of affairs? Verse 3, "The watchmen found me..." These watchmen of the city of God are the watchmen and officers of the church. It is a sad commentary that the Holy Spirit sometimes takes unkind notice of them in this book. Plainly, in 5:7 they turn persecutors. It was Luther's saying, *"Nunquam periclitatur religio nisi inter reverendissimos."* "Never risk things religious unless you are among the reverent." Here they have a gentler temper. Seeing the poor disconsolate soul, they seem to take notice of her condition.

It is the duty of faithful watchmen to take notice of poor, troubled, and deserted souls. They are not to keep at a distance, but be willing to assist. Someone who is truly pressed because of Christ's absence cannot cover her love. She must inquire after him: "Have you seen the one whom my soul loves?" "This is my condition: I have had sweet enjoyment of my blessed Jesus, but he is now withdrawn from me. Can you help me? Can you guide me to my consolation? Are you acquainted with him? When did you see him? How did he seem to you?" All these exertions in his absence are sufficient to reveal the soul's delight in the presence of Christ. Go one step further, to her rediscovery of him, and this delight will be even more evident. Verses 4, 5, "It was but a little while after I passed them, that I found the one whom my soul loves: I held him and would not let him go until I had brought him into my mother's house, and into the chamber of the one who conceived me. I charge you, O you daughters of Jerusalem..."

First, she tells us "She found him." By what ways and means is not expressed. This often happens in our communion with Christ. When private and public means fail, and the soul can do nothing but wait silently and walk humbly, Christ appears, to evidence his grace. Let us not give up when we are in this condition. When all ways are past, and the summer and harvest are gone without relief, when neither bed nor watchmen can assist, let us wait a little, and we will see the Salvation of God. Sometimes Christ honors his immediate and absolute actings with his presence. Though ordinarily he crowns his ordinances, Christ often manifests himself immediately, apart from his ordinances, to those who wait for him in them. Whether he will manifest himself to those who despise those ordinances, I do not know. Though he will meet men unexpectedly in his way, yet he will not meet them at all outside of it. Let us wait as he has appointed. Let him appear as he pleases. How she deals with him when found is neatly declared: "She held him, and would not let him go..." These are all expressions of the greatest joy and delight imaginable.

The sum is this: having at length come once more to enjoy sweet communion with Christ, the soul lays fast hold on him by faith. *"Kratein,"* [OT:270, NT:2722] "to hold fast," is an act of faith. It refuses to part with him any more. In vehement love, it tries to keep him in ordinances in its mother's house, the church of God. And so it uses all means to confirm the mutual love between Christ and her. All the expressions and all the allusions that are used, evidence the utmost capacity of the soul to delight in him. What is it that the saints long for, and that they rejoice in? What is it that completely satisfies them, and that gives sweet contentment to their spirits, in every condition? Whose loss do they fear, and whose absence can they not bear? Is it not their Beloved, and he alone?

They further manifest this by their delight in everything that uniquely belongs to Christ in this world. For his sake, in whom we delight, we also delight in everything that belongs to him. Christ's great interest in this world lies in his people and his ordinances, his household and their provision. Now the saints exceedingly delight in both of these for his sake. Take an example in both these kinds of delight in one man, namely, David. "In the saints and the excellent" (or noble) "of the earth is all my delight; my delight is in them," Ps. 16:3. Christ says of his church that she is "*Hephzibah*," Isa. 62:4, "My delight is in her." Here, David says the same, "*Hephzibah*, "My delight is in them." As Christ delights in his saints, so do they delight in one another, on his account. "Here," says David, "is all my delight." Whatever contentment he took in anyone else, it was nothing in comparison to the delight he took in the people of God. Hence, mention is made of "laying down our lives for the brethren" (1Jn. 3:16), or doing so for any common cause in which the interest of the community of the brethren lies. As for the ordinances, consider David again. Psalms 42, 48, and 84 are replete with testimonies of his delight in them.

This is the first consequential act of conjugal affection in this communion between Christ and believers. He delights in them, and they delight in him. He delights in their prosperity; he takes pleasure in it. They delight in his honor and glory, and in his presence with them. For his sake, they delight in his servants (even though they are condemned by the world) as the most excellent and noble in the world. And they delight in his ordinances, which are foolishness to the world, as the wisdom of God.

CHAPTER 5.

OTHER CONSEQUENTIAL AFFECTIONS

II. The love of Christ consists in *Valuation*.

Christ values his saints; he values believers. Having taken them into communion with himself, he shows this second conjugal affection towards them. I will not need to demonstrate this at length; heaven and earth are full of its evidences. A few considerations will give life to the assertion. If you consider them *absolutely*, and *in comparison to others*, then you will see what valuation he puts on them:

1. *Absolutely* - All that he ever did or does, all that he ever underwent or suffered as mediator, was for the sake of believers. These things were so great and grievous that, if he not valued them beyond expression, he would never have undertaken their performance. Take a few instances:

(1.) For their sakes he was "made flesh," Jn. 1:14, or "manifested in the flesh" 1Tim. 3:16. "Forasmuch then as the children are partakers of flesh and blood, he also himself likewise took part of the same," Heb. 2:14. The apostle aggravates the height of this valuation in verse 16. "Verily he did not take on the nature of angels, but he took on him the seed of Abraham." He had no such esteem of angels. You may take *"epilamtanestai,"* [NT:1949] to mean "take," or "take hold of," as our translators did. They supplied the word "nature," and referred the whole to Christ's incarnation. He took our nature on him, and not the nature of angels. Or you may take it as *"analamtanestai,"* to "help." He did not help or succor fallen angels, but he did help and succor the seed of Abraham. And so consider this as the fruit of Christ's incarnation. It is all the same as it applies to our present business. He prefers the seed of Abraham before that of angels. It plainly expresses his valuing saints above angels. Observe that he came to help the seed of Abraham, that is, believers. His esteem and valuation is for them only.

(2.) For their sakes he was made flesh in such a way that there was an emptying, an exinanition of himself, and an eclipsing of his glory. He became poor for them, 2Cor. 8:9, "You know the grace of our Lord Jesus Christ, that, though he was rich, yet for our sakes he became poor." Being rich in eternal glory with his Father, John 17:5, he became poor for believers. The same person that was rich was also poor. By contrasting it to the poverty he undertook as a man, it is evident that the riches meant here can only be those of the Deity. This is more fully expressed in Phil. 2:6-7. "Who being in the form of

116

God, counted it no robbery to be equal to God, but he emptied himself, taking the form of a servant, and being made in the fashion of a man, and found in form as a man." The "form of God" here is the essence of the Deity. A number of things inevitably evince themselves from this, such as,

[1.] In that form, he was equal to God, that is, his Father. Now, nothing but God is equal to God, not even Christ as mediator in his greatest glory. Nothing but what is infinite is equal to what is infinite.

[2.] The form of God is opposed to the form of a servant. The form of a servant is called the "fashion of a man" in verse 8. That fashion is the one in which he was found when he gave himself to death, in which as a man he poured out his blood and died. "*Morfen doulou laton*," (he "took the form of a servant"), is expounded in the next words, "*en homoiomati antropon genomenos*," an expression used to represent his incarnation, Rom. 8:3. God sent him "*en homoiomati sarkos hamartias*." In taking on true flesh, he was in the "likeness of sinful flesh." Now, in thus doing, it is said "*heautou ekenose*," "he humbled himself, emptied himself, made himself of no reputation." In the very taking on of flesh there was a condescension, a debasing of the person of the Son of God. It could not be any other way. If God humbled himself to "behold the things that are in heaven, and in the earth," Ps. 113:6, then certainly it was an inconceivable condescension and abasement, not only to behold, but to take upon himself our nature in personal union. Though nothing could possibly diminish the essential glory of the Deity, yet by this person appearing in the fashion of a man, and in the form of a servant, the manifestation of the glory of the Deity was eclipsed. He appeared as quite another thing than what indeed he was, and had been from eternity. Hence, he prays that his Father would "glorify him with the glory he had with him before the world was," John 17:5, to manifest that glory. And so, though the divine nature was not abased, the person was.

(3.) For the sakes of the believers, he so humbled and emptied himself by taking on flesh as to become a servant. In the eyes of the world he was of no esteem or account, but he was a true and real servant to the Father. For their sakes, he humbled himself and became obedient. All that he did and suffered in his life comes under this consideration and may be divided into these three areas: [1.] Fulfilling all righteousness. [2.] Enduring all manner of persecutions and hardships. [3.] Doing all manner of good to the point of exhaustion. For their sakes, he took on a life and course that is pointed to in Heb. 5:7, 8. It was a life of prayers, tears, fears, obedience, and suffering; and all of this was done with cheerfulness and delight. He called his employment his "meat and drink," and still professed that the law of this obedience was in his heart, that he was content to do this will of God. The one who will sorely revenge the least opposition to him by others, was content to undergo anything, all things, for believers.

(4.) He does not limit himself to this, but for their sakes he becomes obedient to death, the death of the cross. So he professes to his Father in John 17:19, "For their sakes I sanctify myself." He is saying, "I dedicate myself as an offering, as a sacrifice, to be killed and slain." This was his aim in all the former obedience: that he might die. He was born, and lived, so that he might die. He valued believers above his life. If we pause to consider a little what was in this death that he underwent for them, we would perceive what a price indeed he put upon them. The curse of the law was in it. The wrath of God was in it. The loss of God's presence was in it. It was a fearful cup that he tasted and drank of, that they might never taste it. A man would not for ten thousand worlds be willing to undergo what Christ underwent for us in that one event of desertion from God, even if it were no more distressing than what a mere creature might possibly endure. What our thoughts should be about this, Christ himself tells us in John 15:13. "Greater love has no man than this, that a man lay down his life for his friends." It is impossible to have any greater demonstration or evidence of love than this. What more can anyone do? And yet he tells us in Rom. 5:8 that this act of love is even further heightened. "God commends his love toward us, in that, while we were yet sinners, Christ died for us." When he did this for us we were sinners, and enemies, whom he might justly have destroyed. What more can be done? To die for us when we were sinners! Such a death, in such a manner, attended with such wrath and curses, a death accompanied by the worst that God ever threatened sinners with, argues as high a valuation of us as the heart of Christ himself was capable of.

For one to part with his glory, his riches, his ease, his life, his love from God, to undergo loss, shame, wrath, curse, and death for another, is evidence of a dear valuation. And it was all on our account, we are informed, Heb. 12:2. Certainly Christ had such a dear esteem of believers that rather than let them perish, and not be his, and not partake of his glory, he would part with all he had for their sakes, Eph. 5:25, 26.

There will be no end if I go through all the instances of Christ's valuation of believers, what he has done, what he does in his intercession, what he delivers them from, and what he procures for them. They all point out one thing: believers are the apple of his eye, his jewel, his diadem, his crown.

2. *In comparison to others.* All the world is nothing to Christ in comparison to the saints. They are his garden while the rest of the world is a wilderness. Cant. 4:12, "A garden enclosed is my sister, my spouse; a spring shut up, a fountain sealed." They are his inheritance while the rest are his enemies, and of no regard with him. So it says in Isa. 43:3, 4. "I am the LORD your God, the Holy One of Israel, your Savior: I gave Egypt for your ransom, Ethiopia and Seba for you. Since you were precious in my sight, you have been honorable, and I have loved you, therefore I will give men for you, and people for your life." The reason Christ deals with his church this way, in parting with all others for her, is because he loves her. She is precious and honorable in his sight; thus he puts this great esteem upon her. Indeed, he disposes of all nations and their interests according to the good of believers. Amos 9:9 says that in sifting the nations, the eye of God is upon the house of Israel; not a grain of them will perish. Look to heaven; angels are appointed to minister for them, Heb. 1:14. Look to the world; the nations in general are either blessed for the sake of believers, or destroyed on their account. They are preserved to test them, or rejected for their cruelty towards believers. The nations will receive from Christ their final doom according to their deportment towards these despised ones of his. For the sake of believers, the pillars of the earth are borne up, and patience is exercised towards the perishing world. In a word, there is not the meanest, weakest, poorest believer on earth, that Christ does not prize more than all the world. If our hearts were filled with thoughts of this, it would go far toward consoling us.

In response to this, believers also value Jesus Christ. They esteem him above all the world, and all things in the world. You have been acquainted with this before, in the account that was given of their delight in him and their inquiry after him. In their hearts, they continually say of him, as David did, "Whom do I have in heaven but you? And I desire none upon earth beside you." Ps. 73:25. Neither heaven nor earth will provide them an object to delight in that compares with him.

1. They value him above all other things and persons. Said one, "Christ and a dungeon, Christ and a cross, is infinitely sweeter to their souls than a crown or a scepter without him." So it was with Moses, Heb. 11:26, "He esteemed the reproach of Christ greater riches than the treasures in Egypt." The reproach of Christ is the worst consequence that the wickedness of the world or the malice of Satan can bring upon his followers. In those days, the treasures of Egypt were the greatest in the world. Moses despised the very best of the world, for the worst of the cross of Christ. Indeed, Christ has told believers that if they love anything better than him, father or mother, they are not worthy of him (Matt. 10:37). Despising all things for Christ is the very first lesson of

the gospel. "Give away all, take up the cross and follow me," was the way by which he tried his disciples of old. If there is not the same mind and heart in us, we are none of his.

2. They value him above their lives. Acts 20:24, "My life is not dear, that I may perfect my course with joy, and the ministry I have received of the Lord Jesus." Paul says in effect, "Let life and all go, so that I may serve him, and when all is done, enjoy him, and be made like him." It is known what is reported of Ignatius when he was led to martyrdom: "Let what will come upon me, only so I may obtain Jesus Christ." Hence, those of old rejoiced when whipped, scourged, and put to shame for his sake, Acts 5:41; Heb. 11. All is welcome that comes from him, or for him. The life they have to live, and the death they have to die, is little, is light, upon thinking of the one who is the stay of their life and the purpose of their death. Were it not for the refreshment they receive daily by thoughts of him, they could not live. Their lives would be a burden to them. Their thoughts of enjoying Christ made them cry with Paul, "Oh that we were dissolved!" (2Cor. 5:1). A number of things have rendered this truth clear to men and angels. There are the stories of the martyrs both old and recent, the sufferers witnessing to him under the dragon and under the false prophet, the neglect of life in women and children on his account, and their contempt of torments while his name sweetened all.

3. They value him above all spiritual excellence, and all other righteousness. Phil. 3:7, 8, "Those things which were advantage to me, I esteemed loss for the excellence of the knowledge of Christ Jesus my Lord; for whose sake I have lost all things, and do esteem them common, that I may gain Christ, and be found in him." Paul recounted his excellence, and the spiritual privileges he enjoyed in his Judaism, participation in which made the rest of his countrymen despise the world and look upon themselves as God's only acceptable people. They rested on these things for their righteousness. The apostle tells us of his esteem for these things compared to the Lord Jesus. They are "loss and dung." For many years he had been a zealot of the law, seeking righteousness by works, Rom. 9:32. He instantly served God day and night to obtain the promise, Acts 26:7, He lived in all good conscience from his youth, Acts 23. All the while, he was very zealous for God and his institutions. But now he willingly casts away all these things, and looks upon them as loss and dung. He was not only content to be without them, but for the purpose for which he sought them, he abhorred them all. When men are strongly convinced of their duty, they will labor many years to keep a good conscience. They will pray, and hear, and do good, and deny themselves, and be zealous for God. They will labor with all their might to please him, and so at length come to enjoy him. Men would rather part with all the world, life and all,

than with what they have wrought in this way. You know how unwilling we are to part with anything we have labored and beaten our heads about? How much more is this true when the things are so excellent, such as our duty to God, blamelessness in our life, hope of heaven and the like, which we have beaten our hearts about. But now, when Christ appears to the soul, and when he is known in his excellence, all these things that may have been gained without him have their paint washed off. Their beauty fades. Their desirability vanishes. The soul is not only content to part with them all, but it puts them away as a defiled thing. It cries, "In the Lord Jesus only is my righteousness and glory." Among innumerable testimonies to this is Prov. 3:13-15. "Happy is the man that finds wisdom, and the man that gets understanding. For the merchandise of it is better than the merchandise of silver, and the gain of it than fine gold. She is more precious than rubies. All the things that you can desire are not to be compared to her." The Holy Spirit is speaking of Jesus Christ, the Wisdom of God, the eternal Wisdom of the Father; this is evident from the description that is given in Prov. 8. He and his ways are better than silver and gold, rubies, and all desirable things. As in the gospel, he likens himself to the "pearl in the field" that, when the merchantman finds it, he sells all that he has to purchase it. All goes for Christ; all righteousness without him, all ways of religion; all goes for that one pearl. The glory of his Deity, the excellence of his person, his all-conquering desirability, ineffable love, wonderful undertaking, unspeakable condescensions, effectual mediation, complete righteousness, all of these lie in their eyes, ravish their hearts, fill their affections, and possess their souls.

This, then, is the SECOND mutual conjugal affection between Christ and believers.

On the part of Christ, it may be separated into two categories:

1. All that he parted with, all that he did, all that he suffered, and all that he does as mediator is because of his love for and his esteem of believers. He parted with the greatest glory, underwent the greatest misery, and does the greatest works that ever were, because he loves his spouse, because he values believers. What more can be said? How little we fathom the depth of what has been said! How unable we are to look into its mysterious recesses! He so loves and so values his saints that, having from eternity undertaken to bring them to God, he rejoices his soul in the thoughts of it. He pursues his design through heaven and hell, life and death, by suffering and doing, in mercy and with power; and does not cease until he brings it to perfection.

2. He so values them that he will not lose any of them to eternity, though all the world should combine to take them out of his hand. When in the days of his flesh he foresaw what opposition, what danger,

121

what rocks they would meet with, he cried out, "Holy Father, keep them," John 17:11. "Do not let one of them be lost;" and he tells us plainly in John 10:28, that no man will take his sheep out of his hand. Because he was then in the form of a servant, it could be supposed that he might not be able to hold them. And so he tells them true, as to his present condition of carrying on the work of mediation, his "Father was greater than he." Therefore he committed them to him, and none could take them out of his Father's hand, John 10:29. Although the world with its afflictions and persecutions may be conquered, these are from without. There remains the issue of security against sin from within. By the assistance of Satan, it may prevail against them to their ruin. And so Christ has taken care that sin itself will not destroy them. He has provided against Satan in his promise that the gates of hell will not prevail against them. In this, the depth of his love is to be contemplated. Despite the fact that his holy soul hates every sin (it is a burden, an abomination, and a new wound to him), his poor spouse is sinful. Believers are full of sins, failings, and infirmities. Christ hides them all, covers them all, bears with them all, rather than lose any of the believers. His power to preserve them from such sins is a remedy not provided for in the covenant of grace. Oh, the world of sinful follies that our dear Lord Jesus bears with on this account! Are not our own souls astonished with the thought of it? Infinite patience, infinite forbearance, infinite love, infinite grace, infinite mercy, are all set in motion to this end, to respond to his valuation of us.

On our part, this conjugal affection may also be divided into two categories:

1. That upon discovering Christ, we rejoice to part with all things that we have delighted in or rested our confidence upon. We exchange them for him and for his sake so that we may enjoy him. Sin and lust, pleasure and profit, righteousness and duty will all go, so that we may have Christ.

2. That when we do enjoy him, we are willing to part with all things rather than part with him. To think of parting with peace, health, liberty, relations, wives, and children is offensive. It is heavy, and it grieves the best of the saints. But our souls cannot bear the thought of parting with Jesus Christ; such a thought is as cruel as the grave. The worst fear we have of sin and hell is that we will not enjoy Jesus Christ. We can part with all things freely and cheerfully, no matter how beautiful, so that we may enjoy him here, and hereafter be like him, be ever with him, and stand in his presence.

III. The love of Christ consists in *Pity or Compassion*.

This is the THIRD conjugal affection on the part of Christ. As a man "nourishes and cherishes his own flesh, so does the Lord his church," Eph. 5:29. Christ has a fellow feeling with his saints in all their troubles, just as a man has with his own flesh. This act of conjugal love on the part of Christ relates to the many trials and pressures of afflictions that his saints meet with here below. He does not deal with believers as the Samaritans dealt with the Jews. They fawned on them in their prosperity, but despised them in their trouble. He is like a tender father who, though perhaps loving all his children alike, will take the most pains with and give most of his presence to the ones that are sick and weak. He does so even though such children may be the most froward and, it would seem, the hardest to bear with. He himself suffers with them, and takes a share in all their troubles.

All the sufferings of the saints in this world, in which their head and husband exercises pity, tenderness, care, and compassion towards them, are of two sorts:

    1. Temptations.

    2. Afflictions.

1. Temptations (which includes their tendency to sin), whether from their own infirmities within, or their adversaries without. The frame of Christ's heart, and his attitude towards them in this condition, is given in Heb. 4:15. "We do not have a high priest who cannot be touched with the feeling of our infirmities." We do not have one who cannot. The two negations vehemently affirm that we have such a high priest who can and is touched. The word "touched" comes far short of expressing the original word. It is "*sumpatesai,*" [NT:4834] to "suffer together." "We have," says the apostle, "such a high priest as can, and consequently does, suffer with us and endure our infirmities." In what respect he suffers with us in regard to our infirmities, or has a fellow feeling with us in them, is declared in the next words. "He was tempted as we are," verse 15. It is in respect to our infirmities, our temptations, our spiritual weakness. He has a compassionate sympathy and fellow feeling with us particularly in that. Whatever our infirmities may be so far as temptations go, he suffers with us under them, and he treats us with compassion. Hence, at the last day he says, "I was hungry..." (Matt. 25:35).

There are two ways of expressing a fellow feeling and suffering with another:

    (1.) *Per benevolam condolentiam*, a "friendly grieving."

    (2.) *Per gratiosam opitulationem*, a "gracious supply."

Both of these are eminent in Christ:

(1.) He grieves and labors with us. Zech. 1:12, "The angel of the LORD answered and said, O LORD of hosts, how long will you not have mercy on Jerusalem?" He speaks as one intimately affected by the state and condition of poor Jerusalem. Therefore, he bid all the world to take notice that what is done to them is done to him, chap. 2:8, 9; "the apple of his eye."

(2.) He abounds in the second. Isa. 40:11, "He will feed his flock like a shepherd; he will gather the lambs with his arm, and carry them in his heart, and gently lead those who are with young." Here, we have both together: tender compassion and assistance. The whole frame in which he is described here is a frame of the greatest tenderness, compassion, and condescension that can be imagined. His people are burdened with many infirmities. Some are lambs, some pregnant with young, some very tender, and some burdened with temptations. Nothing in any of them is completely strong or attractive. Christ is a shepherd to them all. He feeds his own sheep and drives them out to pleasant pasture. If he sees a poor weak lamb, he does not shove him on, but takes him into his heart, where he both eases and refreshes him. He leads him gently and tenderly. As Jacob did for those who were burdened with young, so does our dear Lord Jesus with his flock, in the various ways and paths in which he leads them. When he sees a poor soul who is weak, tender, halting, and ready to sink and perish, he takes him into his arms. By some gracious promise administered to him, he carries him and bears him up when he is not able to go one step forward. This is the cause of his great quarrel with those shepherds in Ezek. 34:4, "Woe to you shepherds! You have not strengthened the diseased, nor healed what was sick, nor bound up what was broken, nor brought back what was driven away, nor sought what was lost." This is what our careful, tender husband would have done.

Mention is made of his compassion and fellow suffering with us in Heb. 4:15. In verse 16, it is added that he administers "*charin eis eukairon boeteian*," seasonable grace, grace for help in a time of need. This is evidence of compassion when, like the Samaritan, we afford seasonable help. To lament our troubles or miseries without affording help serves no purpose. Now, Christ does this; he gives "*eukairon boeteian*," seasonable help. Help that meets a need is always excellent, but coming in season puts a crown on it. A pardon to a malefactor when he is ready to be executed is sweet and welcome. Such is the assistance given by Christ. All his saints may take this as a sure rule in both their temptations and their afflictions: when they want these, they will not want relief; and when they can bear them no longer, they will be relieved, 1Cor. 10:13.

It is said emphatically of Christ in Heb. 2:18 that, "Because he has suffered being tempted himself, he is able to succor those who are tempted." It is true. But there is something more in all our temptations than there was in the temptation of Christ. There is something in us that takes part in every temptation. And there is enough in us to tempt us, even if nothing else appeared against us. With Christ it was not so,

John 14:30. But this does not limit his compassion towards us. By all accounts, it increases it. For if he will succor us because we are tempted, the sorer our temptations are, the more ready he will be to succor us. Take some examples of Christ's giving "*eukairon boeteian*," seasonable help, when we are tempted to sin. He does this in several ways:

[1.] By keeping the person who is liable to a particular temptation, and exposed to it, in a strong habitual bent against that sin. So it was in the case of Joseph: Christ knew that Joseph's great trial would be found in his mistress tempting him to lewdness. If he had been conquered in this sin, he would have been undone. And so Christ kept his heart in a steady frame against that sin, as his undeliberated answer argues, Gen. 39:9. In other things, in which he was not so deeply concerned, Joseph's heart was not so fortified by habitual grace. This would appear to be the case when he swore by the life of Pharaoh. This is one way by which Christ gives suitable help to his own, in tenderness and compassion. The saints, in the course of their lives, by the company, society, and business they find themselves in, are exposed to and become liable to temptations both great and violent, some of one kind, some of another. Christ is exceedingly kind and tender to them in fortifying their hearts with an abundance of grace regarding those temptations to sin to which they are most exposed. Perhaps in other things they are very weak, and often surprised.

[2.] By some strong impulse of actual grace, Christ sometimes recovers the soul from the very borders of sin. So it was in the case of David, 1Sam. 24:4-6. "He was almost gone," as he says himself; "his feet had nearly slipped." The temptation was at the point of prevailing, when a mighty impulse of grace recovered him. To show his saints what they are, their own weakness and infirmity, Christ sometimes allows them to go to the very edge of the hill. And then he causes them to hear a word behind them, saying with power and efficacy, "This is the right way, walk in it," and so he recovers them to himself.

[3.] By taking away the temptation itself when it grows so strong and violent that the poor soul does not know what to do. This is called "delivering the godly out of temptation," 2Pet. 2:9. A man is plucked out of the snare, and the snare is left behind to hold another. I have known this to be the case for many in a number of perplexing temptations. They have been quite weary, and tried all means of help and assistance, and yet they have been unable to come to a comfortable resolution. Suddenly and unexpectedly, the Lord Christ, in his tenderness and compassion, rebukes Satan so that they do not hear one word more from him about their temptation. Christ comes in the storm, and says, "Peace, be still."

[4.] By giving fresh supplies of grace as temptations grow or increase. So it was in the case of Paul, 2Cor. 12:9. "My grace is sufficient for you." The temptation, whatever it was, grew high. Paul was earnest for its removal. Despite the growth of the temptation, he receives only this answer that the grace of God is sufficient for his support.

[5.] By giving them wisdom to make a right, holy, and spiritual improvement to all temptations. James bids us "count it all joy when we fall into diverse temptations," James 1:2. This could not be done if there were not a holy and spiritual use to be made of them, which he indicates in the words that follow. There are various uses of temptations that experienced Christians, with suitable assistance from Christ, may make of them. Not the least is that by them we are brought to know ourselves. Hezekiah was left to be tried to know what was in him (2Kgs. 20). By temptation, some heart-hidden corruption is often discovered that the soul knew nothing of before. As it was with Hazael in respect to enormous crimes (2Kgs. 8:13-15), so it is in lesser things with the saints. They would never have believed such lusts and corruptions were in them until they discovered them upon their temptations. Many having been tempted to one sin, have discovered another that they did not think of. Some, being tempted to pride, worldliness, or looseness of life, have been startled by it. This led to a discovery of their neglect of their many duties and communion with God, which they did not think of before. This is from the tender care of Jesus Christ in giving them suitable help, without which no man can possibly make use of or improve a temptation. And this is suitable help indeed. A temptation might otherwise be a deadly wound, but instead it only lances a festered sore. It lets out the corruption that might otherwise have endangered life itself. So we read in 1Pet. 1:6, "If need be, you are in heaviness through various temptations."

[6.] When a believer is being overcome by temptations, Christ in his tenderness relieves him with mercy and pardon, so that he will not completely sink under the burden, 1John 2:1-2.

By one or all of these ways, the Lord Jesus manifests his conjugal tenderness and compassion towards the saints in and under their temptations.

2. Afflictions. Christ is compassionate towards them in their afflictions: "In all their affliction he is afflicted," Isa. 63:9. It seems that all our afflictions (at least in persecutions) are his in the first place, and ours only by participation. We "fill up the measure of the afflictions of

126

Christ," Col. 1:24. Two things evidently manifest this compassion in Christ:

(1.) His interceding with his Father for their relief, Zech. 1:12. Christ intercedes on our behalf, not only in respect to our sins, but also our sufferings. When the work of our afflictions is accomplished, we will have the relief he intercedes for. The Father always hears him. We do not have relief from trouble, recovery of health, ease of pain, or freedom from any evil without the intercession of Jesus Christ. If believers look at their mercies as the dispensing of common providence, then they are unacquainted with their own condition. This may, indeed, be the reason we do not esteem them more, we are not more thankful for them, nor more fruitful in the enjoyment of them. We do not see how, by what means, or on what account, they are dispensed to us. The people of God in the world today are alive and undevoured only because of the intercession of the Lord Jesus. His compassion has been the fountain of their deliverance. Hence, he often rebukes their sufferings and afflictions so their effect on believers is limited while they are under them. He is with them when they pass through fire and water, Isa. 43:2, 3.

(2.) In resolving the matter, he sorely revenges the complaint of their sufferings upon their enemies. He avenges his elect who cry to him, and he does it speedily. The cause of Zion will lead on the day of his vengeance, Isa. 34:8. He looks upon them sometimes in distress, and considers the state of the world in reference to them. "We have walked to and fro through the earth, and, behold, all the earth sits still, and is at rest," say his messengers to him (Zech. 1:11). He sends them to consider the world and its condition during the affliction of his people. This is the common condition of the world in such seasons: "They are at rest and quiet, their hearts are satiated; they drink wine from bowls, and send gifts to one another," Rev. 11:10. Then Christ looks to see who will come to succor them, Isa. 59:16-17. Finding none, he engages himself for their relief by destroying their adversaries. Now, he accomplishes this vengeance two ways:

[1.] *Temporally*, upon persons, kingdoms, nations, and countries as he did upon the old Roman world, Rev. 6:15, 16. You have a type of this in Isa. 63:1-6. And this he also does two ways:

1st. By raising up an eminent opposer, and making him an example to the world. So he dealt with Pharaoh: "For this cause have I raised you up," Exod. 9:16. So he does to this day. He lays his hand upon eminent adversaries, fills one with fury, another with folly, blasts a third, and makes another wither; or he destroys them utterly and terribly. Like a provoked lion, he does not lie down without his prey.

2dly. In general, in the vials of his wrath that in these latter days he will pour out upon the anti-Christian world, and upon all that join them in their thoughts of vengeance and persecution. He will miserably destroy them, and make such work of them in the course of it, that whoever hears of it will have both ears tingle.

[2.] *Eternally;* in eternal vengeance he will answer the adversaries of his beloved, Matt. 25:41-46; 2Thess. 1:6; Jude 15. It is evident from this that Christ abounds in pity and compassion towards his beloved. More examples might be given, but these things are obvious, and occur to everyone.

In response to this pity and compassion, I place in the saints, CHASTITY to Christ in every state and condition. The apostle endeavored that this might be the state of the church of Corinth, 2Cor. 11:2-3. "I have espoused you to one husband, that I may present you as a chaste virgin to Christ. But I fear, lest by any means, as the serpent beguiled Eve through his subtlety, so your minds should be corrupted from the simplicity that is in Christ." And so it is said of the followers of the Lamb on mount Zion in Rev. 14:4. "These are those who were not defiled with women, for they are virgins." What defilement they were free from will be declared later.

Now, there are three things in which this chastity consists:

1. THE FIRST THING is not taking anything into their affections and esteem for those ends and purposes for which they have received Jesus Christ. Here the Galatians failed in their conjugal affection to Christ. They did not preserve themselves chaste to him. They received Christ for life and justification, and him only. But after a while they were overcome with charms, or bewitched. They put the righteousness of the law in the same place as him. How Paul deals with them in this matter is known. How sorely, how pathetically he admonishes them, how severely he reproves them, and how clearly he convinces them of their madness and folly! This, then, is the first chaste affection believers must bear in their heart to Christ. Having received him for their righteousness and salvation before God, for the fountain, spring, and well-head of all their supplies, they must not receive anything else into his room and in his stead.

For one particular example: We receive Christ for our acceptance by God. All that can compete with him for our affections is our own striving for a righteousness to commend us to God. Now, this must be either before we receive him, or after. As for all the duties and endeavors we do to please God before receiving Christ, you know the apostle's attitude from Phil. 3:8-10. He rejects all endeavors, all advantages, and all privileges with indignation. He sees them with

128

abomination, as loss, and as dung. He wraps up all his aims and desires in Christ alone and his righteousness for that purpose. But the works that we do *after* we have received Christ are another consideration. Indeed, they are *acceptable* to God; it pleases him that we walk in them. But as to the purpose for which we receive Christ, they have no more value than our prior works, Eph. 2:8-10. Even the works we do after believing, those we are created to do in Christ Jesus, those that God has ordained believers "should walk in," are excluded from our justification and acceptance by God (i.e. salvation). One day it will appear that Christ abhors the wranglings of men about the place of their own works and obedience in the business of their acceptance by God. The saints will not find any peace in adulterous thoughts of that kind. The chastity we owe to Christ requires another attitude. The necessity, usefulness, and excellence of gospel obedience will be declared later. I marvel to see how hard it is to keep some professors of Christ faithful in this thing. How many disputes have been contrived, distinctions invented, and evasions studied, just so they may dally with that? Those who truly love him have their minds on other things.

Of all things, then, the saints endeavor to keep their affections chaste and loyal to Jesus Christ in this area of trusting in his obedience alone. He is made "righteousness" to them by God (1Cor. 1:30), and they will accept nothing else for that purpose. In fact, sometimes they do not know whether they have any interest in him or not because he withdraws himself. And yet, they still continue in solitude, in a state of widowhood, refusing to be comforted, even though many things offer to replace him in his absence. When Christ is absent from our soul at any time, when we cannot see that we have any interest in him, many lovers will offer themselves to us. Many will woo our affections to get us to rest on this or that thing for relief and succor. But even though our soul mourns ever so long, it will lean upon nothing but Christ. Whenever the soul is in the wilderness, in the saddest condition, it will stay there until Christ comes to gather it up, until it can be brought forth from the wilderness leaning upon him, Cant. 8:5.

The one who has communion with Christ watches diligently over his own heart so that nothing creeps into its affections, and nothing gives it any peace or security before God, except Christ alone. Whenever he asks himself, "With what shall I come before the LORD, and appear before the high God?" he does not think, "I will do this or that;" or, "I will watch here and there, and amend my ways." Instead, he instantly cries, "I have righteousness in the Lord Jesus. My only desire is to be found in him, not having a righteousness of my own," (Phil. 3:9).

2. THE SECOND THING this chastity consists of is cherishing the Spirit, that holy Comforter whom Christ sends to abide with us in his room and in his stead. He tells us that he sends him for that purpose in John 16:7. He gives him to us, *"vicariam navare operam,"* "a substitute to render energetic assistance," says Tertullian. He gives him to abide with us forever, for all those ends and purposes which he has to fulfill toward and upon us. He gives him to dwell in us, to keep us, and to preserve us blameless for him. Christ's name is in him, and with him. Whatever is done to any who belong to Christ is done to Christ, because it is done to those in whom he dwells by his Spirit. This is why the saints preserve their conjugal affections entirely for Christ. They labor by all means not to grieve his Holy Spirit whom he has sent in his stead to abide with them. The apostle puts them in mind of this in Eph. 4:30, "Do not grieve the Holy Spirit."

There are two main purposes for which Christ sends his Spirit to believers:

(1.) For their sanctification;

(2.) For their consolation.

All the particular acts of purging, teaching, anointing, and the rest that are ascribed to him, come under these two headings. So there are two ways by which we may grieve him:

[1.] In respect to sanctification;

[2.] In respect to consolation:

(1.) In respect to sanctification. He is the Spirit of holiness, holy in himself, and the author of holiness in us. He works holiness in us, Tit. 3:5, and he persuades us to be holy by those impulses of his that are not to be quenched. He is carrying on a work in and for us that is so infinitely to our advantage; without it we cannot see God. What primarily grieves the Spirit is when we run at cross-purposes to him, in ways of unholiness, pollution, and defilement. So the words "Grieve not the Holy Spirit" are connected to the obedience of Eph. 4:28-31. Thus Paul bases his powerful and most effectual argument to be holy on the abiding and indwelling of this Holy Spirit, 1Cor. 3:16-17. Indeed, what can grieve a loving and tender friend more than to oppose him and slight him when he is most intent on our good, and a good of the greatest consequence to us. In this, then, believers make it their business to keep their hearts loyal and their affections chaste to Jesus Christ. They instantly labor not to grieve the Holy Spirit by loose and foolish behavior, by careless and negligent walking. Therefore anger, wrath, malice, and envy will no longer dwell in their hearts, because they are contrary to the holy, meek Spirit of Christ, whom he has given to dwell with them. They attend to his impulses, make use of his assistance, and improve his gifts. Nothing lies more upon their spirits than to be worthy of the presence of this holy substitute of the Lord Jesus Christ.

(2.) As to consolation. This is the second great end for which

130

Christ gives and sends his Spirit to us, and for which he is eminently called "The Comforter." To this end he seals us, anoints us, establishes us, and gives us peace and joy. I will speak at large of all this later. For now, there are two ways by which he may be grieved in this end of his mission, and by which we may violate our chastity to Jesus Christ:

[1.] By placing our comforts and joys in other things, and not being filled with joy in the Holy Spirit. When we make creatures or creature comforts our joy and our delight, when we do so with anything other than what we receive by the Spirit of Christ, we are being false with Christ. So it was with Demas who loved the present world (2Tim. 4:10). When the ways of the Spirit of God grieve and burden us, when we say, "When will the Sabbath be past so that we may do our work?" when our delight and refreshment lies in earthly things, that is when we are unsuitable to Christ. May not his Spirit say, "Why do I still abide with these poor souls? I provide them joys unspeakable and glorious, but they exchange them for perishing things. I provide them spiritual, eternal, abiding consolations, and it is all rejected for nothing." Christ cannot bear this. Therefore, believers are exceeding careful not to place their joy and consolation in anything but what is administered by the Spirit. Their daily work is to get their hearts crucified to the world and its things. So that they may not have living affections for dying things, they fabricate looking at the world as a crucified, dead thing that has neither form nor beauty. If at any time they become enamored of creatures and inferior contentments, and lose their better joys, they cry out to Christ, "O restore to us the joys of your Spirit!"

[2.] The Spirit is grieved when, through darkness and unbelief, we will not receive those consolations that he tenders to us, and which he deeply wants us to receive. But I will speak of this later in handling our communion with the Holy Spirit.

3. THE THIRD THING this chastity consists of is the matter and manner of his worship. Christ has married his church to himself, taking us into a marriage relationship. He expresses that, in the main, the church's chaste and choice affections toward him lie in keeping his institutions and his worship according to his appointment. When we breach this fidelity, he calls it "adultery" and "whoredom." He is a "jealous God," and he gives himself that title only in respect to his institutions. The whole apostasy of the Christian church to false worship is called "fornication"; and the church that leads others to false worship is called the "mother of harlots." On this account, those believers who really attend to communion with Jesus Christ, labor to keep their hearts chaste to him in his ordinances, institutions, and worship; and that is done in two ways:

(1.) They will receive nothing, practice nothing, and accept

131

nothing in his worship that is not appointed by him. They know that from the foundation of the world he never allowed the will of the creatures to be the measure of his honor or the principle of his worship, either as to matter or manner. The second commandment forbids the use of images and likenesses. What is so severely forbidden is inventing or finding ways of worship, or ways of honoring God, which are not appointed by him. Believers know how God reacts to all will-worship: "Who has required these things at your hand?" (Isa. 1:12), and, "You worship me in vain, teaching the traditions of men as doctrines," (Matt. 15:9; Isa. 29:13).

I will take leave to say that, when the church believes it has the power to institute anything in the worship of God that goes beyond the orderly circumstances attending the ordinances that Christ himself instituted, it becomes the basis for all the horrible superstition and idolatry, all the confusion, blood, persecution, and wars, that have for so long spread themselves over the face of the Christian world. I do not doubt that the great controversy which God has had with this nation for so many years, and which he has pursued with so much anger and indignation, was upon this account. Contrary to the glorious light of the gospel that shone among us, the wills and fancies of men concerning the ways and worship of God were imposed on men in the name of order, decency, and the authority of the church. All the pretence of glory, beauty, attractiveness, and conformity that was pleaded then, was nothing more than what God describes in the church of Israel as harlotry, Ezek. 16:25. This was how the Spirit of God in prayer was derided, the powerful preaching of the gospel was despised, the Sabbath was decried, and holiness stigmatized and persecuted. And to what end?

To depose Jesus Christ from the sole privilege and power of law-making in his church;

To shove aside the true husband, and embrace the adulterers of his spouse;

To appoint taskmasters that he never authorized over his house, Eph. 4:11;

To introduce a ceremonious, pompous, outward show of worship, drawn from Pagan, Judaical, and Anti-Christian observations, of which there is not one little word or iota in the whole book of God.

Those who hold communion with Christ are therefore careful to admit nothing and practice nothing in the worship of God, whether private or public, unless they have his warrant for it. Unless it comes in his name, with "Thus says the Lord Jesus," they will not hear an "angel from heaven." (Gal. 1:8). They know that the apostles themselves were to teach the saints only what Christ commanded them, Matt. 28:20.

Not long ago, many thousands in this very nation left their native soil and went to a vast and howling wilderness in the farthest reaches of the world [America]. They did so to keep their souls undefiled and chaste to their dear Lord Jesus in this matter of his worship and institutions.

(2.) Positively, to keep their hearts chaste to him in his ordinances, institutions, and worship, they readily embrace, receive, and practice everything that the Lord Christ *does* appoint. They diligently inquire into his mind and will so that they may know what those things are. They go to him for directions, and beg him to lead them in the way that they have not known (Jn. 14:5). The 119th Psalm may be a pattern for this. How the good, holy soul *breathes* after instruction in the ways and ordinances, the statutes and judgments, of God! They are sensitive to whatever is of Christ. They willingly submit to it, accept it, and give themselves up to its constant practice. They refuse whatever comes from anything else.

IV. Finally, the love of Christ consists in *Bounty*.

Christ manifests and evidences his love to his saints through bounty, the rich and plentiful provision that he makes for them. It has "pleased the Father that in him all fullness should dwell," Col. 1:19. That is done for this purpose, that "we might all receive of his fullness, and grace for grace," John 1:16. I will not go into the particulars of the provision that Christ makes for his saints, and all those influences of the Spirit, of life and grace, that they receive from him daily, the bread and refreshment they have from him to the full. I will only observe that the Scripture affirms that he does all things for them abundantly, richly, and bountifully. Whatever he gives us, his grace to assist us, his presence to comfort us, he does it abundantly. You have the general assertion of it in Rom. 5:20, "Where sin abounded, grace did much more abound." If grace abounds much more in comparison to sin, it is abundant grace indeed. This will easily be granted by anyone who considers how flirting with sin abounds in every soul. Hence, he is able to do for us "exceeding abundantly above all that we ask or think," Eph. 3:20, and we are bid to expect that.

Is it pardoning mercy that we receive from him? Well, he does "abundantly pardon," Isa. 55:7; He will multiply or add to pardon. He will add pardon to pardon. Grace and mercy will abound above all our sins and iniquities.

Is it the Spirit that he gives us? He sheds him upon us richly or "abundantly," Tit. 3:6. He not only bids us to drink of the water of life freely, but he also bestows him in such a plentiful measure that rivers of water flow from those who receive him, John 7:38, 39. They will never thirst any more when they have drunk of him.

Is it grace that we receive of him? He gives that in bounty also.

We receive "abundance of grace," Rom. 5:17. He "abounds toward us in all wisdom and prudence," Eph. 1:8. Hence we find that invitation in Cant. 5:1, "Eat, O friends! Drink, yes, drink deeply, O beloved ones!" If we are restricted in anything, it is in ourselves. Christ deals bountifully with us. Indeed, the great sin of believers is that we do not make use of Christ's bounty as we ought to do. We do not take mercy from him in abundance every day. The oil never ceases till the vessels cease. Supplies from Christ fail only when our faith fails in receiving them.

Then our response to Christ is a duty. To this end, two things are required:

1. That we pursue and practice holiness in all its power, because it is obedience to Jesus Christ. Under this formal duty, gospel obedience means, "Whatever Christ commands us," Matt. 28:20. He says in John 15:14, "You are my friends, if you do whatever I command you." We are required to live to the one who died for us, 2Cor. 5:15. We live to him in all holy obedience. We live to him as our Lord and King. I am not suggesting that there are specific precepts and laws from Jesus Christ that justify us by observing them, as the Socinians fancy. The gospel requires no more of us than "to love the Lord our God with all our hearts, and all our souls," which the law also required. The Lord Jesus brought us into acceptance by God. In that condition, our obedience is well-pleasing to him. And we bring honor to Christ as we honor the Father. So, we have a unique regard to him in all our obedience. He has purchased us for himself, Tit. 2:14. And thus, in their obedience, believers consider Jesus Christ,

(1.) As the author of their faith and obedience. It is for his sake that it is "given to them to believe," Phil. 1:29. It is Christ who works that obedience in them by his Spirit. So the apostle says in Heb. 12:1-2. In the course of our obedience, we still look to Jesus, "the author of our faith." Faith is here both the grace of faith, and the fruit of faith in obedience.

(2.) As the one in whom, for whom, and by whom we have acceptance by God in our obedience. Believers know that all their duties are weak, imperfect, and unable to abide the presence of God. Therefore, they look to Christ as the one who bears any iniquity in their holy things, who adds incense to their prayers, pulls out all the weeds from their duties, and makes them acceptable to God.

(3.) As the one who renewed the commands of God to them, with mighty obligations to obedience. And so the apostle says in 2Cor. 5:14-15, "The love of Christ constrains us."

(4.) And they consider him as God, equal with his Father, to whom all honor and obedience is due. So it says in Rev. 5:13. But I have opened these things in another treatise, not long ago, dealing with the worship of Christ as mediator.

In all their obedience, then, the saints have a special regard for their dear Lord Jesus. For these reasons and many others, he is continually in their thoughts. His love for them, his life for them, his death for them, all his kindness and mercy, constrains them to live for him.

2. Our response to Christ requires laboring to abound in fruits of holiness. Just as he deals with us bountifully and abundantly, so he requires that we abound in all grateful, obedient returns to him. We are exhorted to "always abound in the work of the Lord," 1Cor. 15:58. This is what I mean: the saints are never satisfied with the measure they have attained; instead, they continue to press so that they may be more dutiful and more fruitful to Christ.

This is a little glimpse of some of that communion which we enjoy with Christ. It is only a little from someone who has the least experience of it of all the saints of God. And yet I have found in this communion what is better than ten thousand worlds. I desire to spend the residue of the few and evil days of my pilgrimage in pursuit of it, in the contemplation of the excellence, desirability, love, and grace of our dear Lord Jesus, and in returning obedience according to his will. This is the great relief to my soul, that in the midst of the perplexities of this wretched world, and cursed rebellions of my own heart, "He that will come will come, and will not tarry," (Heb. 10:37). "The Spirit and the bride say, Come; and let him that reads say, Come. Even so, come, Lord Jesus," (Rev. 22:17, 20).

CHAPTER 6.

COMMUNION WITH CHRIST IN PURCHASED GRACE –

Our process is now to communion with Christ in purchased grace, "That we may know him, and the power of his resurrection, and the fellowship of his sufferings, and be made conformable to his death," Phil 3:10.

I understand "purchased grace" to be all that righteousness and grace which Christ has procured or worked for us. It is what he has made us partakers of by any means or what he bestows on us for our benefit. It is purchased by anything that he has done or suffered for us, or by anything that he continues to do as our mediator. First, I will consider what this purchased grace is, and then what it consists of. Secondly, I will describe how we hold communion with Christ in this purchased grace.

1. Purchased grace springs from three fountains or CAUSES:

(1.) The obedience of his life.

(2.) The suffering of his death.

(3.) His continued intercession.

All the actions of Christ as mediator which lead to the communication of grace to us, may either be categorized under one of these three, or under something that is dependent on them.

2. The NATURE of this grace, in which we have communion with Christ, may be divided into:

(1.) Grace of *justification*, or acceptance by God, which makes a relative change in our state and condition.

(2.) Grace of *sanctification*, or holiness before God, which makes a real change in our principle of living and way of operating.

(3.) Grace of *privilege*, which is mixed, as I will show when I handle it.

It is evident that we have communion with Christ in this purchased grace, based on this single consideration: there is almost nothing that Christ has done, which is a spring of that grace, that we are not said to do with him. We are "crucified" with him, Gal. 2:20; we are "dead" with him, 2Tim. 2:11; Col. 3:3; and "buried" with him, Rom. 6:4; Col. 2:12; we are "quickened together with him," Col. 2:13; "risen" with him, Col. 3:1. "He has quickened us together with Christ, and has raised us up together, and made us sit together in heavenly places," Eph. 2:5, 6. In Christ's actions as mediator, by virtue of the compact between him and the Father, there is an assured foundation laid for communicating the fruits of those actions to those in whose stead he performed them. Believers are said to participate in those fruits, to have done the same things with him. We may have occasion later to inquire into the life and power of this truth:

(1.) The first fountain and spring of this grace is the obedience of his life: concerning this, it must be declared,

[1.] What it means, and of what it consists.

[2.] What influence it has on the grace of which we speak.

In handling this, I will only observe that, in the order of procurement, the life of Christ necessarily precedes his death. Therefore, we will handle it in the first place. But in the order of application, the benefits of his death are bestowed on us prior to those of his life; and this necessarily follows from our state and condition.

[1.] By the obedience of the life of Christ, I mean the universal conformity of the Lord Jesus Christ, as mediator, to the whole will of God; and his complete actual fulfilling of the whole of every law of God, doing all that God required in them. He might have been perfectly holy by obedience to the law of creation, the moral law, as the angels were. Nor could any more be required of him as a man walking with God. But he also submitted himself to every law or ordinance that was introduced as a result of sin, which he could not be subject to on his own account. It became him to "fulfill all righteousness," Matt. 3:15, as he spoke in reference to a newly instituted ceremony.

That obedience is properly ascribed to Jesus Christ as mediator. The Scripture is witness, both as to the title and the performance, in Heb. 5:8, "Though he was a Son, yet he learned obedience..." In fact, he was obedient in his sufferings. It was what gave life to his death, Phil. 2:8. He was obedient to death, for in that "he made his soul an offering for sin," Isa. 53:10, or "his soul made an offering for sin," as it is interpreted in verse 12. "He poured out his soul to death," or, "his soul poured out itself to death." And he not only sanctified himself to be an offering, John 17:10, but he also "offered himself up," Heb. 9:14, an "offering of a sweet savor to God," Eph. 5:2. Hence, as to the whole of his work, he is called the Father's "servant," Isa. 42:1, 19. And he professes that he "came into the world to do the will of God, the will of him that sent him," for which he manifests "his great readiness," Heb. 10:7. All of this evinces his obedience. I suppose I do not need to prove that Christ, in his work of mediation, was obedient and did what he did willingly and cheerfully, in obedience to God.

Now, this obedience of Christ may be considered two ways:

1st. As to its habitual root and source.

2dly. As to its actual parts or duties:

1st. The habitual righteousness of Christ, as mediator in his human nature, was the absolute, complete, and exact conformity of the soul of Christ to the will, mind, or law of God. It was his perfect habitually inherent righteousness. He necessarily had this from the grace of his union of God and man; and it is why what was born of the virgin was a "holy thing," Luke 1:35. It was consequentially necessary to be holy, although effecting it was by the free operations of the Spirit, Luke 2:52. He had an all-fullness of grace on all accounts. The apostle describes this in Heb. 7:26, "Such a high priest became holy, harmless, undefiled, and separate from sinners." He was to be in every way separate and distant from sin and sinners, which is why he is called "The Lamb of God, without spot or blemish," 1Pet. 1:19. This habitual holiness of Christ was inconceivably above that of the angels. "He who charges his angels with folly," Job 4:18; "who puts no trust in his saints; and in whose sight the heavens" (or their inhabitants) "are not clean," chap. 15:15. The Father always embraces him in his heart, and is always "well pleased with him," Matt. 3:17. The reason for this is that every other creature is never so holy, having the Spirit of God given to them by measure. But the Spirit was not given to Christ "by measure," John 3:34. It pleased the Spirit that in him "all fullness should dwell," Col. 1:19. This habitual grace of Christ is not absolutely infinite, but by comparison to any other creature, it is like the water of the sea to the water of a pool. All other creatures are limited from perfection by this. They subsist as a created, dependent being. And so the fountain of what is communicated to them is outside of themselves. But the human nature of Christ subsists in the person of the Son of God. And so his nature has the fountain of its holiness strictly united with itself.

2dly. The actual obedience of Christ, as was said, was his willing, cheerful, obedient performance of everything, duty or command, that God required by virtue of any law that we were liable to; and moreover, to the specific law of the mediator. This, then, has two parts:

(1st.) He did and fulfilled whatever was required of us by virtue of any law. This includes whatever was required of us by the law of nature in our state of innocence; whatever kind of duty was added by morally positive or ceremonial institutions; and whatever is required of us by righteous judicial laws. He did it all. Hence he is said to be "made under the law," Gal. 4:4. He was subject to all its precepts or commands. So in Matt. 3:15, he said it became him to "fulfill all righteousness," "*pasan dikaiosunen*," [NT:3956,1343] all manner of righteousness whatever; that is, everything that God required as evident from the application of that general axiom to the baptism by John. I will not need to go to particular instances for this in the duties of the law of nature to God and his parents, morally positive

138

duties in the Sabbath and other acts of worship, the ceremonial law, circumcision, observation of all the rites of the Judaic church, judicial duties in paying tribute to governors, etc. It will suffice, I presume, that on the one hand he "did no sin, neither was guile found in his mouth," (1Pet. 2:22), and on the other, that he "fulfilled all righteousness." Based on this, the Father was always well pleased with him. This was what he engaged himself to do. He came to do the will of God; and he did it.

(2dly.) There was a specific law of the Mediator that applied only to him. It contained all those acts and duties of his that are not for our imitation. So the obedience that he showed in dying was unique to this law. John 10:18, "I have power to lay down my life, this commandment have I received of my Father." As mediator, he received this unique command from his Father to lay down his life and take it up again; and he was obedient to this command. Hence we say that, as mediator, he did some things merely as a man, subject to the law of God in general. And so he prayed for his persecutors, those who put him to death, Luke 23:34; He did some things as mediator. And so he prayed for his elect only, John 17:9. There were none worse in the world than many of those who crucified him, and yet, as a man, and subject to the law, he forgave them, and he prayed for them. When he prayed as mediator, his Father always heard him and answered him, John 11:41; and in his other prayers, he was accepted as someone performing his duty exactly.

This, then, is the obedience of Christ; which was the first thing considered in the obedience of his life. The next thing is,

[2.] That it has an influence on the grace of which we speak, and in which we hold communion with him, namely, our free acceptance by God. What that influence is must also follow in its order.

1st. For his habitual and inherent righteousness, I will only propose two considerations:

(1st.) That it was necessary to have a mediator who was God and man in one person. Because it could not be otherwise, it was necessary that he be holy. Although there is one primary and necessary effect of the hypostatical union (which is the subsistence of the human nature in the person of the Son of God), it was also necessary that he be a "holy thing," completely holy.

(2dly.) That the relation which this righteousness of Christ has to the grace we receive from him is only that by his righteousness he was "*hikanos*," or fit to do all that he had to do for us. This is the intent of the apostle in Heb. 7:26. Such a one "became us." It was necessary that he be such a one, so that he might do what he had to do. And there are two reasons for this:

[1st.] Had he not been completely furnished with habitual grace, he could never have actually fulfilled the righteousness which was required at his hands. It was because he was completely furnished that he was able to do all that he did. So he lays down the presence of the Spirit with him as the foundation of his work, Isa. 61:1. "The Spirit of the Lord is upon me..."

[2dly.] Without such righteousness, he could not have been a complete and perfect sacrifice, nor could he have resolved all the types and figures of him, completely and without blemish. But having this habitual righteousness, he would have been a fit sacrifice and offering even if he had never actively continued in obedience to the law. Therefore his subsequent obedience has another use besides fitting him for an offering, for which he was fit without it.

2dly. The next influence on our grace comes from Christ's obedience to the law of mediation, which is not tied to his inherent obedience. It was requisite to discharge his office as mediator. His obedience as mediator is not imputed to us as though we had done it, even though the "*apotelesmata*" (the official acts) and its fruits are. Instead, the nature of his intercession provides the good things we need, at least subserviently to his offering and intercession. More will be said of this afterward.

3dly. There is some doubt about his actual fulfilling of the law, or doing all the things required of us. There are three opinions:

(1st.) This *active obedience* of Christ has no other influence on our justification and acceptance by God than as preparation for his blood-shedding and offering. It is the sole cause of our justification. The whole righteousness that is imputed to us arises from that obedience.

(2dly.) That his fulfilling of the law may be considered as pure obedience in preparation for his offering as mentioned. But it may also be considered as to its punishment for sin. Because it was accomplished with suffering as part of his humiliation, that suffering is imputed to us, and becomes part of the basis on which we are justified.

(3dly.) That this obedience of Christ, being done for us, is reckoned to us graciously by God. Because of it, we are accepted as righteous before him.

My intent is not to treat this difference as a controversy, but to give such an understanding of the whole as to lead to the practice of godliness and consolation. I will do this in the ensuing observations:

[1st.] The obedience that Christ yielded to the law in general is not only to the specific law of the mediator, even though he yielded it as mediator. He was incarnate as mediator, Heb. 2:14; Gal. 4:4. All

140

that he did afterward was as our mediator. That was the reason "he came into the world" (1Tim. 1:15; Heb. 10:5). So there is a twofold sense of mediator here. It may refer strictly to his obedience in assuming the office of the mediator; and it may refer to his obedience as a man who was subject to all the laws. He was obedient to those laws because he was the mediator.

[2dly.] Whatever Christ did as mediator, he did for those he mediated for, in whose stead and for whose good he executed the office of a mediator before God. The Holy Spirit witnesses to this in Rom. 8:3, 4. "What the law could not do, in that it was weak through the flesh, God sending his own Son in the likeness of sinful flesh, and for sin, condemned sin in the flesh, that the righteousness of the law might be fulfilled in us." We could not come to God and be freed from the condemnation of the law, because of our weakened condition caused by sin. Therefore, God sent Christ as a mediator, to do and suffer whatever the law required at our hands for that purpose. This was so that we might not be condemned, but be accepted by God. It was all to this end, "That the righteousness of the law might be fulfilled in us," meaning, fulfilling what the law required of us, consisting in duties of obedience. Christ performed these duties for us. The apostle says, "God sending his own Son in the likeness of sinful flesh, and for sin, condemned sin in the flesh," Rom. 8:3. If you add Gal. 4:4 to this, then he was sent *"hupo nomou genomenos,"* "made under the law." That is, he was liable to the law, and he was to yield all the obedience that the law required. This comprises the whole of what Christ did or suffered; and the Holy Spirit tells us that all of this was for us, Rom. 8:4.

[3dly.] The purpose of this active obedience of Christ cannot be to prepare him for his death and offering. For by his union and habitual grace he was already in every way *"hikanos"* [NT:2425] (fit to be made an offering for sin). So, if the obedience of Christ was not done on our account, and reckoned to us, then there is no just reason why he should have lived in the world as long as he did in perfect obedience to all the laws of God. He was already perfectly innocent and holy because of his habitual grace, infinite virtue, and worth from the dignity of his person. Surely he did not yield that long course of obedience unless it was for some great and special purpose relating to our salvation.

[4thly.] If the obedience of Christ had not been for us, he might have been required to yield obedience to the law of nature, the sole law which he would be liable to as a man. For an innocent man in a covenant of works, as he was, needs no other law. Nor did God ever give any other law to such a person. The law of creation is all that an

141

innocent creature is liable to. And yet his subjection to this law was also voluntary. This was not only the result of being born of his own choice, but also because as mediator, God and man, he was not obliged to that law. He was exempted and lifted above that law by the hypostatical union. Yet, when I say that his subjection to the law was voluntary, I do not mean that it was optional, and that he had a choice whether to yield obedience to it or not. Once he undertook to be a mediator, it was necessary to submit to the law voluntarily and willingly, and so he really became subject to its commands. But then Jesus Christ yielded perfect obedience to all those other laws that came upon us by the occasion of sin, such as the ceremonial law. These were the very institutions that signified the washing away of sin, and repentance from sin, such as the baptism of John which he had no need of himself. Therefore, it must have been done for us.

[5thly.] The obedience of Christ cannot be part of his sufferings. Instead, it is clearly distinct from it in all its formalities. Doing is one thing, and suffering is another. They take place in different circumstances and cannot be coincident.

Let us briefly see what we have learned from these considerations. Then I will intimate what results from this first spring or fountain of purchased grace, and what influence it has on it:

First, by the obedience of the life of Christ you see what is intended. You see his willing submission to every law of God, and his perfect and complete fulfilling of what the saints of God were obliged to fulfill. It is true that almost every act of Christ's obedience, from the blood of his circumcision to the blood of his cross, was accompanied by suffering. His whole life might be called a death in that regard. Yet, looking at his willingness and obedience, his obedience is distinguished from his specific sufferings, and it is called his active righteousness. This active righteousness is the complete and absolutely perfect accomplishment of the whole law of God by Christ, our mediator. He not only "did no sin, neither was there guile found in his mouth," but he also most perfectly fulfilled all righteousness, as it became him to do (Matt. 3:15).

Secondly, this obedience was performed by Christ not for himself, but for us, and in our stead. It is necessarily true that while he lived in the flesh he must be most perfectly and absolutely holy. Yet the prime intent of his accomplishing this holiness was no less for us than his suffering death was for us. The apostle tells us this is so in Gal. 4:4, 5. "God sent forth his Son, made of a woman, made under the law, to redeem those who were under the law." This Scripture must be examined a little further. He was made of a woman, and he was made under the law. That is, he was obedient to the law *for us*. That is what must be understood here by the phrase "made under the law", "*hupo nomou genomenos.*" He was made in such a condition that he must yield subjection and obedience to the law. The end here, of both the incarnation and Christ's obedience to the law, was to redeem us. In these two expressions, "made of a woman" and "made under the law," the apostle does not knit together his incarnation and death while excluding the obedience of his life. He was made under the law just as those whom he was to redeem were made under the law. Now, we were not only liable to its penalties, but bound to all its duties. This is our existence "under the law," as the apostle informs us in Gal. 4:21. "Tell me, you that desire to be under the law." It was not the *penalty* of the law that they desired to be under, but its duties of obedience. If you take away the end, you destroy the means. If Christ was not made incarnate for himself, and he was not made under the law for himself, then he did not yield obedience for himself. It was all for us, and for our good. Let us now look forward, and see what influence this has on our acceptance.

Thirdly, then, this perfect and complete obedience of Christ to the law is reckoned to us. There is truth in the promise that, "The day you eat of it you shall die." Death is the reward of sin, and so we cannot be freed from death but by the death of Christ, Heb. 2:14, 15. It is no less true that we may, "Do this, and live," (Lk. 10:28). Life cannot be obtained unless everything that the law requires is done. And that is still true. "If you will enter into life, keep the commandments," Matt. 19:17. They must, then, be kept either by us or by our surety. It is useless to object that if Christ yielded perfect obedience to the law for us, then are we no longer bound to yield obedience ourselves. For by his death, which was the penalty of the law, we are supposedly freed from the duty. I answer by asking, "How did Christ undergo death?" Merely as it was penal. How, then, are we delivered from death? Merely as it is penal. We still must die. We must die as the last conflict with the effects of sin, and as the passage to our Father. Well, then, Christ yielded perfect obedience to the law. But how did he do it? Purely as it stood in that condition to, "Do this, and live." He did it in the strength of the grace that he received. He did it as a means to procure life, as the tenor of a covenant. Are we, then, freed from this obedience? Yes, but how far? From doing it in our own strength; from doing it to obtain everlasting life. It is foolish to say confidently that we must still work for life. It is the same as saying we are still under the old covenant. We are not freed from obedience as a way of *walking with God,* but we are freed from it as a way of *working to come to him.*

Rom. 5:18, 19, "By the righteousness of one, the free gift came upon all men to justification of life: by the obedience of one many will be made righteous," says the Holy Spirit. By his obedience to the law

143

we are made righteous; it is reckoned to us for righteousness. It is false that the *passive obedience* of Christ is all that is intended here:

First, it is opposed to the disobedience of Adam, which was active. The "*dikaioma*" (righteousness) is opposed to "*paraptomati*" (the fault) [NT:1345, 3900]. The fault was an active transgression of the law. The obedience opposed to it had to be an active fulfillment of the law. Besides, the nature of obedience denotes actions that conform to the law. Christ came not to destroy but to fulfill the law, Matt. 5:17. That was the design of his coming, and so his obedience was for us. He came to fulfill the law for us, Isa. 9:6, and he was born to us, Luke 2:11. This was also the will of the Father, which he came to accomplish out of his infinite love.

Secondly, properly speaking, there is no such thing as passive obedience. Obeying is doing, to which passion and suffering cannot belong. I know it is commonly called passive obedience when men obey until they suffer, but it is not properly so.

The same distinction is found in Phil. 3:9. "And be found in him, not having my own righteousness, which is of the law, but what is through the faith of Christ, the righteousness which is of God by faith." The righteousness we receive is opposed to our own obedience to the law. It is opposed to it, not as something of another kind, but as something of the same kind. It excludes our righteousness from the result that the obedience of Christ obtains. He is thereby "made righteousness to us," 1Cor. 1:30.

In Rom. 5:10, the issue in the *death* of Christ is reconciliation. "For if, when we were enemies, we were reconciled to God by the death of his Son, much more, being reconciled, we will be saved by his life." That is, he removes the enmity and restores us to that condition of peace and friendship that Adam had before his fall. But is there no more to be done? Despite Adam's freedom from wrath, he had to obey if he was to enjoy eternal life. Likewise, there is something more to be done in respect to us if we are to enjoy life after reconciliation. "Being reconciled by his death," we are saved by that perfect obedience which he yielded to the law of God in his life. Distinct mention is made of being reconciled through a non-imputation of sin, as found in Ps. 32:1, Luke 1:77, Rom. 3:25, 2Cor. 5:19; and we are justified through an imputation of righteousness, as found in Jer. 23:6, Rom. 4:5, 1Cor. 1:30. These two things are far from being separate. They reciprocally affirm one another. If not identical, they are eminently joined. And this justification is what we have by the life of Christ.

This is fully expressed in the typical representation of our justification before the Lord in Zech. 3:3-5. It indicates two things belong to our free acceptance before God: taking away the guilt of our

144

sin, represented by removing our filthy robes; this is done by the death of Christ. Remission of sin is its proper fruit; but something more is required for our acceptance. That something more is righteousness, which gives us a right to eternal life. This is represented by the "Change of raiment." The Holy Spirit expresses it again in Isa. 61:10, where he calls it plainly "The garments of salvation," and "The robe of righteousness." This is made ours only by the obedience of Christ, just as the other is made ours only by his death.

Objection: "If we have his righteousness, then we are as righteous as Christ himself."

Answer: There is a great difference between what is his and what we receive. First, this righteousness was inherent in Christ, and it was properly his own. It is only reckoned or imputed to us; it is freely bestowed on us. We are made righteous with what is *not* our own. Secondly, Christ was not righteous for himself, but for us. So there can be no comparison. We may only say that we are made righteous with his righteousness, which he completely worked for us.

This obedience of Christ is the origin of the purchased grace of which we speak; and this is its influence on our acceptance by God. The guilt of our sin, and our liability to be punished for it, is removed and taken away by the death of Christ. But besides taking away the guilt of our sin, we need complete righteousness if we are to be accepted by God. This obedience of Christ, through the free grace of God, is imputed to us for that purpose.

All I will insist on for the present is that the passive righteousness of Christ is only imputed to us in the non-imputation of sin. As for exalting the condition of our faith and new obedience into the place of the righteousness of Christ, that is something I am unfamiliar with in communion with Christ.

(2.) The second cause or spring of our communion with Christ in purchased grace is his death and offering. He lived for us. He died for us. He was ours in all he did and suffered. I will be brief in handling this, because I have addressed all its concerns elsewhere.

The death of Christ is a spring of that purchased grace in which we have communion with him. It is presented in the Scripture under three considerations: [1.] price [2.] sacrifice, and [3.] penalty.

In regard to price, the proper effect of his death is full payment for our redemption; in regard to the sacrifice he offered up, his death produces reconciliation or atonement; and in regard to the penalty required for sin, it yields satisfaction. These are the great ingredients of that purchased grace by which we have communion with Christ in the first place.

[1.] It is a price. "We are bought with a price," 1Cor. 6:20. We are "not redeemed with silver and gold, and corruptible things, but with the precious blood of Christ," 1Pet. 1:18-19. In that sense, it mirrors those things found in other contracts. He came to "give his life a ransom for many," Matt. 20:28. It was the price of redemption, 1Tim. 2:6.

The proper effect and result of the death of Christ, as a price or ransom, is redemption, as I said. Redemption is delivering anyone from bondage or captivity, and from the miseries that attend it. It is accomplished by intervening with or interposing a price or a ransom. It is paid by the redeemer to the one with the authority to detain the captive:

1st. In general, it is a deliverance. Hence Christ is called "The Deliverer," Rom. 11:26. He gives himself to "deliver us," Gal. 1:4. He is "Jesus, who delivers us from the wrath to come," 1Thess. 1:10.

2dly. It is the delivery of someone from bondage or captivity. Without Christ we are all prisoners and captives, "bound in prison," Isa. 61:1, "sitting in darkness, in the prison house," Isa. 42:7, 49:9. We are "prisoners in the pit in which there is no water," Zech. 9:11, "the captives of the mighty, and the prey of the terrible," Isa. 49:25. We are under a "captivity that must be led captive," Ps. 68:18, in "bondage," Heb. 2:15.

3dly. The person who commits us to prison and bondage is God himself. We owe "our debts" to him Matt. 6:12, 18:23-27. Our offenses are against him, Ps. 51:4. He is the judge and lawgiver, James 4:12. To sin is to rebel against him. He imprisons men who continue in disobedience, Rom. 11:32; and he will cast both the body and soul of the impenitent into hell-fire, Matt. 10:28. Men are liable to his wrath, John 3:36. They lie under it by the sentence of the law, which is their prison.

4thly. The miseries that attend this condition are innumerable. They are summed up in bondage to Satan, sin, and the world. We are delivered from all this by the death of Christ, paid as a price or ransom. "God has delivered us from the power of darkness, and has translated us into the kingdom of his dear Son; in whom we have redemption through his blood," Col. 1:13-14. And he "redeems us from all iniquity," Tit. 2:14; "from our vain life," 1Pet. 1:18-19; even from the guilt and power of our sin. He purchased us for himself "a peculiar people, zealous of good works," Tit 2:14. And so he died for the "redemption of transgressions," Heb. 9:15, redeeming us from the world, Gal. 4:5.

5thly. All of this comes by the payment of a price into the hand of God, by whose supreme authority we are detained as captives under the sentence of the law. The debt is owed to the great

146

householder, Matt. 18:23-24; and the penalty is his curse and wrath, from which we are delivered by Christ's death, Rev. 1:5.

The Holy Spirit frequently emphasizes all of this. Rom. 3:24-25, "Being justified freely by his grace, through the redemption that is in Christ Jesus; whom God has set forth to be a propitiation through faith in his blood, to declare his righteousness for the remission of sins." See also 1Cor. 6:20, 1Pet. 1:18; Matt. 20:28; 1Tim. 2:6; Eph. 1:7; Col. 1:13; and Gal. 3:13. This is the first consideration of the death of Christ. The price paid influences the procurement of that grace in which we hold communion with him.

[2.] His death was also a sacrifice, an offering. He had a body prepared for him (Heb. 10:5), one in which he was to accomplish what the typical sacrificial offerings of the law prefigured. And he offered that body, Heb. 10:10. Indeed, he offered his whole human nature, for "his soul" was also made "an offering for sin," Isa. 53:10. For that reason, he is said to offer himself, Eph. 5:2; Heb. 1:3, 9:26. He gave himself as a sacrifice to God, a sweet-smelling savor. He did this willingly, as became the one who was to be a sacrifice. The law of this obedience was written in his heart, Ps. 40:8. That is, he was ready, willing, and desirous to perform it.

Now, the purpose of sacrifices such as his, being bloody and for sin, was atonement and reconciliation (Rom. 5:10; Heb. 2:17). This purpose is ascribed to them throughout the Scripture. They made atonement in a way that was suitable to their nature. And this is the tendency of the death of Christ. It was a sacrifice, atonement, and reconciliation with God. Sin had broken friendship between God and us, Isa. 63:10, for which his wrath was on us, John 3:36. We are liable to it by nature, Eph. 2:3. This wrath is taken away by the death of Christ, *because* it was a sacrifice, Dan. 9:24. "When we were enemies, we were reconciled to God by the death of his Son," Rom. 5:10. And thereby we "receive the atonement," verse 11. For "God was in Christ reconciling the world to himself, not imputing to them their sins and their iniquities," 2Cor. 5:19-21; Eph. 2:12-16. And this sacrificial aspect is the second consideration of the death of Christ. I merely name it, having discussed it at large elsewhere.

[3.] It was also a punishment - a punishment in our stead. "He was wounded for our transgressions, he was bruised for our iniquities, the chastisement of our peace was upon him," Isa. 53:5. God made all of our iniquities (that is, their punishment) "to lay upon him," verse 6. "He bore the sins of many," verse 12. "He bore our sins in his own body on the tree," 1Pet. 2:24; and in doing so, he "who knew no sin, was made sin for us," 2Cor. 5:21. In the Scripture, what it means to bear sin may be found in Deut. 19:15, 20:17; Numb.

14:33; and Ezek. 18:20. I have discussed the nature, kind, matter, and manner of this punishment elsewhere.

Now, being punished tends to satisfy the one who was offended, and who inflicted the punishment because of it. Justice can desire no more than a punishment proportional to the offense. And this is what was inflicted on our dear Lord Jesus. He voluntarily undertook to be our mediator. The righteous Judge, allowing Christ to substitute himself in our place, is properly satisfied by that.

This is the threefold consideration of the death of Christ as a principal fountain of that grace in which we have communion with him. As it will soon appear, the single most eminent part of purchased grace is nothing more than the natural outworking of the threefold effect of the death of Christ.

This, then, has been the second cause of purchased grace, which we will see if we hold communion with Christ. It is his death and blood-shedding under this threefold notion of price, offering, and punishment.

(3.) This is not all. The Lord Christ goes further still. He does not leave us in this state, but carries on the work to completion. "He died for our sins, and rose again for our justification." He rose again to carry on the complete work of purchased grace by his intercession. This is the third effect of it. He is said to be "able to completely save those who come to God by him, seeing he forever lives to make intercession for them," Heb. 7:25.

Now, the intercession of Christ, in respect to its influence on purchased grace, is considered two ways:

[1.] As a continuance of his offering to convey all its fruits and effects to us. This is called his "appearing in the presence of God for us," Heb. 9:24. That is, the high priest, having offered the great offering for expiation of sin, carries its blood into the most holy place, which was the representation of the presence of God. This is to perfect the atonement he made for himself and the people. In the same way, the Lord Christ, having offered himself as a sweet-smelling sacrifice to God, and being sprinkled with his own blood, appears in the presence of God. It is as if to remind the Father of his engagement to redeem sinners by his blood, and to convey the good things to them that his sacrifice procured. And so his appearance has an influence on purchased grace in that he puts in his claim for it in our behalf.

[2.] He procures the Holy Spirit for us to effectively collate and bestow all this purchased grace upon us. We have his engagement to do this for us in John 14:16. "And I will pray the Father, and He will give you another Helper, that He may abide with you forever." This is purchased grace, in respect to its source, which I will not handle now,

148

because I will handle it at large in the communion we have with the Holy Spirit.

CHAPTER 7.

THE NATURE OF PURCHASED GRACE

The fountain of that purchased grace in which the saints have communion with Christ has been revealed. Next we may consider the *nature* of this grace. As said earlier, it has three parts: 1. Grace of acceptance by God. 2. Grace of sanctification from God. 3. Grace of privileges with and before God.

1. The first part is *acceptance by God.* Outside Christ, we are alienated from God, accepted neither personally nor in our services. Sin makes a separation between God and us. It is not my business here to unfold that state of separation with all its consequences. The first issue of purchased grace is to restore us to a state of acceptance. This is done two ways: (1.) By removing what we are refused for, the cause of the enmity. (2.) By bestowing what we are accepted for.

All the causes of the quarrel were to be taken away, so that we would not be under God's displeasure. And what makes us the objects of God's delight and pleasure was to be given to us, the lack of which distanced us from God:

(1.) It removes what we are refused for, which is the guilt of sin and all its circumstances. The first effect of purchased grace is to take away the guilt of sin, so that it will not bind the soul to its wages, which is death.

How this is accomplished by Christ, was evidenced in the close of the foregoing chapter. It is the fruit and effect of his death for us. The guilt of sin was the only cause of our separation and distance from God, as has been said. This made us liable to wrath, punishment, and the whole displeasure of God. Because of it, we were imprisoned under the curse of the law, and given over to the power of Satan. This is the state of our unacceptance. By his death, Christ delivers us from this condition. He bore the curse, underwent the punishment that was ours, and paid the ransom that was due. Thus far the death of Christ is the sole cause of our acceptance by God; all cause for the quarrel and our rejection is taken away. To that end, his sufferings are reckoned to us. Being "made sin for us," 2Cor. 5:21, he is made "righteousness to us," 1Cor. 1:30.

But this will not complete our acceptance by God. The old quarrel may be laid aside, but no new friendship has begun. We may not be sinners, but we are not so far righteous as to have a right to the kingdom of heaven. Adam had no right to life because he was innocent. He must "do this," and *then* he will "live." He must not only have a negative righteousness (not guilty of anything), but he must also have a positive righteousness (he must do all things).

(2.) In the second place then, to our complete acceptance, we must not only escape the imputation of sin, but also be reckoned righteous. Now, this is what we have in the obedience of the life of Christ. This was also revealed in the last chapter. The obedience of the life of Christ was done for us; it is imputed to us; and it is our righteousness before God. By his obedience we are "made righteous," Rom. 5:19. The role that our obedience of faith plays will be declared later.

These two things, then, complete our grace of acceptance. Because sin is now removed, and righteousness bestowed, we have peace with God. We are continually accepted before him. There is nothing to charge us with. It is taken out of the way by Christ and nailed to his cross. It is fastened there. It is publicly and legally cancelled so that it can never be admitted as evidence again. What court of men would admit evidence that has been publicly cancelled and nailed up for all to see? This is how Christ has dealt with what was against us. Not only has he done this, but he also puts the very thing upon us for which we are received into God's favor. He makes us attractive through *his* beauty. He gives us *his* white raiment to stand before the Lord. This is the first part of purchased grace in which the saints have communion with Jesus Christ. It consists in the remission of sin and the imputation of righteousness. It arises from the death of Christ, as a price, sacrifice, and a punishment, and from the life of Christ spent in obedience to the law. It is the great product of the Father's righteousness, wisdom, love, and grace. It is the great and astonishing fruit of the love and condescension of the Son. It is the great discovery of the Holy Spirit in the revelation of the mystery of the gospel.

2. The second part of the nature of grace is *grace of sanctification*. He not only makes us accepted, but also acceptable. He not only purchases love for his saints, but he also makes them lovely. He did not come by blood alone, but by water and blood. He not only justifies his saints from the guilt of sin, but he also sanctifies and washes the filth of sin from them. The first is from his life and death as a sacrifice of propitiation. It is from his death as a purchase, and his life as an example. So says the apostle in Heb. 9:14 and Eph. 5:26, 27.

Two things are eminent in this issue of purchased grace: (1.) The removal of defilement; (2.) The bestowing of cleanness in actual grace.

(1.) The first issue, removal of defilement, has three components:

[1.] The habitual cleansing of our nature. We are naturally unclean, defiled, and habitually so. "Who can bring a clean thing

151

out of an unclean thing?" Job 14:4; "What is born of the flesh is flesh," John 3:6. We are born polluted in our blood, Ezek. 16, completely defiled. The grace of sanctification, purchased by the blood of Christ, removes this defilement of our nature. "Such were some of you; but you are washed, you are sanctified," 1Cor. 6:11. "He has saved us by the washing of regeneration, and the renewing of the Holy Spirit." Tit. 3:3-5. We do not need to dispute how far this original, habitual pollution is removed. It is certain that the soul is made fair and beautiful in the sight of God. Although the sin that defiles remains in us, its habitual defilement is taken away. But handling this is not my aim.

[2.] Removal means taking away the pollution of all our actual transgressions. There is a defilement that accompanies every actual sin. Our own clothes make us abhorrent, Job 9:31. A spot, a stain, rust, wrinkle, filth, blood, attends every sin. In 1John 1:7 we read that, "The blood of Jesus Christ cleanses us from all sin." Besides purging the defilement of our nature (Tit. 3:5), he takes away the defilement created by our actual follies. "By one offering he perfected forever those who are sanctified." He "purged our sins" before he sat down at the right hand of the Majesty on high, Heb. 1:3.

[3.] In the best performances of our duties, we still have defilement, Isa. 64:6. Self, unbelief, and formality, drop themselves into all that we do. We may rightly be ashamed of our best performances. God has promised that the saints' good works will follow them. Truly, if they were measured by the rule as they come from us, and weighed in the balance of the sanctuary, it might be better for us if they were buried forever. But as our high priest, the Lord Christ first bears the iniquity, guilt, and provocation that attends them in severe justice."So it shall be on Aaron's forehead, that Aaron may bear the iniquity of the holy things which the children of Israel hallow in all their holy gifts; and it shall always be on his forehead, so that they may be accepted before the LORD." Ex 28:38. Not only that, he washes away all their filth and defilements. He is like a refiner's fire, purging both the sons of Levi and their offerings. Moreover, he adds sweet incense to them so that they may be accepted.

Whatever is of the Spirit, of Christ, or of grace remains. Whatever is of the self, the flesh, or unbelief, he consumes, wastes, and takes away. Thus, the saints' good works will meet them one day with such a changed appearance that they will scarcely know what they have done. What seemed to them to be black, deformed, and defiled, will appear beautiful and glorious. They will not be afraid to acknowledge them, but will rejoice to see and trace them.

This cleansing of our nature, person, and duty, has its whole foundation in the death of Christ. Hence, our washing and purifying, our cleansing and purging, is ascribed to his blood and its meritorious sprinkling. Sprinkling the blood of Christ proceeds from the communication of the Holy Spirit, which he purchased for us and promises to us. The Spirit is the pure water with which we are sprinkled from all our sins. He is that spirit of judgment and burning that takes away the filth and blood of the daughters of Zion.

This cleansing of our defilement is the first thing in the grace of sanctification. There will be more about this issue later.

(2.) The second issue in this purchased grace is bestowing cleanness as to actual grace. The blood of Christ not only takes away defilement, it also gives purity. And that also takes place in a threefold gradation:

[1.] His blood gives us the Spirit of holiness to dwell in us. By procuring the Spirit of sanctification for us, "He is made sanctification to us," 1Cor. 1:30. Our renewing is done by the Holy Spirit, who is shed on us through Christ alone, Tit. 3:6. The apostle insists in Rom. 8 that the primary gift of sanctification that we receive from Christ, is the indwelling of the Spirit, and our following his guidance. But what concerns the Spirit must be deferred until I discuss our communion with him.

[2.] Christ gives us habitual grace. That is a principle of grace by which we choose to live, as opposed to the principle of lust that is in us by nature. This is the grace that dwells in us, and makes its abode with us. It is called various things according to the distinct faculties of our souls through which it operates, or according to the distinct objects of its exercise. It is a whole new principle of life. In our understanding, it is light. In our will, it is obedience. In our affections, it is love. In all, it is faith. When it leads the soul to rest on Christ, it is faith. When it transports us to delight in him, it is love. But it is still one and the same habit of grace.

[3.] Christ gives us the actual influence we need to perform every spiritual duty. After the saints have been given both the Spirit and habitual grace, Christ still tells them that, "they can do nothing" without him, John 15:5. They are still dependent on him for new influences of grace, or supplies of the Spirit. They cannot live on and spend the old stock. For every new act, they must have new grace. He must "work in us to will and to do of his good pleasure," Phil. 2:13.

It is in these three briefly described aspects of sanctification in purchased grace, looking at purity and cleanness, that we have communion with Christ.

3. The third part of the nature of grace consists in our privileges to stand before God. These privileges are of two sorts, primary and consequential. The primary privilege is adoption, receiving the Spirit of adoption. Consequential privileges are all the favors of the gospel, which only the saints have a right to. But I will speak of this when I come to communion with the Holy Spirit.

These are the things in which we have communion with Christ as to purchased grace in this life. Take them to perfection, and you have what we call everlasting glory. Perfect acceptance, perfect holiness, perfect adoption, the full inheritance of sons: that is glory.

CHAPTER 8.

ACCEPTANCE BY GOD THROUGH COMMUNION WITH CHRIST –

Next is to look at how we hold communion with Christ in these things of purchased grace.

I. How we hold communion with him in the obedience of his life and merit of his death, as to our acceptance by God the Father.

II. How we hold communion with Christ in his blood, in the habits and acts of grace, as to the Spirit of sanctification. (Chap. 9)

III. How we hold communion with him as to the privileges we enjoy. (Chap. 10)

These last two will be treated in the ensuing chapters.

I. Communion with Christ from the OBEDIENCE OF HIS LIFE and the EFFICACY OF HIS DEATH, as to our acceptance by God. This involves discovering what is required on Christ's part and what is required on our part to have fellowship and communion together.

First, on the part of Christ only two things are required:

(1.) That what he did, he did not do for himself, but for us.

(2.) That what he suffered, he did not suffer for himself, but for us.

That is, his intention from eternity, and when he was in the world, was that all that he did and suffered was and should be for us and for our advantage to ensure our acceptance by God. He still continues to make use of what he so did and suffered for that end and purpose. This is most evident:

(1.) What he did, he did for us, and not for himself: "He was made under the law, that we might receive the adoption of sons," Gal. 4:4, 5. He was made under the law. That is, he was made liable to the will and commands of the law. And why was this? To what end? Was it for himself? No. It was to redeem us. That was the aim of all that he did, the purpose of all his obedience. And he accomplished that. He acquaints us with this in John 17:19, "For their sakes I sanctify myself, that they may be sanctified through the truth." He is saying, "I sanctify myself, dedicate myself, and set myself apart, to do all that work I have to do. I did not come to do my own will. I came to save what was lost; to minister and not be ministered to; and to give my life as a ransom." This was the testimony he gave about all he did in the world. This intent of his should especially be seen. From eternity he thought of what he would do for us, and delighted in that. And when he was in the world, in all he did, he still thought, "This is for them, for my beloved."

155

When he went to be baptized, John said, "I need to be baptized by you, and you come to me?" Matt. 3:14, 15. It was as if he said, "You have no need to be baptized at all." But Christ replies, "Let it to be so, now; for it becomes us to fulfill all righteousness." He is saying, "I do it for those who have no righteousness at all, and I am obliged to all of it."

(2.) In what he suffered. This is more clear, In Dan. 9:26 we read, "Messiah will be cut off, but not for himself." The apostle lays the following down as the main difference between Christ and the high priests of the Jews: when the priests made their solemn offerings, they offered for themselves first, and then for the people. But Jesus Christ only made an offering for others. He had no sin, and therefore he could not make a sacrifice for his own sin. He could only do it for others. He "tasted death for every man," Heb. 2:9, "gave his life as a ransom for many," Matt. 20:28. The "iniquity of us all was placed on him," Isa. 53:6; "He bore our sins in his own body on the tree," 1Pet. 2:24; he "loved the church, and gave himself for it," Eph. 5:25; Gal 2:20; Rom. 4:25; Rev. 1:5, 6; Tit. 2:14; 1Tim. 2:6; Isa. 53:12; John 17:19. It is exceedingly clear and admitted that Christ's only intent in his suffering and oblation was for the good of his elect, and their acceptance by God. He suffered for us, "the just for the unjust, that he might bring us to God."

Secondly, to complete this communion on the part of Christ, it is required,

(1.) That there be added to what he has done, the complete righteousness and acceptance by God which arise from his perfect obedience and sufferings. The tendering of this acceptance is twofold:

[1.] It is declaratory rather than meritorious in the conditional promises of the gospel. Mark 16:15; Matt. 11:28, "He that believes will be saved;" "Come to me, and I will give you rest;" "As Moses lifted up the serpent...;" "Christ is the end of the law for righteousness to every one that believes," Rom. 10:4; and many other places. Now, declaratory tenders are very precious. They are filled with kindness. If they are rejected, they will be the "savor of death to death." But the Lord Christ knows that the outward letter of the law will not enable any of his people to receive his righteousness. And his righteousness is necessary to gain them that acceptance. Therefore,

[2.] In this tender of acceptance by God, because of what he has done and suffered, a law is established, that whoever receives his righteousness will be accepted. But Christ knows the condition and state of those who belong to him in this world. This will not do. If he does not effectively *invest* them with his righteousness, then all is lost. Therefore,

(2.) He sends them his Holy Spirit to quicken them, John 6:63, to cause those who are "dead to hear his voice," John 5:25, and to work in them whatever is required of them to make them partakers of his righteousness, and to be accepted by God.

This is how Christ deals with his people: he lives and dies with an intention to work out and complete the necessary righteousness for them, for their enjoyment of it, which leads to a perfect acceptance before God. Then he tenders it to them. He declares the usefulness and preciousness of it to their souls. He stirs them up to desire and value it. And lastly, he effectively bestows it on them. He reckons it to them as if it was their own, so that by it, for it, and with it, they will be perfectly accepted by his Father.

Thus, for our acceptance by God, two things are required:

First, that satisfaction be made for our disobedience, for whatever we did that might damage the justice and honor of God. And that God be reconciled towards us. This could only result from someone undergoing the penalty of the law. This is done by the death of Christ, as I have clearly shown. God "made him to be sin for us," 2Cor. 5:21, a "curse," Gal. 3:13. On this account, we have our absolution. We have our acquittal from the guilt of sin, the sentence of the law, and the wrath of God, Rom. 8:33, 34. We are justified, acquitted, freed from condemnation, because it was Christ who died. "He bore our sins in his own body on the tree," 1Pet. 2:24.

Second, that the righteousness of the law be fulfilled, and the obedience be performed that is required of us. And this is done by the life of Christ, Rom. 5:18, 19.

So, in answer to our fallen state, and the condition of our acceptance by God, there are two parts: one is our absolution from the guilt of sin, so that our disobedience is not charged against us. We have this by the death of Christ. Our sins are imputed to him and will not be imputed to us, 2Cor. 5:21; Rom. 4:25; Isa. 53:12. The other is the imputation of righteousness, so that we may be considered perfectly righteous before God. We have this by the life of Christ. His righteousness in yielding obedience to the law is imputed to us.

And thus our acceptance by God is complete. Being discharged from the guilt of our disobedience by the death of Christ, and having the righteousness of the life of Christ imputed to us, we have friendship and peace with God. This is what I call our grace of acceptance by God, in which we have communion with Jesus Christ.

What remains is to show how believers hold distinct communion with Christ in this grace of acceptance. I will show how they can keep a sense of it alive, and renew the comfort of it every day. Without this, life is a hell. We cannot partake of any peace or joy that does not arise from this grace of acceptance. Look at what grounds we have to be persuaded of our acceptance by God, and that he is at peace with us.

This is the revenue of our peace, comfort, joy, and holiness itself, proportioned to our confidence in the truth of it.

But before I handle our practical communion with the Lord Jesus in this thing, I must remove two considerable objections. One of them speaks against the discharge of our guilt by Christ's death, the other against the imputation of Christ's righteousness by his life.

Objection 1. It may be said, that "if the elect were absolved, reconciled, and freed by the death, blood, and cross of Christ, then from what were they not actually absolved? Because from the time they were born, and for a long while afterward, many of them lived under the wrath of God in this world as unbelievers. They were under the sentence and condemning power of the law (John 3:36). Why were they not immediately freed when the price was paid and reconciliation was made for them?"

Objection 2. "If the obedience of the life of Christ is imputed to us, and that is our righteousness before God, then why do we need to yield any obedience ourselves? Is all of our praying, laboring, watching, fasting, and giving to charity done in vain? Are all the fruits of holiness, done in purity of heart and contributing to a useful life, done without purpose? Who, then, will care or need to be holy, humble, righteous, meek, temperate, patient, good, and peaceable? Who will abound in good works in the world?"

Answer 1. I shall, God assisting, briefly remove these two objections, and then proceed to the topic of our communion with Christ:

(1.) Jesus Christ undertook the work of our reconciliation with God by coming into the world, and he accomplished this work by his death. To do that, he was constituted and considered a common, public person who stood in the place of those for whom he suffered. Hence he is the "mediator between God and man," 1Tim. 2:5. That is, he is one who undertook our responsibilities to God. This is what the next words show in verse 6, "Who gave himself a ransom for all," and the "surety of the better covenant," Heb. 7:22. He undertook on behalf of those with whom that covenant was made. Hence, he is said to be given "for a covenant of the people," Isa. 42:6; and a "leader," 55:4. For all the ends and purposes of righteousness, he was the second Adam to his spiritual seed, 1Cor. 15:45, 47, just as the first Adam was the cause and source of sin to his natural seed, Rom. 5:15-19. "For as by one man's disobedience many were made sinners, so also by one Man's obedience many will be made righteous," (verse 19).

(2.) Being a common person chiefly resulted from these things:

[1.] In general, it results from the covenant he entered into with his Father for this purpose. The terms of this covenant are extensively listed in Isa. 53, and summed up in Ps. 40:7, 8; Heb.

10:8-10. The Father came to be his God, which is a covenant expression, Ps. 89:26; Heb. 1:5; Ps. 22:1, 40:8, 45:7; Rev. 3:12; Mic. 5:4. He was assigned to this work by his Father, Isa. 42:1, 6, 49:9; Mal. 3:1; Zech. 13:7; John 3:16; 1Tim. 1:15. Thus the "counsel of peace" came to be "between them both," Zech. 6:13, that is, the Father and the Son. The Son rejoices from eternity in the thought of this undertaking, Prov. 8:22-30. The command given him to this purpose, the promises made to him, and the assistance afforded to him, I have handled elsewhere.

[2.] It results from the sovereign grant, appointment, and design of the Father, in giving and delivering the elect to Jesus Christ in this covenant. He was to redeem and reconcile them to the Father. "Yours they were, and you gave them me," John 17:6. They were God's by eternal designation and election. He gave them to Christ to be redeemed. Hence, before they were called or they believed, he called them his "sheep," John 10:15, 16. He laid down his life for them as his sheep. And so we are said to be "chosen in Christ," Eph. 1:4. We are designed to obtain all the fruits of the love of God by Christ, and we are committed into his hand for that end and purpose.

[3.] His being a common person results from undertaking to suffer the penalty that was due the elect, and to do what was required of them, so that they might be delivered, reconciled, and accepted by God. He undertook to give in to the Father, without loss or miscarriage, to fulfill what he was assigned to do by the Father, John 17:2, 12, 6:37, 39. He did so just as Jacob did with the cattle he received from Laban, Gen. 31:39, 40. I have treated both of these things somewhat at large elsewhere, in handling the covenant between the Father and the Son. I will not repeat it here.

[4.] The elect being given to him, Christ undertook to do and suffer what was required on their part. He received on their behalf all the promises of mercies, grace, good things, and privileges that they would receive as a result of his undertaking. Because of this, eternal life is said to be promised by God "before the world began," Tit. 1:2. That is, it was promised to the Son of God for us when he undertook these things on our behalf. Grace, too, is said to be given to us "before the world began," 2Tim. 1:9. That is, grace is given to us in Christ, who is our appointed head, mediator, and representative.

[5.] Christ thus was a common person, a mediator, surety, and representative of his church. Upon undertaking this office, his actual performance of his responsibilities on our behalf was efficacious and meritorious, and solemnly declared so. He was acquitted, absolved, justified, and freed from all and everything that was or could be charged against him on behalf of the elect. I say, as to the efficacy and merit of his undertakings, he was immediately absolved upon his faithfulness in first taking the engagement. Thereby all the saints of the Old Testament were saved by his blood no less than we are saved by it.

As to the solemn declaration of his absolution, he was absolved when the "pains of death being loosed," he was "declared to be the Son of God with power, by the resurrection from the dead," Rom. 1:4. God says to him, "You are my Son; this day have I begotten you," Ps. 2:7. And Christ expresses his confidence in his absolution in Isa. 1:5-9. He was "justified," 1Tim. 3:16. What I mean by this absolution of Christ as a public person is this: God made him under the law for those who were also made under the law, Gal. 4:4. In their stead, he was made liable to the punishment that was due to them for their sin. He was made sin for them, 2Cor. 5:21. And so God gave justice, and law, and all the consequences of the curse of the law, power against him, Isa. 53:6. Upon undergoing what was required of him, Isa. 53:12, God releases the pains and the power of death, accepts him, and is well pleased with him as to the performance and discharge of his work, John 17:3-6. He pronounces Christ free from his obligation, and gives him a promise of all the good things he aimed at, and which his soul desired, Acts 13.

All the promises God made to Christ, and their accomplishment, are founded and built upon executing his office as surety and mediator. All the encouragements given to Christ to ask the Father for the things that he was originally engaged for, Ps. 2:8, (and which he accordingly asked for, John 17), were based on that. This is the certain, stable foundation of our absolution, and of our acceptance by God. Christ in our stead, acting for us as our surety, is acquitted and absolved. He is solemnly declared to have answered the whole debt that was incumbent on him to pay. And having made satisfaction for all the injury we had done, a general pardon is sealed for us all, to be sued out particularly in God's appointed way.

[6.] Christ thus being absolved as a public person, it became a righteous thing for God to bestow on those whom Christ represented all the fruits of his death, and to be reconciled to them, Rom. 5:8-11. According to the covenant between God and the mediator, as Christ received the general acquittal for them all, so they would enjoy it, every one of them respectively. This is evident everywhere in those passages which express a commutation designed by God in this matter; as 2Cor. 5:21; Gal. 3:13; 1Pet. 2:21, 24. More will be said of this afterward.

[7.] In the covenant of the Mediator, the elect are said to be circumcised with him, to die with him, to be buried with him, to rise with him, and to sit with him in heavenly places. Christ being acquitted in this covenant, and the elect being personally acquitted in the covenant of grace, it was determined by the Father, Son, and Holy Spirit, that their actual personal deliverance from the sentence and curse of the law should be done in a way that might lead to the praise of the glorious grace of God, Eph 1:5-7. God's design is that they be adopted as his children. The means of doing so is by Jesus Christ. The unique way of bringing it about is through the redemption that is in Christ's blood. The purpose is for the praise of God's glorious grace.

[8.] Until their actual deliverance is accomplished, God determined and appointed for them, in their several generations, that they be under the curse of the law personally. Because of that, they are legally liable to the wrath of God, from which they will certainly be delivered. I say they are personally liable to the law and its curse, but not at all with its primitive intention of being executed. Instead, it is a means appointed to help forward their acquaintance with Christ, and their acceptance by God on his account. When this is accomplished, that whole type of obligation ceases. It is continued in a design of love. Their final condition is such that, without love, they cannot participate in Christ to the praise of the glorious grace of God.

[9.] The purpose of the dispensation of grace being to glorify the whole Trinity, the appointed order in which this is to be done is by ascending to the Father's love through the work of the Spirit and the blood of the Son. The emanation of divine love to us begins with the Father. It is carried on by the Son. And then it is communicated by the Spirit. The Father designs, the Son purchases, and the Spirit effectually works. Our participation comes first by the work of the Spirit, which gains us an actual interest in the blood of the Son, for which we have acceptance by the Father.

This, then, is the order by which we are brought to acceptance by the Father, for the glory of God through Christ:

1st. So that the Spirit may be glorified, he is given to us to enliven us, convert us, and work faith in us, Rom. 8:11; Eph. 1:19, 20. This is done according to all the promises of the covenant, Isa. 4:4, 5; Ezek. 11:19, 36:26.

2dly. This being done, and for the glory of the Son, we thereby actually gain an interest under the covenant in the blood of Christ. We gain an interest in the benefits that he has procured for us by his blood. This very work of the Spirit is itself a fruit and a part of the purchase of Christ. But our sense of it is that the communication of the Spirit comes prior to that.

3dly. To the glory of the Father, we are accepted by him. We are justified, freed from guilt, and pardoned; we have "peace with God," Rom. 5:1. Thus, "through Christ we have access by one Spirit to the Father," Eph. 2:17. And thus the Father, Son and Holy Spirit are glorified in our justification and acceptance by God. The Father is glorified in his free love, the Son in his full purchase, and the Holy Spirit in his effectual working.

[10.] All of this, in all its parts, is as fully procured for us, and as freely bestowed on us, as if we had all been immediately translated into heaven upon Christ's death. It is all done for Christ's sake, on his account, as part of his purchase and merits. This way of deliverance and freedom is fixed on glorifying the whole Trinity.

This may suffice in answer to the first objection. Though our reconciliation with God is fully and completely procured and accomplished by the death of Christ, we actually enjoy it by the means and in the order mentioned, for the praise of the glorious grace of God.

Answer 2. The second objection is, "If the righteousness and obedience of Christ to the law is imputed to us, then why do we need to yield obedience ourselves?" To this, also, I will return an answer as briefly as I can in the ensuing observations:

(1.) We need to place our gospel obedience on the right foot. It may not be exalted into a state, condition, use, or end, that is not given to it by God. Nor may any reason, cause, motive, end, or need for it be taken away, weakened, or impaired. This is a matter of great importance. Some make our obedience (the works of our faith) the basis or cause of our justification. Some make it the condition for imputing the righteousness of Christ to us. Some make it the qualification for being justified. Others exclude the need for works altogether, and turn the grace of God into lasciviousness. It is not my present business to debate these differences. I will only say that our obedience is of great importance in walking with God.

(2.) By no means do we give the same place, condition, state, and use to our personal obedience as we do to the obedience of Christ that is imputed to us. They are inconsistent with one another. Therefore, those who say that our obedience is the condition or cause of our justification, will at the same time deny the imputation of the obedience of Christ to us. The righteousness of Christ is imputed to us so that we are accepted and esteemed as righteous before God. We are really considered such, though not for anything inherent in us. We are as truly righteous with the obedience of Christ imputed to us as Adam was, or could have been, by a complete righteousness of his own performance. So according to Rom. 5:18, by Christ's obedience we are made righteous; truly so, and accepted so. And by the disobedience of Adam we are made trespassers; truly so and considered so. This is the condition that the apostle desires to be found in, in opposition to his own righteousness, Phil 3:9. But our own obedience is not the righteousness by which we are accepted and justified before God.

Nonetheless, God wants us to abound in obedience and personal righteousness.

The apostle evidently delivers and confirms this distinction, so that nothing can be more clearly revealed: Eph. 2:8-10, "For by grace are you saved through faith: and that not of yourselves: It is the gift of God: not of works, lest any man should boast. For we are his workmanship, created in Christ Jesus for good works, which God has ordained before that we should walk in them." We are saved (or justified) "by grace through faith," which receives Jesus Christ and his obedience; "not of works, lest any man should boast." "But what works does the apostle mean?" He means the works of believers, as indicated in the next few words: "For *we* are..." It is we believers, our obedience, and our works, of which he speaks. "What need, then, is there of works?" There is still a need, for "We are his workmanship..."

The apostle intimates two things in these words:

[1.] There is a reason why we cannot be saved by works. It is because we do not do them in our own strength. They must be done in our own strength if we are to be saved or justified by them. "But this is not so," says the apostle; "for we are the workmanship of God..." All our works are wrought in us by full, effectual, undeserved grace.

[2.] Good works are necessary, notwithstanding that we are not saved by them. God has ordained that we will walk in them. This is sufficient ground for our obedience, whatever its use.

If you ask, "What are the proper grounds, reasons, uses, and motives for our gospel obedience to encourage us to abound and be fruitful in that?" I say, there are so many, and they lie so deep in the mystery of the gospel and the dispensation of grace, and they are so spread throughout the whole revelation of the will of God to us, that to handle them fully and distinctly, I would have to turn aside from my topic. I will only give you some brief summaries:

1st. Our universal obedience and good works are indispensably necessary because they are the sovereign appointment and will of God the Father, Son, and Holy Spirit.

In general "This is the will of God, even your sanctification" (or holiness), 1Thess. 4:3. This is what God wills. He requires that we be holy, that we be obedient, that we do his will just as the angels do in heaven. The equity, necessity, profit, and advantage of this reason for our obedience might be examined extensively. If there was no other reason, this one might suffice alone. It is the will of God; it is our duty:

(1.) The Father has ordained or appointed it. It is the will of the Father, Eph 2:10. The Father is spoken of personally, and Christ is mentioned as mediator.

(2.) The Son has ordained and appointed it as mediator. John

15:16, "'I have ordained that you should bring forth the fruit' of obedience, and that it should remain."

(3.) The Holy Spirit appoints and ordains believers to works of obedience and holiness, and to work holiness in others. So, in particular, in Acts 13:2 he appoints men to the great work of obedience in preaching the gospel. And in sinning, men sin against *him.*

2dly. Our holiness, obedience, and work of righteousness, is an important and special end of the unique dispensation of the Father, Son, and Spirit. It exalts the glory of God in our salvation. It is an intended result of the electing love of the Father, the purchasing love of the Son, and the operative love of the Spirit:

(1.) It is a special end of the electing love of the Father, Eph 1:4, "He has chosen us, that we should be holy and without blame." So too in Isa. 4:3, 4. His aim and design in choosing us was that we should be holy and blameless before him in love. This he will accomplish in those who are his. "He chooses us to salvation, through sanctification of the Spirit, and belief of the truth," 2Thess. 2:13. This is what the Father designed as the first and immediate end of his electing love. He proposes that we consider his love as a motive for holiness, 1John 4:8-10.

(2.) This is also true of the exceeding love of the Son. The Scriptural testimonies of it are innumerable. I will only give one or two: Tit. 2:14, "Who gave himself for us, that he might redeem us from all iniquity, and purify for himself a special people, zealous of good works." This was his aim and his design in giving himself for us. Eph. 5:25-27, "Christ loved the church, and gave himself for it; that he might sanctify and cleanse it with the washing of water by the word; that he might present it to himself a glorious church, not having spot, or wrinkle, or any such thing; but that it should be holy, and without blemish" 2Cor. 5:15; Rom. 6:11.

(3.) It is the product of the love of the Holy Spirit. His whole work on us, in us, and for us, consists in preparing us for obedience. He enables us to obey, and brings forth its fruits in us. He does this in opposition to any righteousness of our own, Tit. 3:5. I need not insist on this. The fruits of the Spirit in us are known, Gal. 5:22, 23.

And thus have we a twofold basis for the necessity of our obedience and personal holiness: God requires it, and it is an immediate and important result of the dispensation of God in the work of our salvation. If God's sovereignty over us is to be accepted, and if his love towards us is to be regarded, and if the whole work of the Trinity in us has any importance, then our obedience is necessary.

3dly. It is necessary in respect to its purpose; and that is true whether you consider God, ourselves, or the world:

(1.) The purpose of our obedience in respect to God is his glory and honor, Mal. 1:6. And God's honor is all that we can give him. It is true that God will *take* his honor from the stoutest and proudest rebel in the world. But all that we can *give* him is our obedience. Glorifying God by our obedience is all that we are, or can be. Particularly,

[1st.] Our obedience is the glory of the Father. Matt. 5:16, "Let your light so shine before men, that they may see your good works, and glorify your Father in heaven." By walking in the light of faith glory arises to the Father. The fruits of his love, grace, and kindness are seen in us; and God is glorified on our behalf.

[2dly.] The Son is glorified by our obedience. It is the will of God that just as all men honor the Father, they should honor the Son, John 5:23. How is this done? By believing in him, John 14:1; and obeying him, John 15:10; he says he is glorified in believers, John 17:10; He prays for an increase of grace and unity for them so that he may be more glorified, and so that all might know that he was sent by God as mediator.

[3dly.] The Spirit is also glorified by it. He is grieved by our disobedience, Eph. 4:30; and therefore his glory is in our bringing forth the fruit of obedience. He dwells in us as in his temple, which is not to be defiled. Holiness becomes his habitation forever.

Now, if what has been said is insufficient to evince the necessity for our obedience, then we must be speaking with the sort of men who disregard the sovereignty, love, and glory of God. Even if God completely ignored our obedience, his glory would still be a sufficient ground for yielding our obedience to him. I speak only of the gospel grounds for obedience, not the natural and legal grounds, which are indispensable for all of mankind.

(2.) For ourselves, the purpose for our obedience is threefold. It is for our own honor, peace, and usefulness.

[1st.] *Honor.* It is by holiness that we are made like God, and by which his image is renewed in us. This was our honor at our creation. This is what exalted us above all our fellow-creatures below. We were made in the image of God. We lost this image by sin, and we became like the beasts that perish. We are exalted to this honor again, of conforming to God and bearing his image, by holiness alone. "Be holy," says God, "for I am holy," 1Pet. 1:16. "Be perfect" (that is, in doing good), "just as your Father in heaven is perfect," Matt. 5:48. This is how the image of God is renewed. We "put on the new man, which is created after God in righteousness and holiness of truth," Eph. 4:23, 24. What was originally attended with power and dominion, is still all that is beautiful or attractive in the world. It might easily be proved how it makes men honorable and precious in the sight of God, angels, and men. It is the only thing that is not despised, and has value before the Lord. What contempt and scorn he has for those in whom it is not found. They and all their ways are an abomination to him.

[2dly.] *Peace.* By holiness we have communion with God, and it is solely by holiness that we enjoy peace. "The wicked are like the troubled sea, that cannot rest. 'There is no peace for them' says my God," Isa. 57:20; 21. There is no peace, rest, or quietness, in being distanced, separated, or alienated from God. He is the rest of our souls. In the light of his countenance we have life and peace. "If we walk in the light, as he is in the light, we have fellowship one with another," 1John 1:7. "*Truly our fellowship is with the Father, and with his Son Jesus Christ,*" verse 3. Someone who walks in the light of new obedience has communion with God; in his presence is fullness of joy forever. Without obedience, there is nothing but darkness, wandering, and confusion.

[3dly.] *Usefulness.* A man without holiness is good for nothing. "Ephraim," says the prophet, "is an empty vine, that brings forth fruit to itself." And what is such a vine good for? Nothing. Says another prophet, "A man cannot make so much as a pin of it, to hang a vessel on." A barren tree is good for nothing but to be cut down for the fire. Men who serve the providence of God in their generations are seemingly useful. I could easily show that, although the world and the church might want them, in themselves they are good for nothing. Only the holy man serves the common good.

(3.) Its purpose in respect to others in the world is various:

[1st.] It serves to convict and silence some of the enemies of God, both here in this world, and hereafter at the Judgment:

1. *Here.* 1Pet. 3:16, "Having a good conscience; when they speak evil of you, as evil-doers, they may be ashamed who falsely accuse your good life in Christ." By keeping a good conscience, men will be made ashamed of their false accusations. Their malice and hatred of God's ways has provoked them to speak all manner of evil of the saints' profession; but the holiness and righteousness of the saints convicts and shames them. It is like a thief when he is taken, and driven to acknowledge that God is among them, and that they are wicked themselves, John 18:23.

2. *Hereafter.* It is said that the saints will judge the world. Their good works, righteousness, and holiness will be manifested to all the world, and the righteousness of God's judgments against wicked men will be proven by them. "See," Christ will say, "these are the ones whom I own, whom you so despised and abhorred; and see their works following them. They have done this and that when you wallowed in your abominations," Matt. 25:42, 43.

[2dly.] The conversion of others. 1Pet. 2:12, "Keep your behavior honest among the Gentiles; so that in what they say against you as evil-doers, they may, by your good works, which they will watch, glorify God on the day of visitation," Matt. 5:16. Even revilers, persecutors, and evil-speakers have been overcome by the constant holy walking of professors of Christ. And when their day of visitation has come, they have glorified God because of it, 1Pet. 3:1, 2.

[3dly.] The benefit of all. The benefit comes partly from keeping judgments off the remainder of men, just as ten good men would have preserved Sodom [Gen. 18:32]. It comes partly by their real communication of good to those with whom they deal in their generation. Holiness makes a man a good man, and useful to all; others eat of the fruits of the Spirit that he continually brings forth.

[4thly.] It is necessary in respect to the condition of those who are justified, whether you consider their acceptance or their sanctification:

First. They are accepted and received into friendship with a holy God, a God of purer eyes than to behold iniquity, and a God who hates every unclean thing. Is it not necessary that those who are admitted into his presence, who walk in his sight, and who lie in his heart, should be holy themselves? Should they not cleanse themselves from all pollution of flesh and spirit with all diligence, and mature in holiness in the fear of the Lord?

Secondly. In respect to sanctification. We have a new creature in us, 2Cor. 5:17. This new creature is fed, cherished, nourished, and kept alive by the fruits of holiness. To what end has God given us new hearts, and new natures? Is it that we should kill them? Are we to stifle the creature that is found in us in the womb? Should we give him to the old man to be devoured?

[5thly.] It is necessary in respect to the proper place of holiness in the new covenant. That is threefold:

First. It is a means to an end. God has appointed holiness as the means, the way to that eternal life which, in itself is his gift by Jesus Christ. But with regard to his constituting our obedience as the means of attaining eternal life, eternal life is a reward, and God is bestowing it as a reward. Even though holiness is not the cause, the matter, nor the condition of our justification, it is the way God has appointed for us to obtain salvation. And therefore, someone who has hope of eternal life purifies himself, just as God is pure. No one will ever come to eternal life who does not walk that way; for without holiness it is impossible to see God.

Secondly. It is a testimony and pledge of adoption, a sign and evidence of grace, that is, of acceptance by God.

Thirdly. It is the whole expression of our thankfulness.

Now, each of these reasons for the necessity of our obedience, good works, and personal righteousness would require a larger to explain than I have allotted to proposing them. And there are innumerable others of the same import that I cannot take time to name. If someone thinks universal holiness and obedience are not indispensably necessary for these reasons, or if he wants them to replace the obedience and righteousness of Christ, then let him remain filthy.

It now remains to show what is required on our part to complete our fellowship with Christ in this purchased grace, as to our acceptance by God. It consists of the ensuing particulars:

1. The saints cordially approve of this righteousness of Christ as the only thing that is absolutely complete and able to make them acceptable before God. This supposes six things:

(1.) Their clear and full conviction of the necessity of a righteousness with which to appear before God. This is always in their thoughts; this in their whole lives they take for granted. Many men spend their days in obstinacy and hardness, adding drunkenness to thirst [Dt. 29:19], never once inquiring what their condition will be when they enter into eternity. Others trifle away their time and their souls, sowing the wind of empty hopes, and preparing to reap a whirlwind of wrath [Hos. 8:7]. But for the saints, this conviction of the need for Christ's righteousness lies at the bottom of all their communion with him. It is a deep, fixed, resolved persuasion of the absolutely indispensable need for a righteousness with which to appear before God. The holiness of God's nature, the righteousness of his government, the severity of his law, and the terror of his wrath are always before them. They have all been convinced of sin, and they look at themselves as ready to sink under the vengeance it provokes. They have all cried, "What shall we do to be saved?" "With what shall we come before God?" And they have all concluded that it is useless to flatter themselves with hopes of escaping their nature. If God is holy and righteous, and has purer eyes than to behold iniquity, then they must have a righteousness with which to stand before him. They know that one day the cry of those who now depend on themselves will be far different, Isa. 53:1-5; Mic. 6:6, 7.

(2.) They weigh their own righteousness in the balance, and find it wanting. It is wanting in two ways:

[1.] In general - When men are convinced of the necessity of a righteousness with which to stand before God, they catch at everything that presents itself for relief. Like drowning men, they grab at anything to save themselves. Sometimes it proves to be a rotten stick that sinks with them. That is what the Jews did. They caught hold of the law, but it would not relieve them, Rom. 9:31-32.

They perished with it, the apostle says, Rom. 10:1-4. The law led them to set up a righteousness of their own. This kept them doing, and in hope, but it kept them from submitting to the righteousness of God. Here is where many perish, and never get any nearer to God all their days. The saints renounce this self-righteousness. They have no confidence in the flesh. They know there is nothing they can do, or the law can do, to avail them. They are both weakened through the flesh. See what judgment Paul makes of man's own righteousness, Phil 3:8-10. The saints bear this in mind daily. They fill their thoughts with the fact that nothing they have personally done will ever make them acceptable to God, or justified thereby. This keeps their souls humble and full of a sense of their own vileness all their days.

[2.] In particular – The saints weigh their particular actions in the balance daily, and find them wanting. They are incomplete on their own to be accepted by God. "Oh!" says a saint, "if I had nothing to commend me to God but this prayer, this duty, this conquest of a temptation, in which I myself see so many failings and so much imperfection, how could I appear with any confidence before him? Will I piece together a garment of righteousness from my best duties? It is all a defiled cloth," Isa. 64:6. These thoughts accompany all their duties, even their best performances. "Lord, what am I when I am doing my best? My best duties are little suited to your holiness! Spare me when considering the best thing that I ever did in my life!" Neh. 13:22. When a man who lives on such convictions has some improvement in his duties, some conquest over a sin or temptation, he hugs himself, like Micah did when he got a Levite to be his priest. Surely it will be well with him now; surely God will bless him. His heart is eased; he has peace in what he has done, Judg. 17:13. But the one who has communion with Christ, despite achieving great success in sanctification and holiness, clearly understands that he has gained little to commend him to God. He rejects every thought in his heart that is satisfied in letting his peace depend on these acts. He says to his soul, "Do these things seem like something to you? No! You are dealing with an infinitely righteous God who sees through all that vanity, which you are so little acquainted with. If he dealt with you according to your best works, you would perish."

(3.) The saints approve of, value, and rejoice in Christ's righteousness for their acceptance. The Lord Jesus has worked it out and provided it for them. This being revealed to them, they approve of it with all their hearts, and they rest in it. "Surely, one will say, in the LORD I have righteousness and strength," Isa. 45:24. Once the righteousness of God in Christ is made known to them, they say

169

"Here is righteousness indeed; here I have rest for my soul. Like the merchant in the gospel (Matt. 13:45, 46) who finds the pearl of great price, I had been searching up and down. I looked this way and that for help, but it was far away. I spent my strength for what was not bread. Here is that pearl, indeed, which makes me rich forever!" When a poor laboring soul, who has fought for rest and found none, first discovers the righteousness of Christ for acceptance by God, he is surprised and amazed. He cannot contain himself. In his heart he approves of this righteousness for two reasons:

[1.] Because it is full of infinite wisdom. "To those who believe," says the apostle, "Christ crucified is 'the wisdom of God,'" 1Cor. 1:24. He sees infinite wisdom in this way of being accepted by God. "I was in such darkness," he says, "such straits, and such entanglements! I could not see through the fog and perplexities that enclosed me! I looked inwards, and saw nothing but sin, horror, fear, and tremblings; I looked upwards, and saw nothing but wrath, curses, and vengeance. I knew that God was a holy and righteous God, and that no unclean thing could abide before him. I knew that I was a poor, vile, unclean, and sinful creature. What I did not know, was how to bring these two together in peace. But, in the righteousness of Christ, a world of wisdom opens itself, dispelling all difficulties and darkness, and reconciling all of this." "O the depth of the riches both of the wisdom and knowledge of God!" Rom. 11:33; Col. 2:3.

[2.] Because it is full of grace. He knows that sin barred the way of grace towards him. God wants nothing more than to manifest his grace, but because of sin, this man was completely cut off from it. Now, it delights the soul to have complete righteousness provided, and abundant grace manifested. His thoughts are consumed by God's dealing with him entirely by grace, and dealing with his righteousness entirely by justice. God assures us everywhere that this righteousness is of grace. It is "by grace, and no more of works," Rom 11:6, just as the apostle lays it out in Eph. 2:7-9. It is from his riches of grace and kindness that the provision of this righteousness is made. It is of mere grace that it is bestowed on us. It is not at all of works. Although in itself it is a righteousness of works, to us it is of mere grace. So it says in Tit. 3:4-7. "But after that, the kindness and love of God our Savior toward man appeared, not by works of righteousness which we have done, but according to his mercy he saved us, by the washing of regeneration, and the renewing of the Holy Spirit, which he shed on us abundantly through Jesus Christ our Savior, that being justified by his grace, we should be made heirs according to the hope of eternal life."

The source of all this dispensation is kindness and love, which is grace, as verse 4 indicates. The way it is communicated, negatively speaking, is *not* by works of righteousness that we have done. Instead, positively, it is by the communication of the Holy Spirit to us, verse 5. The means of the Spirit's procurement is Jesus Christ, verse 6. And the work itself is by grace, verse 7. Here use is made of almost every word by which the exceedingly rich grace, kindness, mercy, and goodness of God may be expressed. They all join together in describing this work. For example, these words:

1. "*Chrestotes*," meaning his goodness, benignity, readiness to communicate of himself and his good things that may profit us.

2. "*Philanthropia*," meaning his mercy, love, and propensity to help, assist, and relieve those of whom he speaks, and towards whom he is so affected.

3. "*Eleos*," meaning mercy forgiveness, compassion, and tenderness toward those who suffer; and

4. "*Charis*," which is free pardoning bounty, and undeserved love.

All of this is said to be "*tou Theou soteros*" [to God our Savior]. He exercises all these properties and attributes of his nature towards us so that he may save us. And in bestowing it, in giving us the Holy Spirit, it is said, "*exeche-en*," he poured him out as water out of a vessel, without stop or hesitation. And that was done not in a small measure, but "*plousios*," richly and in abundance. As to the work itself, it is emphatically said, "*dikaiotentes te ekeinou chariti*," we are justified by the grace of the one who is gracious, kind, and merciful. And in their communion with Christ, the saints of God greatly rejoice that the way of acceptance is a way of grace, kindness, and mercy. They rejoice that they might not boast in themselves, but in the Lord and his goodness. They cry, "How great is your goodness! How great is your bounty!"

(4.) They approve of this righteousness, and rejoice in it, as a haven of great peace and security to themselves and their own souls. They remember their condition while they tried to set up a righteousness of their own, and were not subject to the righteousness of Christ. They remember how miserably their thoughts and emotions were tossed up and down. Sometimes they had hope, and sometimes they were full of fear. Sometimes they thought themselves in a good condition, and later were at the very brink of hell. Their consciences were racked and torn with sin and fear. But now, "being justified by faith, they have peace with God," Rom. 5:1. All is quiet and serene. Not only is that storm over, but they are in the haven where they want to be. They have abiding peace with God. Hence that description of Christ given to a poor soul in Isa. 32:2, "And a man will be as a hiding-place from the wind, and a covert from the tempest; as rivers of water in a dry place, as the shadow of a great rock in a weary land." Wind and tempest, drought and weariness, nothing now troubles the one who is in Christ. He has a hiding-place, a covert, rivers of water, and the shadow of a great rock for his security. This is the great mystery of faith, in our acceptance by God through Christ. Although the believer finds enough in himself to tear the very membrane of his heart, to fill him with fears, terror, and disquiet all his days, yet through Christ he is at perfect peace with God, Isa. 26:3; Ps. 4:6-8. Hence believers magnify Jesus Christ, because they can behold the face of God with boldness, confidence, peace, joy, and assurance. They can call him Father, rest themselves on his love, walk up and down in quietness, and without fear. How glorious the Son of God is in this grace! They remember the wormwood and bitterness that they have eaten, Deut. 29:18; the vinegar and tears they have drunk, Ps. 69:21; the trembling of their souls, like an aspen leaf that is shaken with the wind. Whenever they thought of God, they contrived to hide, fly, and escape! To be brought to a settlement now, and security, must greatly affect them.

(5.) They cordially approve of this righteousness because it is a way to exalt and honor the Lord Jesus, whom they love. Once acquainted with Jesus Christ, their hearts desire nothing more than to honor and glorify him to the utmost, and to give him pre-eminence in all things. Now, what can advance and honor him more in our hearts, than to know that he is "made wisdom and righteousness to us by God?" 1Cor. 1:30. He is not *part* of our acceptance by God; he is the *whole* of it. The saints know that, because he worked out their acceptance by God,

[1.] He is honored by God his Father. Phil. 2:7-11, "He made himself of no reputation, and took upon him the form of a servant, and was made in the likeness of men: and being fashioned as a man, he humbled himself, and became obedient to death, even the death of the cross. Wherefore God also has highly exalted him, and given him a name which is above every name, that at the name of Jesus every knee should bow, of things in heaven, and things in earth, and things under the earth; and that every tongue should confess that Jesus Christ is Lord, to the glory of God the Father." It does not matter whether that word "wherefore" denotes a cause or only a consequence. It is evident that because of his suffering, and as its purpose, he was honored and exalted by God to an inexpressible pre-eminence, dignity, and authority. This was according to God's promise to him, Isa. 53:11, 12; Acts 2:36, 5:30, 31. And therefore it is said, that when "he had purged our sins, he sat down at the right hand of the Majesty on high," Heb. 1:3.

[2.] For this great work of bringing sinners to God, he is honored above all the angels in heaven; for they not only bow down and desire to look into the mystery of the cross, 1Pet. 1:12, but they always worship and praise him on this account, Rev. 5:11-14. "I heard the voice of many angels round about the throne, and the living creatures and the elders: and their number was ten thousand times ten thousand, and thousands of thousands; saying with a loud voice, 'Worthy is the Lamb that was slain to receive power, and riches, and wisdom, and strength, and honor, and glory, and blessing.' And every creature which is in heaven and earth, and under the earth, and those that are in the sea, and all that are in them, I heard saying, 'Blessing, and honor, and glory, and power, be to him that sits upon the throne, and to the Lamb forever and ever.' And the living creatures said, Amen. And the twenty-four elders fell down and worshipped him that lives forever and ever." The reason given for this glorious and wonderful doxology, this attribution of honor and glory to Jesus Christ by the whole host of heaven, is because he was the Lamb that was slain. That is, it is because of the work of our redemption and our being brought to God. And it is refreshing and joyous to the saints to know that all the angels of God, the whole host of heaven, who never sinned, still continually rejoice and ascribe praise and honor to the Lord Jesus for bringing the saints to peace and favor with God.

[3.] He is honored by his saints all over the world. Indeed, if they do not honor him, who should? If they do not honor him just as they honor the Father, then they are the most unworthy of men. But see what they do in Rev. 1:5-6. "To him that loved us, and washed us from our sins in his own blood, and who has made us kings and priests to God and his Father; to him be glory and dominion forever and ever. Amen." Rev. 5:8-10, "The four living creatures and the twenty-four elders fell down before the Lamb, every one of them having harps and golden vials full of fragrant aromas, which are the prayers of the saints. And they sung a new song, saying, 'You are worthy to take the book, and to open its seals: for you were slain, and have redeemed us to God by your blood, out of every kindred, and tongue, and people, and nation; and have made us kings and priests to our God: and we will reign on the earth.'" The great, solemn worship of the Christian church consists in this assignation of honor and glory to the Lord Jesus. Thereby they love him, honor him, and delight in him, as Paul does in Phil. 3:8; and so too the spouse in Cant. 5:9-16.

(6.) They cordially approve of this righteousness, this way of acceptance, as something that brings glory to God. When they labored under the guilt of sin, what most perplexed them was that their safety was inconsistent with the glory and honor of the great God. His justice, faithfulness, and truth were all engaged to destroy sin. They could not see how to avoid this jeopardy without the loss of their honor. But now, having the revelation of this righteousness from faith to faith, they plainly see that all the properties of God are magnificently glorified in the pardon, justification, and acceptance of sinners, as shown before.

This is the first way by which the saints hold daily communion with the Lord Jesus in this purchased grace of acceptance by God. They consider, approve of, and rejoice in the way of gaining acceptance, its means, and the acceptance itself.

2. They actually exchange their sins for Christ's righteousness.

(1.) They continually keep alive in their hearts a sense of the guilt and evil of sin. They do this even when they are comfortably persuaded of their personal acceptance by God. The sense of pardon takes away the horror and fear of sin, but not a due sense of the guilt of it. The daily exercise of the saints of God is to consider the great provocation that is in their sins, both of their nature and of their lives. They render themselves vile in their own hearts and thoughts because of it. They compare it with the terror of the Lord, and judge themselves continually. "My sin is ever before me," says David. Likewise, the saints set their sin before them, not to terrify and frighten their souls, but to keep alive in their hearts a due sense of the evil of it.

(2.) They clearly and specifically gather up in their mind the sins for which they have not made a particular reckoning with God in Christ. There is nothing more dreadful for a man than to digest his convictions of sin, to have sin look him in the face and perhaps terrify him, and then put off coming to a full trial of his sin through distractions or delays. This is what the saints do: they gather up their sins, place them on the scales of the law, see them for what they are, consider their weight and consequences, and then,

(3.) They make this exchange I speak of with Jesus Christ.

[1.] They seriously consider, and then by faith conquer all doubt, that Jesus Christ, by the will and appointment of the Father, has really undergone the punishment that was due for those sins which now lie under his eye for consideration, Isa. 53:6; 2Cor. 5:21. He has certainly, and really, satisfied the justice of God for these sins, just as if the sinner had been cast into hell for them at that instant.

[2.] The saints respond to the voice of Christ calling them to come to him with their burden, "Come to me, all you that are weary and heavy laden," Matt. 11:28. "Come with your burdens; come to me, you poor soul, with your guilt of sin." Why? To do what? "Why, this burden is mine." says Christ; "I made this agreement with my Father to come and take away your sins; they were my responsibility. Give me your burden, give me all your sins. You do not know what to do with them. I know how to dispose of them in a way that glorifies God, and delivers your soul." And so,

[3.] They lay down their sins at the cross of Christ. They place them on his shoulders. This is faith's great and bold venture, founded on the grace, faithfulness, and truth of God, to stand by the cross and say, "Ah! He is bruised for my sins, and wounded for my transgressions, and the chastisement for my peace is upon him. He is thus made sin for me. Here, I give up my sins to the one who is able to bear them. He requires it of me, so I will be content to have him take them from me. I heartily consent to that." Isa. 53:5; 2Cor. 5:21. This is every day's work. I do not know how any peace can be maintained with God without doing this. If it is our work to receive Christ as one who is made sin for us, then we must receive him as one who takes our sins upon him. It is not as though he could die any more, or suffer any more than he did. The faith of the saints of old made present what had not yet come to pass, as if done before their eyes, Heb. 11:1. So faith now makes present what was already accomplished many generations ago. This is what it means to know Christ crucified.

[4.] Having thus, by faith, given up their sins to Christ, and having seen God lay all their sins on him, the saints draw close, and take from Christ that righteousness which he has worked out for them. They are fulfilling the whole of what the apostle says in 2Cor. 5:21, "He was made sin for us, that we might be made the righteousness of God in him." They consider him offering himself and his righteousness as their righteousness before God. They take it, and accept it. They complete this blessed bartering and exchange of faith. Anger, curse, wrath, death, the guilt of sin - he takes it all away. We leave with him everything of this nature, and receive from him righteousness, love, life, and peace.

Objection. It may be said, "Surely this cannot be acceptable to Jesus Christ. Will we come to him every day with our filth, our guilt, and our sins? Will he not tell us to keep them to ourselves? They are our own. Will we always give him our sins and take his righteousness?"

Answer. There is nothing that Jesus Christ more delights in, than having his saints hold communion with him in this business of giving and receiving.

1. This greatly honors him, and gives him the glory that is his due. Many, indeed, cry "Lord, Lord," and mention him, but do not honor him. How? They take his work out of his hands, and ascribe it to other things. They think their repentance, their duties, will bear the

175

burden of their iniquities. They do not say so, but that is what they do. The exchange they make, if any, is with themselves. All their bartering about sin is with their own souls. The work that Christ came to do in the world was to "bear our iniquities," and to lay down his life as a ransom for our sins. The cup he had to drink was filled with our sins and their punishment. What greater dishonor can be done to the Lord Jesus, than to ascribe this work to anything else, to think we can get rid of our sins by any other means? Christ is honored indeed when we go to him with our sins by faith, and say to him, "Lord, this is your work. This is why you came into the world. This is what you have undertaken to do. You call for my burden which is too heavy for me to bear. Take it, blessed Redeemer. You offer your righteousness; that is my portion." Christ is honored, and the glory of mediation is ascribed to him, when we walk with him in this kind of communion.

2. This greatly endears the saints to him. It constrains them to put a due value on him, his love, his righteousness, and grace. When they make this exchange daily, then they rightly value him. Who would not love him? "I have been with the Lord Jesus," may the poor soul say. "I have left my sins, my burden, with him; and he has given me his righteousness, with which I am going with boldness to God. I was dead, and now I am alive; for he died for me. I was cursed, and now I am blessed; for he was made a curse for me. I was troubled, but now I have peace; the chastisement for my peace was on him. I did not know what to do, nor how to relieve my sorrow; by him I have received unspeakable and glorious joy. If I do not love him, delight in him, obey him, live to him, die for him, I am worse than the devils in hell." The great aim of Christ in the world is to have a high place and esteem in the hearts of his people. It is to have the pre-eminence in all things, not to be shuffled among other things. He is to be all, and in all. The saints of God esteem him this way by engaging in this communion with him.

Objection. You may say, "If this is so, then why do we need to repent or amend our ways? Making this exchange with him means our sin will just go to Christ by faith anyway. And so we may sin more so that grace may grow more."

Answer. I judge no one, but I must say that I do not understand how anyone truly acquainted with Christ could accept this objection in cold blood, unless he was under a temptation or accidental darkness. However, I am certain that this communion in itself produces quite different effects than those supposed.

1. I assume it is gospel repentance that is intended. As for legal repentance, it is born of bondage. It is full of dread, awe, terror, self-love, and shock at the presence of God. I admit that this communion takes such repentance away. It precludes it, and casts it out along with its bondage and fear. But as for gospel repentance, its nature consists

in having a godly sorrow for sin, and relinquishing it. It proceeds from faith, love, and abhorrence of sin, on the account of the Father, Son, and Spirit, because of both the law and their love. It is impossible for such repentance to be hindered by this communion. I told you that the foundation of this communion is laid in a deep, serious, and daily consideration of the guilt of sin, its vileness and abomination. A sense of it is to be kept alive in the heart of everyone who would enjoy this communion with Christ. Without a sense of the guilt of our sin, we would have no value or esteem for Christ. Is it possible for someone to be a stranger to godly sorrow if he fills his heart daily with thoughts of how vile his sin is? It does not matter whether he considers it vile because of the law, love, grace, the gospel, love of life, or fear of death. He will be filled with self-abhorrence because of it. Here is the mistake made in this objection: the foundation of this communion is laid in the very thing that this objection supposes it overthrows. Communion drives us to repentance.

2. But what will we say for obedience? "If Christ is so glorified and honored by taking our sins, the more we bring to him, the more he will be glorified." We can only suppose that this objection would not be made unless the Holy Spirit, who knows what is in a man's heart, has made it for them, as in Rom. 6:1-3. And the very same doctrine that I have delivered is found in Rom. 5:18-20, where the same objection is made to it. For those who think the objection has any weight, I refer them to the answer given there by the apostle. Our obedience is necessary, notwithstanding the imputation of the righteousness of Christ.

But you will ask, "How should we perform this duty? What path are we to take?"

Faith exercises itself in obedience, three ways especially:

(1.) In meditations. The heart goes over its thoughts concerning sin severally and jointly. Sometimes it fixes primarily on one thing, sometimes on another, and sometimes going over the whole. Perhaps the soul mostly considers its own sinfulness, and so it fills itself with shame and self-abhorrence for it. Sometimes it is filled with thoughts of the righteousness of Christ, and with unspeakable and glorious joy on that account. Especially when grieved and burdened by negligence, or a burst of corruption, the soul goes over the whole work. It drives things to an issue with God, and then it takes up the peace that Christ has worked out for it.

(2.) In considering the promises of the gospel. The soul considers the excellence, fullness, and suitability of the righteousness of Christ, the rejection of all false righteousness, and the exchange that was made in the love of God.

(3.) In prayer. The saints go through this work of prayer day by

177

day. All the saints have this communion with the Lord Jesus, as to their acceptance by God. This was the first thing proposed for consideration under the graces of communion.

CHAPTER 9.

COMMUNION WITH CHRIST IN HOLINESS –

II. Our communion with the Lord Jesus as to that grace of SANCTIFICATION and PURIFICATION may be neatly considered in two parts. We have made mention of this earlier in its several distinctions and degrees. We must show

1. What the specific acts of the Lord Christ are as to this communion, and

2. What the duties of the saints are in this communion.

The sum will be how we hold communion with Christ in holiness as well as in righteousness.

1. There are several acts ascribed to the Lord Jesus in reference to this. Briefly,

(1.) He intercedes with the Father by virtue of his offering on behalf of his saints; and this is to bestow the Holy Spirit on them. I choose to enter here, because I have spoken before of the offering of Christ itself. Everything else flows from that spring. It is the foundation of all spiritual mercies, as I will show later. Now, the Spirit is part of the purchase of Christ. To us, he is a Spirit of grace, holiness, and consolation. Receiving him is the great promise of the new covenant, Ezek. 11:19, "I will put a new spirit within you;" also Ez. 36:27; Jer. 32:39, 40; and a number of other places. Christ is the mediator and "surety of this new covenant." Heb. 7:22, "Jesus was made surety of a better testament," or covenant (a testament needs no surety). He undertakes what he does on the part of both God and man. On the part of man, he gives satisfaction for sin. On the part of God, he bestows the whole grace of the promise, as in Heb. 9:15, "For this cause he is the mediator of the new covenant, so that by means of death, for the redemption of transgressions that were under the first covenant, those who are called might receive the promise of eternal inheritance."

He satisfied for sin, and he procured the promise. He procures all the love and kindness that are the fruits of the covenant. He is, himself, the original promise of the covenant, Gen. 3:15. The whole of this is so "ordered in all things, and made sure," 2Sam. 23:5, that the remainder of its effects all derive from him, depend on him, and are procured by him. It is done "so that he, in all things, might have the pre-eminence," Col. 1:18. This is according to the agreement made with him, Isa. 53:12. These fruits are all purchased by his blood, and therefore the Spirit is too, as promised in that covenant, 1Cor. 1:30.

Now, the whole fruit and purchase of his death derives from the Father upon Christ's intercession. John 14:16-18, "And I will pray the Father, and He will give you another Helper, that He may abide with you forever — the Spirit of truth, whom the world cannot receive, because it neither sees Him nor knows Him; but you know Him, for He dwells with you and will be in you. I will not leave you orphans; I will come to you." He promises his disciples that he will pursue the work which he has in hand on their behalf. He will intercede with the Father for the Spirit as a fruit of his purchase. Therefore he tells them that he will not pray the Father for his love for them, because the eternal love of the Father is not the fruit but the fountain of his purchase. Instead he will pray for the Spirit, which is a fruit. And as mediator, what Christ asks the Father to bestow on us is part of his purchase. It is promised to him upon his undertaking to do the will of God.

This is the first thing to be considered in communion with the Lord Jesus. He intercedes with his Father, so that the Spirit may be bestowed on us as a fruit of his death, of his blood shed on our behalf. This is the relation of the Spirit of holiness, as bestowed on us, to the mediation of Christ. The Spirit is the great foundation of the covenant of grace. He is everlastingly destined and freely given to purchase all the good things of that covenant. Receiving the Holy Spirit according to the promise, Acts 2:33, he sheds him abroad on his own, Rom. 5:5. Faith considers this. It fixes on it and dwells upon it. For,

(2.) His prayer being granted (because the Father "always hears him") he actually sends his Spirit into the hearts of his saints to dwell in his stead. The Spirit does all things for them and in them that Christ himself does. Secondly, the Lord Christ is to be seen in this by faith. That is not only in respect to the first provision of his Holy Spirit, but also the continuing supplies of the Spirit. Christ draws out and stimulates more effective operations and acts of that indwelling Spirit. Hence, although John 14:16 says the Father will give them the Comforter, Christ affirms that he sends the Spirit himself. The original and sovereign dispensation is in the Father's hand. It is executed by him upon the intercession of Christ. Yet, the Spirit is not bestowed immediately upon us. He is given into the hand of Christ for us. Christ actually bestows him. Jn. 15:26, "I will send the Comforter to you, from the Father." He receives him from his Father, and actually sends him to his saints. So to in John 16:7, "I will send him." And in verses 14-15 he shows how he will send him. He will equip him with what is Christ's to bestow upon them: "He will take of mine [of what is properly and uniquely mine as mediator, the holy fruit of my life and death], and give it to you." But more of these things afterward.

This, then, is the second thing that the Lord Christ does, and which is to be seen in him: He sends his Holy Spirit into our hearts to abide with us, and to dwell in us. This is the efficient cause of all holiness and sanctification. The Spirit quickens, enlightens, and purifies the souls of his saints. How our union with Christ flows from this communication of the Spirit to us, with all the benefits that depend on it, I have declared elsewhere at some length. This reference to the Spirit is to be considered in Christ by faith.

(3.) There is what we call habitual grace. This means the fruits of the Spirit, the spirit which is born of the Spirit, John 3:6. What is born of, or produced by, the Holy Spirit, in the heart or soul of a man when he is regenerate, and what makes him regenerate, is spirit. It is in opposition to the flesh, or that enmity against God which is in us by nature. It is faith, love, joy, hope, and the rest of the graces of the gospel, in their root or common principle. Concerning habitual grace, two things are to be observed:

[1.] Although many particular graces are mentioned, we do not have different habits or qualities in us. Several distinct principles do not exist for each. There is only the same habit or spiritual principle that expresses itself in various operations or ways of working. And it does so according to the variety of objects which it addresses. So it is distinguished in respect to its actual exercise in relation to its objects, rather than those objects being inherent in it. It is one root which has many branches.

[2.] What I mean by this habit of grace is a new, gracious, spiritual life, or principle, that is created and bestowed on the soul. By this principle, the soul is changed in all its faculties and affections. It is fitted and enabled to progress in the way of obedience to every divine object that is proposed to it according to the mind of God. For instance, the mind can discern spiritual things in a spiritual manner; and in that ability, this principle acts as a light, or illumination. The whole soul joins with Christ for righteousness and salvation, as promised of the gospel. Faith, being the principal work of grace, is often given as the title for the whole. So when faith rests in God, in Christ, with delight, desire, and contentment, it is called love. It is the principle that suits all the faculties of our souls for spiritual and living operations, according to their natural use. Now, habitual grace differs from several other things.

1st. It differs from the Spirit dwelling in the saints, because it is a created quality. The Spirit dwells in us as a free agent in holy habitation. This grace, as a quality, remains in us as something that does not have any subsistence, but is capable of being roused or restrained in great degree.

2dly. It differs from actual grace, which is transient. Habitual grace makes its residence in the soul. Actual grace is a passing of divine influence and assistance to work any spiritual act or duty in the soul. It does not pre-exist the act, nor continue after it. "God working in us, both to will and to do." But habitual grace is always resident in us. It causes the soul to be a fit vehicle for all those holy and spiritual operations which are to be performed by actual grace.

3dly. It is capable of growing and shrinking by degree, as was said. In some people, it is larger and more effectual than in others. In the same person, it may be more effectual at one time than it is at another. Hence, the Scripture frequently mentions how we die, decay, spoil, recover, complain, and rejoice depending on the vigor of this habitual grace.

These things being said as to its nature, let us now consider what we are to see *in the Lord Jesus* in reference to habitual grace. This will be an introduction to our communion with him in this, as things performed by him or on his part:

First, as I said of the Spirit, I say of this grace. It is a purchase of Christ, and it is to be seen as such. "It is given to us for his sake to believe on him," Phil. 1:29. Because it is purchased and procured by him for us, the Lord bestows faith, and (by same rule) all grace upon us. "We are blessed with all spiritual blessings in heavenly places in him," Eph. 1:3. "In him" means it is the result of his mediation for us. His offering and intercession lie at the bottom of this dispensation. If grace were not procured by them, it would never be enjoyed by anyone. All grace is from this fountain. In receiving it from Christ, we must still consider what it cost him. The lack of this weakens faith. His whole intercession is founded on his offering, 1John 2:1-2. What he purchased by his death may be bestowed, neither more nor less. And he prays that all his saints may have this grace we are speaking of, John 17:17. If we continually consider all grace as the fruit of the purchase of Christ, it would greatly endear our spirits. Without this consideration, according to the tenor of the gospel, we cannot ask for or expect any grace. It does not prejudice the free grace of the Father to look at anything as the purchase of the Son. It was from the Father's free grace that Christ made that purchase. In receiving grace from God, we do not have communion with Christ, the treasury of the God's grace, unless we look upon it as his purchase. He obtained it so that we would be sanctified throughout, so that we would have life, be humble, holy, believing, and so that we would divide the spoil with the mighty, by destroying the works of the devil in us (Isa. 53:12; 1Jn. 3:8).

Secondly. The Lord Christ actually communicates this grace to his saints. He bestows it on them: "Of his fullness have all we received, and grace for grace," John 1:16. For,

(1st.) The Father, by compact and agreement, actually invests him with all the grace he has purchased (just as he received the promise of the Spirit). This is everything that is useful to bring his many sons to glory. "It pleased the Father that all fullness should dwell in him," Col. 1:19. It pleased him that Christ should be invested with the fullness of grace that is needed for his people. Christ calls this the "power of giving eternal life to his elect," John 17:2. This power is not only his ability to do it, but also his right to do it. Hence, all things are delivered to him by his Father. This is the basis for inviting sinners to come to him for refreshment: "All things are delivered to me of my Father," Matt. 11:27. "Come to me, all that labor and are heavy laden, and I will give you rest," Matt. 11:28.

The covenant of the Father with him, and his promise to him, is that upon making "his soul an offering for sin, he would see his seed, and the pleasure of the LORD would prosper in his hand," Isa. 53:10. "Pouring out his soul to death, and bearing the sins of many," Isa. 53:12, is the foundation and procuring cause of our justification and sanctification:

1. Of justification: "By his knowledge he will justify many," Isa. 53:11.

2. Of sanctification; in "destroying the works of the devil," 1 Jn. 3:8.

Thus our merciful high priest comes to be the great possessor of all grace, so that he may give to us according to his own pleasure, quickening whom he will. He has this grace in him really, as our head, in not receiving that Spirit by measure (John 3:34). The Spirit is the bond of union between him and us, 1Cor. 6:17. By holding the head, we are filled with his fullness, Eph. 1:22, 23; Col. 1:19. He has this grace as a common person. He is entrusted with it on our behalf, Rom. 5:14-17. "The last Adam is made a quickening Spirit" to us, 1Cor. 15:45. He is also a treasury of this grace in a moral and legal sense. This is not only because "it pleased the Father that all fullness should dwell in him," Col. 1:19, but also because the whole dispensation of grace is founded on his mediation.

(2dly.) Being actually vested with this power, privilege, and fullness, he intends the Spirit to take from this fullness and give it to us: "He will take of mine, and will show it to you," John 16:15. The Spirit takes of the fullness that is in Christ, and in Christ's name, he actually bestows it on those he is sent to sanctify. More will be

183

said later concerning the manner and efficacy of the Spirit in doing this.

(3dly.) As for actual grace, which is that influence or power by which the saints are enabled to perform particular duties according to the mind of God, there is no need to further discuss it. What concerns our communion with the Lord Christ was said before.

I now proceed to the way by which we carry on communion with the Lord Jesus in all of these things. They may be considered first in respect to their bestowal, and secondly in respect to their degrees of continuance and increase.

In the Spirit's communication of grace to the soul, raising it from death to life, the saints have no communion with Christ beyond a passive reception of that life-giving, quickening Spirit and power. They are like the dead bones mentioned in the prophet; the wind blows on them and they live. They are like Lazarus in the grave; Christ calls, and they come forth, because the call is accompanied with life and power. It is in the second respect, the efficacy of the Spirit in continuing and increasing our habitual and actual grace, that we become more holy and more powerful in walking with God. We have more fruit in our obedience and more success against temptations. This brings us to our duties in communion with Christ.

2. The duties of the saints in this communion with Christ.

The saints continually eye the Lord Jesus as the great Joseph, who has charge of all the granaries of the kingdom of heaven committed to him. He is the one in whom it pleased the Father to gather all things under one head, Eph. 1:10, so that from him all things might be dispensed to the saints. All treasures, all fullness, and the Spirit without measure are in him. And they eye this fullness, in reference to their condition, in these three particulars:

(1.) In the preparation of the dispensation mentioned – in the expiating, purging, and purifying efficacy of his blood itself. It was a sacrifice not only of atonement as offered, but also of purification as poured out. The apostle presents this eminently in Heb. 9:13, 14. "For if the blood of bulls and of goats, and the ashes of a heifer, sprinkled on the unclean will purify the flesh, then how much more will the blood of Christ, who through the eternal Spirit offered himself without spot to God, purge your conscience from dead works to serve the living God?" This blood of his is what satisfies all the types of sacrifices instituted for carnal purification. And therefore it has a spiritually purifying, cleansing, and sanctifying virtue in itself, as offered and poured out. Hence, it is called, "A fountain for sin and for uncleanness," Zech. 13:1; that is, it washes them and takes them away. It is "a fountain opened;" It is already prepared, virtuous, and efficacious in itself, before anything is put into it. It is poured out, instituted, and appointed for that purpose.

The saints see that they are still greatly defiled. Indeed, to be able to see the *defilements* of sin is a more spiritual discovery than to have only a sense of the *guilt* of sin. This follows every conviction, and it is commensurate to the revelation of the purity and holiness of God and all his ways. Upon this discovery, they cry with shame, within themselves, "Unclean, unclean," unclean in their natures, unclean in their persons, unclean in their lives; they are completely soaked in the blood of their defilements. Their hearts by nature are a cesspool, and their lives a dung hill. They know, also, that no unclean thing will enter the kingdom of God, or have a place in the New Jerusalem. They know that God is of purer eyes than to behold iniquity. They cannot endure to look at themselves. How will they dare to appear in his presence? What remedies will they now use? "Though they wash themselves with lye, and use much soap, yet their iniquity will continue marked," Jer. 2:22. With what, then, will they come before the Lord?

To remove this defilement, I say, they look first to the purifying virtue of the blood of Christ, which is able to cleanse them from all their sins, 1John 1:7. It is the spring from which flows all the purifying virtue that will take away all their spots and stains, "make them holy and without blemish, and in the end present them glorious to himself," Eph. 5:26, 27. They dwell on this with thoughts of faith. They roll it around in their minds and spirits. Here faith obtains new life, new vigor, when this sense of vileness has overwhelmed it. Here is a fountain opened: draw close and see its beauty, purity, and efficacy. This is where a foundation is laid for that work we long to be accomplished. One moment's communion with Christ by faith in this is more effective to purge the soul, and to increase grace, than the self-endeavors of a thousand ages.

(2.) They eye the blood of Christ as the blood of sprinkling. When they come to "Jesus, the mediator of the new covenant," they come to the "blood of sprinkling," Heb. 12:24. The stain of Christ's shed blood will not take away pollution in itself. Not only is there "*haimatekchusia*," a "shedding of blood" for the remission of sin, Heb. 9:22, but there is also "*haimatos rantismos*," a "sprinkling of blood," for the actual purification. The apostle largely describes this in Heb. 9:19, "When Moses," he says, "had spoken every precept to all the people according to the law, he took the blood of calves and of goats, with water, and scarlet wool, and hyssop, and sprinkled both the book and all the people, saying, 'This is the blood of the testament which God has enjoined to you.' Moreover, he likewise sprinkled with blood both the tabernacle, and all the vessels of the ministry. Almost all things are by the law purged with blood. It was therefore necessary that the patterns of things in the heavens should be purified with these; but the heavenly things themselves with better sacrifices than these," verses 19-23.

The apostle had previously compared the blood of Christ to the blood of sacrifices, in respect to the petition and the purchase it made. Now he does it to the blood as sprinkled, in respect to its application for purification and holiness. He tells us how this sprinkling was performed. It was by dipping hyssop in the blood of the sacrifice, and dashing it on the things and people to be purified, just as instituted with the Paschal lamb, Exod. 12:7. Hence, David, in a sense of the pollution of sin, prays that he may be "purged with hyssop," Ps. 51:7. It is evident that this specifically referred to the uncleanness and defilement of sin. That is because there is no mention made of sprinkling blood with hyssop in any sacrifice other than those for purification of uncleanness. This was true in the case of leprosy, Lev. 14:6, and any other defilements, Numb. 19:18. For the latter, it is not a sacrifice of blood, but the water of separation. This is also typical of the blood of Christ, which is the fountain for separation for uncleanness, Zech. 13:1.

Now, this bunch of hyssop, by which the blood of purification was prepared to sprinkle the unclean, is (to us) the free promises of Christ. The cleansing virtue of the blood of Christ lies in the promises, just as the blood of sacrifices lies in the hyssop. It is ready to pass out to those who draw close to it. Thus, the apostle takes us from receiving the promise, to universal holiness and purity: "Therefore, having these promises, dearly beloved, let us cleanse ourselves from all filthiness of the flesh and spirit, perfecting holiness in the fear of God," 2Cor. 7:1. This, then, is what the saints do: they eye the blood of Christ as it is found in the promise, ready to spray out upon the soul to purify it. This is how its purging and cleansing virtue is communicated to them. By the blood of Christ, they are purged from all their sins, 1John 1:7. Thus far, this purifying blood is only prepared and made ready for its purpose. Although the bunch of hyssop is drenched with it in the promises, the soul may not yet partake of it. And so,

(3.) The saints look upon Christ as the only dispenser of the Spirit, and the source of all grace of sanctification and holiness. They consider that, by his intercession, it is granted to him to make all the fruits of his purchase effective, to sanctify, purify, and make glorious in holiness, his whole people. They know that this is actually to be accomplished by the Spirit, according to the innumerable promises given to that end. He is to sprinkle that blood upon their souls. He is to create the holiness in them that they long for. He is to be a well of water in them, springing up to everlasting life. In this state, they look to Jesus. Faith fixes itself here, expecting him to give out the Spirit for all these ends and purposes. They mix the promises with faith, and so they become actual partakers of all this grace. This is their way. This is their communion with Christ. This is the life of faith, as to grace and holiness. Blessed is the soul who exercises it: "He will be like a tree planted by the waters, that spreads out her roots by the river, and will not notice when heat comes, but her leaf will be green; and will not be afraid in the year of drought, neither will she cease from yielding fruit," Jer. 17:8.

People convicted of their sin, who do not know Christ nor the fellowship of his sufferings, would create holiness out of their own depths; they would work it out in their own strength. They start with difficult striving, and then follow it with vows, duties, resolutions, and commitments, sweating at it all day long. They continue this way for a season, until their hypocrisy ends for the most part in apostasy. The saints of God, at the start of their walk with him, desire three things:

[1.] the Spirit of holiness to dwell in them.

[2.] a habit of holiness to be infused in them.

[3.] actual assistance to work out all their duties;

If these continue to be lacking, they can never, with all their might, power, and endeavors, perform a single act of holiness before the Lord. They know that they are insufficient in themselves. Without Christ, they can do nothing. Therefore, they look to him, the one who is entrusted with a fullness of all these things on their behalf. In doing so, by faith, they derive from him an increase of what they need.

In this, I say, the saints have communion with Christ as to their sanctification and holiness. From him they receive the Spirit to dwell in them. From him they have the new principle of life which is the root of all their obedience. From him they have actual assistance for every duty they are called to perform. They spend their lives and time with him in waiting for, expecting, and receiving these blessings. Looking for help from other mountains is pointless. Spending our strength in pursuing righteousness is also pointless if this communion is wanting. Fix your soul here; you will not be ashamed. This is the way, the only way, to obtain full and effectual manifestations of the Spirit's indwelling. This is the only way to have our hearts purified, our consciences purged, our sins mortified, and our graces increased. This is the way our souls are made humble, holy, zealous, believing, and Christ-like. This is the only way to make our lives fruitful, and our deaths comfortable. Let us abide in this, absorbing the stain of Christ by faith, being conformed to him to the extent allotted to us in this world, so that when we see him as he is, we may be like him.

CHAPTER 10.

COMMUNION WITH CHRIST IN PRIVILEGES –

III. The third thing in which we have communion with Christ, as the third part of purchased grace, is the grace of privilege before God. The privileges we enjoy by Christ are great and innumerable. Specifying each of them would take a lifetime of work, not a few sheets. I will present them only in summary. The spring and fountain from which they all arise and flow is our adoption: "Beloved, now we are the sons of God," 1John 3:2. This is the great fountain of our privilege. What is the source of our adoption? It is from the love of the Father. 1John 3:1, "Behold, what manner of love the Father has bestowed upon us, that we should be called the sons of God!" But from whom do we immediately receive this honor? As many as believe on Christ, he gives them this power to become the sons of God, John 1:12. Christ was appointed to be the first-born among many brothers, Rom. 8:29. Taking us as his brothers, Heb. 2:11, makes us become the children of God. God is our Father by being the Father of Christ, and we are his children by being the brothers of Christ. This being the sum of all the honor, privilege, right, and title that we have, let us consider a little the nature of our adoption. It is the act by which we are invested with this state and title.

Adoption is the authoritative translation of a believer, by Jesus Christ, from the family of the world and Satan, into the family of God. It invests him with all the privileges and advantages of that family.

To complete the adoption of any person, five things are required:

1. That he actually, in his own right, belongs to a family other than the one into which he is adopted. [Orphans are the rightful, if solitary, members of their own family].

2. That there is a family to which he has no inherent right to belong, into which he must be grafted. If he has an inherent personal right, he does not need adopting. If a man who is a distant cousin comes into the family inheritance by the death of the nearer heirs, even though his previous right was little better than nothing, he is still a son born of that family. A person does not need adopting if he has any right of succession.

3. That there is an authoritative, legal translation of him from one family into another, by someone with the power to do it. Under the law of old, people did not have the power to adopt when and whom they would. It had to be done by the authority of the sovereign power.

4. That the adopted person be freed from all the obligations he has to the family from which he is translated. Otherwise he cannot be

useful or serviceable to the family into which he is grafted. He cannot serve two masters, much less two fathers.

5. That, by virtue of his adoption, he is invested with all the rights, privileges, advantages, and title to the whole inheritance of the family into which he is adopted, as fully as if he had been born a son in that family.

All these things agree and are found in the adoption of believers:

1. Believers, by their own original right, belong to a family other than that into which they are adopted. They are "by nature the children of wrath," Eph. 2:3, sons of wrath. They belong to that family whose inheritance is "wrath," called "the power of darkness," Col. 1:13. From this family, God "translated them into the kingdom of his dear Son." By nature, believers are of the world and of Satan. Whatever is to be inherited in that family, such as wrath, curse, death, and hell, is what they have a right to. They cannot of themselves, or by themselves, get free of this family: an armed strong man keeps them in subjection (Lk. 11:21). Their natural estate is a family condition. It is attended with all the circumstances of a family, family duties and services, rights and titles, relations and observances. They belong to the black family of sin and Satan.

2. There is another family into which they are to be translated, and to which they have neither right nor title. This is the family in heaven and earth, the great family of God, which is named after Christ, Eph. 3:15. God has a house and family for his children. Some he maintains on the riches of his grace, and some he entertains with the fullness of his glory. This is the house of which the Lord Christ is the great dispenser. The Father was pleased to "gather together all things in him, both those in heaven, and those on earth," Eph. 1:10. In this house live all the sons and daughters of God, spending largely on the riches of his grace. They have no right nor title to this family in themselves; they are wholly alienated from it, Eph. 2:12, and they can lay no claim to anything in it. God drove fallen Adam out of the garden, and closed off all the ways back with a flaming sword, ready to cut him off if he should attempt it. God abundantly declares that Adam, and all his offspring, had lost all right to approach God in any family relationship. Our corrupted and cursed nature is not vested with any right to anything of God. Therefore,

3. Believers have an authoritative translation from the one family to the other. It is not done in a private, underhanded way, but by way of power or authority. John 1:12, "As many as received him, to them he gave power to become the sons of God." Investing them with the power, excellence, and light of the sons of God, is a forensic act. It is a legal proceeding. It is "making us fit to partake of the inheritance of the saints in light," Col. 1:12; It judicially exalts us into membership in that

family, where God is the Father, and Christ is the elder brother. All the saints and angels are brothers and fellow-children. And the inheritance is a crown that is immortal and incorruptible; it does not fade away, 1Pet. 1:4; 5:4.

This authoritative translation of believers from one family into another has two parts:

(1.) An effectual declaration and proclamation of a believer's immunity from all his obligations to the former family to which he was related by nature. This declaration has a threefold object:

[1.] Angels. It is declared to the angels because they too are the sons of God, and members of the family into which the adopted person is to be admitted. Therefore it concerns them to know who is invested with the rights of that family, so that they may discharge their duty towards them. It is declared to them that believers are freed from the family of sin and hell, to become fellow-sons and servants with them. And this is done two ways:

1st. Generally, by the doctrine of the gospel. Eph. 3:10, "The manifold wisdom of God is made known to the principalities and powers in heavenly places by the church." This wisdom is made known to the angels by the church, either as the doctrine of the gospel is delivered to it, or as the doctrine gathers it. What is this wisdom of God that is thus made known to principalities and powers? It is that, "the Gentiles should be fellow-heirs and of the same body with us," Eph. 3:6. This wisdom is the mystery of adopting sinners from the Gentiles. It is taking them from their slavery in the family of the world, so that they might have a right of heirship, and become sons in the family of God. How was it made known? It was "revealed by the Spirit to the prophets and apostles," Eph. 3:5.

2dly. It is declared particularly, by immediate revelation. When anyone is freed from the family of this world, it is revealed to the angels. "There is joy in the presence of the angels of God" (that is, among the angels, and by them) "over one sinner that repents," Luke 15:10. Now, the angels cannot absolutely know the true repentance of a sinner themselves; it is a work done in that cabinet to which none has a key but Jesus Christ. It is revealed by him to the angels when the specific care and charge of a believer is committed to them. These things are transacted before the angels, Luke 12:8, 9. Christ confesses the names of his brothers before the angels, Rev. 3:5. When he admits them into the family, Heb. 12:22-24, he declares to the angels that those he names are sons, so that the angels may discharge their duty towards them, Heb. 1:14.

[2.] It is denounced in a judicial way to Satan, the great master of the family to which they were formerly in subjection.

When the Lord Christ delivers a soul from the power of that strong armed one, he binds Satan. He prevents him from exercising that power and dominion which he held over the person before. By this means, Satan knows that the person has been delivered from his family. Any future attempts to dominate the believer will encroach on the possession and inheritance of the Lord Christ.

[3.] It is announced to the conscience of the person adopted. The Spirit of Christ testifies to the heart and conscience of a believer that he is freed from all obligations to the family of Satan, and that he has become the son of God, Rom. 8:14, 15. This enables him to cry, "Abba, Father," Gal. 4:6. I will speak later of the particulars of this testimony of the Spirit, and of its absolving the soul from its old alliance.

(2.) There is an authoritative and actual grafting of a believer into the family of God, investing him with the whole right of sonship. This has a number of acts:

[1.] Giving a believer a new name on a white stone, Rev. 2:17. Those who are adopted take new names. They change the name they had in their old family to the name of the family into which they are translated. This new name is, "A child of God." That is the new name given in adoption. No one knows what is in that name except the one who receives it. This new name is given and written on a white stone. That is the *tessera* 4 of our admission into the house of God. It is a stone of judicial acquittal. Our adoption by the Spirit is based on our absolution in the blood of Jesus. Therefore the new name on the white stone is a privilege based on discharge. The white stone quits the claim of the old family; the new name gives entrance to the other.

[2.] Enrolling the believer's name in the catalogue of the household of God. This admits him to fellowship in that household. It is called the "writing of the house of Israel," Ezek. 13:9. That is, it is the roll in which all the names of Israel, the family of God, are written. God has a catalogue of his household. Christ knows his sheep by name. When God writes up the people, he counts that "this man was born in Zion," Ps. 87:6. This is an extract of the Lamb's book of life.

[3.] Testifying to the believer's conscience that he is accepted by God, thus enabling him to behave himself as a child, Rom. 8:15; Gal. 4:5, 6.

4. The two last things required for adoption are that the adopted person be freed from all his obligations to the family from which he is translated, and be invested with the rights and privileges of the family into which he is translated. Now, because these two comprise the whole issue of adoption in which the saints have communion with Christ, I

will handle them together. I am addressing their concerns under four categories: (1.) Liberty. (2.) Title, or right. (3.) Boldness. (4.) Correction. These are the four things that he receives by his adoption, and in which he holds communion with the Lord Jesus:

(1.) Liberty. The Spirit of the Lord that was on the Lord Jesus anointed him to proclaim liberty to the captives, Isa. 61:1; and "where the Spirit of the Lord is" (that is, the Spirit of Christ, given to us by Christ because we are sons), "there is liberty," 2Cor. 3:17. All spiritual liberty is from the Spirit of adoption. Whatever else is pretended, is licentiousness. The apostle argues this in Gal. 4:6, 7, "He has sent forth his Spirit into their hearts, crying, 'Abba, Father.' Hence, you are no longer servants;" Bondage is ended. Believers have the liberty of sons in respect to,

[1.] The family from which he is translated. Liberty is being set free from all the obligations of that family. In this sense, the liberty which the saints have by adoption is either from what is real, or from what is pretended:

1st. What is real involves a twofold issue of law and sin. The unchangeable moral law of God, and sin, are in conjunction with each other. There is a twofold issue here:

(1st.) The instituted law of ordinances, which keeps those to whom it was given in bondage, Col. 2:14.

(2dly.) The "natural" pressure of the law, with its power and efficacy against sin. These are three components of that pressure:

[1st.]   It is rigorous and terrifying in its commands.

[2dly.] It is impossible to accomplish, and insufficient to achieve its primitively appointed end.

[3dly.] The penalties for transgressing it are the Curse, and Death. I will speak very briefly of these, because they are commonly handled and granted by all.

2dly. What is pretended is that there is anything which has power over the conscience once we are made free by Christ:

(1st.) Believers are freed from the instituted law of *ordinances*. The apostles testify that the law was a yoke which neither we nor our fathers (in the faith) could bear, Acts 15:10. Therefore, Christ "blotted out this handwriting of ordinances that was against them, which was contrary to them, and took it out of the way, nailing it to his cross," Col. 2:14. After a long dispute concerning the liberty that we have from that law, the apostle concludes with this instruction, "Stand fast in the liberty with which Christ has made us free," Gal. 5:1.

(2dly.) In reference to the *moral* law:

[1st.] The first thing we have liberty from is the law's rigor

192

and terror in commanding us. Heb. 12:18-22, "We have not come to the mount that might be touched, and that burned with fire, to the whirlwind, darkness, and tempest, to the sound of the trumpet, and the voice of words, which those who heard begged that they might hear it no more; but we have come to mount Zion..." We are freed from the administration of the law, given out with dread and terror, that exacts its obedience with rigor. We are not called to that estate.

[2dly.] We are freed from the moral law as the instrument of righteousness. It is impossible to accomplish and insufficient to achieve its primitive end because of sin, Rom. 8:2, 3; Gal. 3:21-23. And it being impossible to obtain life by the law, we are exempt from the law for that purpose. This exemption comes through the righteousness of Christ, Rom. 8:3.

[3dly.] We have liberty from the consequence of its transgression. The first consequence is *Curse*. There is a solemn curse in the wrath of God that the law contains for its transgression. We are completely freed from this, Gal. 3:13, "Christ has redeemed us from the curse of the law by being made a curse for us."

The second consequence we are delivered from is *Death*, Heb. 2:15, and the power of Satan, Heb. 2:14, Col. 1:13. We are delivered from sin, Rom. 6:14, 1Pet. 1:18, and from our relationship with the world, Gal. 1:4. We are delivered from all the circumstances, advantages, and claims these have on us, Gal. 4:3-5, Col. 2:20. Without this deliverance, we could not live one day.

What is claimed by some is that we are freed from the power of having our conscience bound by any laws and constitutions that are not from God, Col. 2:20-22. In truth, we were never in bondage to these things, but we are indeed hereby set free from them.

[2.] Believers have liberty as sons in the family of God, as well as liberty from the family of Satan. Sons are free. Their obedience is a free obedience. They have the Spirit of the Lord, and where he is, there is liberty, 2Cor. 3:17. As a Spirit of adoption, he is opposed to the spirit of bondage, Rom. 8:15. This liberty that we have as children in our Father's family, is a spiritual largeness of heart. In this open atmosphere, the children of God pursue all holy obedience in Christ freely, willingly, and genuinely, without fear, terror, bondage, or constraint.

There are Gibeonites who outwardly attend the family of God, who serve his house as if it is the drudgery of their lives (Josh. 9:21). The principle by which they yield obedience is a spirit of bondage to fear, Rom. 8:15. The rule that governs them is the law in all its dread and rigor. It exacts the utmost obedience from them, without mercy or mitigation. The reason they obey is to fly from the wrath to come and to pacify their consciences. They seek righteousness as if it could be obtained by the works of the law. Thus, all their days they servilely, painfully, and fruitlessly, serve their conviction of sin.

The saints, by adoption and in contrast, have a largeness of heart in all holy obedience. Says David, "I will walk at liberty, for I seek your precepts," Ps. 119:45. See also Isa. 61:1; Luke 4:18; Rom. 8:2, 21; Gal. 4:7, 5:1, 13; James 1:25; John 8:32, 33, 36; Rom. 6:18; 1Pet. 2:16. Now, this son-like freedom of the Spirit in obedience, consists in a number of things:

1st. Freedom consists in the principles behind all spiritual service, which are life and love. The one regards the *matter* of their obedience, giving them power. The other regards the *manner* of their obedience, giving them joy and sweetness in it:

(1st.) Life is what gives them power in the matter of obedience. Rom. 8:2, "The law of the Spirit of life in Christ Jesus sets them free from the law of sin and death." Life frees them. It enables them to freely obey so that "they walk after the Spirit," Rom. 8:1. "Christ lives in me; and the life which I now live in the flesh, I live by the faith of the Son of God," Gal. 2:20. It is saying that the life which I now live in the flesh, that is, the obedience which I yield to God while I am in the flesh, comes from a principle of life. And that principle is Christ living in me. There is power, then, for everyone who lives to God; and that power comes from Christ living in them. The Spirit of life from Christ carries them out to that life. The fruits of a dead root are only dead excrescences. The fruits of a principle of life are living acts.

Hence, there is a difference between the liberty that slaves receive, and the liberty that children have as a right:

[1st.] Slaves take liberty *from* duty; children have liberty *in* duty. There is no greater mistake in the world, than to think that the liberty of the sons of God means they can either perform duties, or omit them; they can serve in the family of God, or choose not to. That would be a liberty stolen by slaves, not a liberty given by the Spirit to sons.

The liberty of sons is found in the inward spiritual freedom of their hearts to naturally and kindly fulfill all the ways and worship of God. When they find themselves restricted and enclosed in them, they wrestle with God for enlargement. They are never content with doing a duty unless it is done as in Christ, with free, genuine, and enlarged hearts. To repeat, the liberty that servants have is *from* duty; the liberty given to sons is *in* duty.

[2dly.] The liberty of slaves or servants is from mistaken and deceptive conclusions; the liberty of sons is from the power of the indwelling Spirit of grace. The liberty of servants is from outward, dead conclusions; the liberty of sons is from an inward, living principle.

(2dly.) Love, in the *manner* of their obedience, gives them delight and joy. John 14:15, "If you love me," says Christ, "keep my commandments." Love is the basis of all their duties. Hence, our Savior distills all obedience into the love of God and our neighbor. On the same grounds, Paul tells us "that love is the fulfilling of the law," Rom. 13:10. Where love is contained in any duty, it is made complete in Christ. How often David, with admiration, expresses this principle of his walk with God! "O," he says, "how I love your commandments!" The saints delight that the commandments of Christ are not a burden to them. Jacob's hard service was not a burden because of his love for Rachel. And no duty of a saint is a burden to him because of his love for Christ. Saints do all things with delight and contentment. Hence they long to walk with God, and pant after more ability. This is a great part of their son-like freedom in obedience. It gives them joy. 1John 4:18, "There is no fear in love; but perfect love casts out fear." When their soul is motivated by love to obedience, it expels the fear that results from bondage of the spirit. Now, when life and love act together, there is freedom, liberty, and largeness of heart. This is far from that narrow and bandaged frame that others walk in all their days who do not know adoption as sons.

2dly. The object of believers' obedience is seen as desirable, while to others it is terrible. In drawing near to God, they see him as a Father. They call him Father, Gal. 4:6, not in the form of words, but in the spirit of sons. God in Christ is continually before them not only as one who deserves all the honors and obedience he requires, but also as one who is to be delighted in greatly. He is all-sufficient to satisfy and satiate all the desires of the soul. While others napkin their talents because they deal with an austere master, believers exercise their strength to its fullest because they draw close to a gracious rewarder. From the principle of life and love, they go to the heart of a living and loving Father. They are only returning the strength they receive to its fountain, to the ocean.

3dly. Their motive to obey is love, 2Cor. 5:14. From an apprehension of love, they are led to surrender themselves to the one who is love. What a freedom this is! What a largeness of spirit exists in those who walk according to this rule! Darkness, fear, bondage, conviction, and mere hopes of righteousness accompany others in their ways. But the sons of God, by the Spirit of adoption, have light, love, and contentment in their walk with God. The frame of the children of God in their Father's house is completely foreign to the world.

4thly. The manner of their obedience is willingness. "They yield themselves to God, as those who are alive from the dead," Rom. 6:13. They yield themselves, surrender themselves, willingly, cheerfully, and freely. "With my whole heart," says David (Ps. 119:10). "They present themselves a living sacrifice," Rom. 12:1, and a willing sacrifice.

5thly. The rule that guides their walk with God is the law of liberty, divested of all its terrifying, threatening, killing, condemning, and cursing power. In the blood of Jesus, it is rendered sweet, tender, useful, instructive, and helpful as a rule of walking in the life they have received, not the way of working for the life they do not have. These may be sufficient examples of the liberty of obedience that sons and daughters have in the family of God, which Gibeonites are not acquainted with.

(2.) The second thing which the children of God have by adoption is title. They have title and right to all the privileges and advantages of the family into which they are translated. This is the pre-eminence of the true sons of any family. The ground on which Sarah pleads for the ejection of Ishmael was that he was the son of the bond woman, Gen. 21:10. He was not a genuine child of the family, and therefore he could have no right of heirship with Isaac. The apostle's argument is, "We are no longer servants, but sons; and if sons, then heirs," Rom. 8:14-17; "then we have right and title: not being born to this (for by nature we are the children of wrath), we have this right by our adoption."

The saints have a double right and title:

1st. They have proper and direct title in respect to *spiritual* things.

2dly. They have consequential title in respect to *temporal* things:

[1.] In respect to *spiritual* things, their title is to:

1st. A *present* place, name, and room, in the house of God, with all its privileges and administrations.

2dly. A *future* abundance of the great inheritance of glory, a kingdom purchased for their whole family:

1st. *They have title to, and an interest in, the whole administration of the family of God here in this world*. The main idea of the supreme administration of the house of God by the Lord Christ, in instituting ordinances and dispensing the Spirit, is to activate those ordinances in the lives of believers, and to make them effective in obtaining the end for which they were instituted. Believers are the prime objects of this administration. All of this is done for them. It is exercised towards them. God has made Jesus Christ the "head over all things to the church, which is his body," Eph. 1:22, 23. He has made him the head over all these spiritual things, and committed their authoritative administration to him, for the use and benefit of the church, the family of God. He does all this for the benefit and advantage of the many sons he will bring to glory, Heb. 2:10.

The aim of the Lord Jesus in establishing gospel administrations, and administrators, is "for the perfecting of the saints, the work of the ministry..." Eph. 4:8-13. All of this is done for the family of God. Christ is faithful to all the house of God in this, Heb. 3:2. Hence, the apostle tells the Corinthians, 1Cor. 3:22, 23, that all these gospel administrations and ordinances are theirs, and for them. Even though the world benefits by the things of the gospel, it is designed for the children of this family. This, then, is the aim and intent of the Lord Christ in the institution of all gospel ordinances and administrations. They are used for the house of God, and all his children and servants in that house.

It is true that the word is preached to all the world to gather the children of God's purpose who are scattered around the world, and to leave the rest without excuse. But the primary purpose is to gather the heirs of salvation to enjoy a feast of the sumptuous things that the Lord Christ has prepared for them in his house.

Again, only believers have a right and title to gospel administrations and to the privileges of the family of God. This is because these are offered to his church according to his mind. The church is the "house of God," 1 Tim. 3:15; Heb. 3:6. This is where he keeps and maintains his whole family, ordering them according to his mind and will. Who else would have any rights in the house of God besides his children? If we allow rights only to our own children in our houses, why would we think God allows rights to any but his own children in his house? Is it good to "take the children's bread and cast it to the dogs?" Matt. 15:26. We will see that only children have a right or title to the privileges and advantages of the house of God if we consider,

(1st.) The nature of that house. It is such that it is impossible for any but adopted children to have a right to a place in it. It is composed of "living stones," 1Pet. 2:5, a "chosen generation, a royal priesthood, a holy nation, a unique people," verse 9; "saints and faithful in Christ Jesus," Eph. 1:1; "saints and faithful brothers," Col. 1:2; a people that are "all righteous," Isa. 60:21. Its whole fabric is glorious, chap. 54:11-14. The way of the house is "a way of holiness," which the unclean will not pass through, chap. 35:8. Expressly stated, they are the "sons and daughters of the Lord Almighty," and they alone, 2Cor. 6:17-18. All others are excluded, Rev. 21:27. It is true that others may sneak into the great house of God; and so there are

197

"not only vessels of gold and silver, but also of wood and of earth...,"
2Tim. 2:20. But they only sneak in, Jude says in verse 4. They have
no right or title to it.

(2dly.) The privileges of the house will not suit or profit any
other. What good will it do to give food to a dead man? Will he grow
or become stronger by it? The things of the family and house of God
are food for living souls. Only God's children are alive; all others are
dead in trespasses and sins. What will outward signs avail, if life and
power are missing? The saints' enjoyments in the family of God are
all suited to believers. If bestowed on the world, they would be pearls
in the snout of a swine.

Only the sons of the family have this right. They have fellowship
with one another, with the Father, and with the Son Jesus Christ. They
proclaim the Lord's death until he comes, 1Cor. 11:26. They are
entrusted with all the ordinances of the house, and their
administration. Who will deny them the enjoyment of this right, or
keep them from what Christ has purchased for them? In the end, the
Lord will give them hearts everywhere to make use of this title
accordingly, and not to wander on the mountains, forgetting their
resting-place.

**2dly. *They have a title to the future fullness of the
inheritance that is purchased for this whole family by Jesus
Christ*.** This is what the apostle argues in Rom. 8:17. "If children, then
heirs..." All God's children are "first-born," Heb. 12:23, and therefore
they are heirs. Hence, the whole weight of glory that is prepared for
them is called the inheritance. "The inheritance of the saints in light."
Col. 1:12. "If you are Christ's, then you are Abraham's seed, and heirs
according to the promise," Gal 3:29. We are heirs of the promise,
meaning heirs of everything promised to Abraham in and with Christ.

There are three things that the children of God are said to be
heirs to:

(1st.) They are heirs to the promise, as in Gal. 3:29 and Heb.
6:17. God shows "the heirs of the promise, the immutability of his
counsel;" Abraham, Isaac, and Jacob are said to be "heirs of the same
promise," Heb. 11:9. From the foundation of the world, God made a
most excellent promise in Christ, containing a deliverance from all
evil, and an engagement to bestow all good things upon them. It
contains a deliverance from all the evil that the guilt of sin and the
dominion of Satan had brought upon them. It invested them with all
spiritual blessings in heavenly things in Christ Jesus. Hence, in Heb.
9:15, the Holy Spirit calls it a "promise of the eternal inheritance."
This is what the adopted children of God are primarily heirs to.
They are heirs to the promise that God made at the beginning to
fallen man, and that he has solemnly renewed and confirmed by his

oath. Their claim for their inheritance is accepted in the courts of heaven.

(2dly.) They are heirs of righteousness, Heb. 11:7. Noah was an heir of the righteousness which comes by faith. Peter calls it being "heir of the grace of life," 1 Pet. 3:7. James puts both of these together, chap. 2:5, "Heirs of the kingdom which God has promised." That is, they are heirs of the kingdom of grace and its righteousness. In this respect, the apostle tells us that "we have obtained an inheritance," Eph. 1:11, which he also places with the righteousness of faith, Acts 26:18. Now, this righteousness, grace, and inheritance, not only means that righteousness which we actually partake of here, but the purpose and accomplishment of that righteousness in glory. And so,

(3dly.) They are "heirs of salvation," Heb. 1:14, and "heirs according to the hope of eternal life," Tit. 3:7. Peter calls this an "incorruptible inheritance," 1Pet. 1:4. Paul calls it the "reward of the inheritance," Col. 3:24. That is, salvation is the result of the inheritance of light and holiness which they already enjoy. Thus, full salvation by Christ is founded on the promises; the means of salvation is righteousness and holiness; and the purpose of salvation is eternal glory. The sons of God have a right and title to all of this because they are made heirs with Christ.

In sum, the saints' main title and right by adoption, is that the Lord is their portion and inheritance, and they are the inheritance of the Lord. What they have is a large portion, and nicely divided.

[2.] Besides this principal right, the adopted sons of God have a second consequential right to the things of this world. They have a right to all the portions of this world that God is pleased to entrust them with. Christ is the "heir of all things," Heb. 1:2. The Lord, by his sovereignty, originally granted all things here below for man's use. He appointed the works of his hands to be used for man's benefit. Sin reversed this whole grant and institution. All right and title to the things of creation was lost and forfeited by sin. All things were freed from their subjection to man. Yet that freedom, which removes the purposes for which they were originally appointed, is part of their vanity and curse. It is evil for anything to be separated from the purposes for which it was created. And so the whole creation is released from any subordinate ruler. Man, having lost the title by which he held his dominion over the creatures, has no interest in any of them, nor can he lay any claim to them.

But now the Lord, taking a portion for himself from fallen mankind, and appointing them heirs of salvation, reserves the works of creation for their use in their pilgrimage. To this end, he invests the second Adam with the right and title to what the first Adam had lost. He appoints him "heir of all things." Thereupon, his adopted ones, being "fellow-heirs with Christ," also have a right and title to the things of this creation. To clear up what this right is, I must make a few observations:

1st. The right that the adopted sons have is not the right that Christ has. What Christ has is sovereign and supreme, to do what he will with his own. But what the adopted sons have is subordinate. They are accountable for the use of those things to which they now have a right and title. The right of Christ is the right of the Lord of the house; the right of the saints is the right of servants.

2dly. All the children of God have a right to the whole earth, which is the Lord's, and the fullness of it, 1Cor. 10:26. This is in two regards:

(1st.) The sovereign Lord of the earth preserves it merely for their use, and for their account. All others are *maalae fidei possessores* [wrongful occupants], invading a portion of the Lord's territories without his permission.

(2dly.) Christ has promised to give them the kingdom and dominion over it in such a way that the government of the earth is exercised to their advantage.

3dly. This right to the whole earth is a spiritual right, not a civil interest. It only sanctifies the right and interest that is bestowed. God has providentially set the civil bounds of the inheritance of men, Acts 17:26, allowing the men of the world to enjoy a portion here. Often that portion is very large. Yet, for his children's sake, the beasts of the forest that are made to be destroyed, may not take over the whole possession. Hence,

4thly. No adopted person has any right, by virtue of his adoption, to any portion of earthly things to which he does not have a right and title based upon a civil interest that has been given to him by the providence of God. But,

5thly. What they do have by their adoption are these:

(1st.) A right to whatever portion God is pleased to give them, as it is reinvested in Christ and not as it lies under the curse and vanity of sin. Therefore, the sons of God can never be called to account for usurping what they have no right to. But all the sons of men who violently grasp those things which God has liberated from their dominion because of sin will indeed be called to account.

(2dly.) By this right, they are led to a sanctified use of what they do enjoy. These things are pledges of the Father's love, washed in the blood of Christ, and inspirations to live to his praise, who gives them all things to richly enjoy.

Hence, I dare say that unbelievers have no true, unquestionable right to the temporal things they possess. It is true that they have a civil right in respect to others, but they do not have a sanctified right in

200

respect to their own souls. They have a right and title that will be upheld in the courts of men, but not a right that will hold up in the court of God, nor in their own conscience. One day it will be sad for them when they give an account of their enjoyments. They will be reckoned with for abusing what they have possessed by not using it for the glory of the one who is the true owner, but for laying their hands on the creatures of God, and keeping these things from the ones for whose sakes alone these unbelievers are preserved from destruction.

The God of glory will come to them, either in their consciences here, or in the judgment that is to come. He will say with the terror of a vengeful judge, "I have allowed you to enjoy corn, wine, and oil, and a great portion of my creatures. You have rolled yourselves in wealth and prosperity, when the rightful heirs of these things lived poor, low, and mean next door. Give now an answer for what and how you have used these things. What have you used for the service and advancement of the gospel? What have you given to those for whom nothing was provided? What contribution have you made for the poor saints? Have you had a ready hand and willing mind to lay down everything for my sake?"

They will be compelled to answer truthfully, "Lord, we indeed had a large portion in the world. But we thought it was our own, and that we could do what we wanted with our own. We ate the fat and drank the sweet, and left the rest of our substance for our children. We spent some on our lusts, and some on our friends. But the truth is, we cannot say that we used this unrighteous mammon to advance the gospel, or to minister to your poor saints. And now, look, we must die..." The Lord will proceed further, and question not only the use of these things, but also their title to them. He will tell them, "The earth is mine, and the fullness of it. I did, indeed, make an original grant of these things to man, but that was lost by sin. I have restored that grant only for my saints. Why, then, have you laid your fingers of prey on what was not yours? Why did you compel my creatures to serve you and your lusts, when I freed them from your dominion? Give me my flax, my wine, and wool. I will make you as naked as the day of your birth, and revenge upon you your rapine, and unjust possession of what was not yours." What will men do when that happens?

(3.) The third thing which the children of God have by adoption is boldness. But I have spoken of this at large before, in treating the excellence of Christ in respect to our approach to God through him. So I will not reconsider it here.

(4.) The fourth thing which the children of God have by adoption is affliction. Affliction is the privilege of children, because it proceeds from love. It leads to spiritual advantages, such as being conformed to Christ, and being sweetened with his presence, Heb. 12:3-6. But I will not elaborate on this.

Adoption is the source of all the privileges which Christ has purchased for us, and in which we have fellowship with him:

fellowship in name; we are sons of God (as he is).

fellowship in title and right; we are heirs, and co-heirs with Christ.

fellowship in likeness and conformity; we are predestined to be like the firstborn.

fellowship in honor; he is not ashamed to call us brothers.

fellowship in sufferings; he learned obedience by what he suffered, and every son that is received is to be scourged.

fellowship in his kingdom; we will reign with him.

I must speak of all these things specifically in another place, so I will not draw out the discourse concerning them any further here.

202

PART 3. COMMUNION WITH THE HOLY SPIRIT.

CHAPTER I.

THE FOUNDATION OF OUR COMMUNION WITH THE HOLY

SPIRIT –

The foundation of all of our communion with the Holy Spirit consists in his mission as our comforter, being sent for that purpose by Jesus Christ. This dispensation will be the first thing considered, so that we have a correct understanding of its truth. The main promise and chief considerations, including the good received and the evil prevented by it, are given in the beginning of the 16th chapter of John. I will view its state as proposed there.

Our blessed Savior, being ready to leave the world, acquainted his disciples with what they were likely to encounter. He explains the reason why he gave them the doleful tidings of his departure. He does so considering how sad and dispirited they were when he mentioned it. Verse 1, "I have spoken these things to you, so that you would not stumble." He is saying, "I have acquainted you with these things beforehand (that is, the things which will come upon you, which you are to suffer), so that you poor souls, who expected another state of affairs, would not be surprised by it, or be offended at me and my doctrine, and thus fall away from me. You are now forewarned, and know what to look for." He says in verse 2, "having said in general that you will be persecuted, I tell you plainly that there will be a combination of all men against you, and all sorts of men will use their power for your ruin." "They will cast you out of the synagogues; in fact, the time comes that whoever kills you will think that he does service to God." He says, "The ecclesiastical power will excommunicate you. They will put you out of their synagogues; and so that you may not expect relief from the power of the magistrate against their perversity, they will kill you; and so that you may know that they will do it for that purpose, without check or control, they will think that in killing you they are doing God good service; this will cause them to act rigorously, and extremely."

"But this is a shaking trial," they might reply (Heb. 12:26). "Is our condition such that men, in killing us, will think to approve their consciences to God?" "Yes, they will," says our Savior; "Yet, so that you will not be mistaken, or trouble your consciences about their confidence, know that their blind and desperate ignorance is the cause of their fury and persuasion." Verse 3, "These things they will do to you, because they have not known the Father, nor me."

This, then, was the state of the disciples. But why did our Savior tell them at this point? To add fear and anxiety to their grief and sorrow? What advantage would they gain by that? Their blessed Master essentially says in verse 4, "There are weighty reasons why I tell you these things. Chiefly, I provided them to you so that when they happen, you may be supported with the consideration of my Deity and omniscience, because I told you all these things before they came to pass." Verse 4: "But these things I have told you, so that when the time comes, you may remember that I told you of them." "But if they are so necessary, why is it that you have not told us before? Why not in the beginning, at our first calling?" "Because," says our Savior, "there was no need for that; for while I was with you, you had protection and direction at hand." "'And I did not say these things at the beginning, because I was present with you:' but now the state of things is altered; I must leave you," verse 4. "And for your part, you are so stunned with sorrow, that you do not ask me 'where I go;' which would certainly relieve you, because I go to take possession of my glory, and to carry on the work of your salvation: but your hearts are filled with sorrow and fears, and you do not so much as inquire after relief," verses 5, 6. At this point, he adds that wonderful assertion in verse 7, "Nevertheless I tell you the truth; It is expedient for you that I go away: for if I do not go away, the Comforter will not come to you; but if I depart, I will send him to you."

This verse, then, is the foundation of what will be declared later. It must be considered as to its words and their interpretation.

1. In the preface to his statement:

(1.) The first word, "*alla*," is adversative. It does not negate what goes before, but creates a transition: "I know you have sad thoughts of these things; but nevertheless..."

(2.) "*Ego ten aleteian lego humin*," "I tell you the truth." The words are very emphatic. They denote some great thing to follow.

First, "*Ego*," "I tell it you, what will now be spoken; I who love you, who take care of you, who am now about to lay down my life for you; these are my dying words, so that you may believe me; I who am truth itself, I tell you." And,

Second, "*Ego ten aleteian lego*," "I tell you the truth." "You have in your sad, misgiving hearts many misapprehensions of things. You think if I would abide with you, then all these evils might be prevented. But you do not know what is good for you, nor what is expedient. 'I tell you the truth;' this is truth itself; quiet your hearts in it." A great deal of evidence is needed to comfort their souls. They are dejected and disconsolate, apprehensive about Christ's absence from them, whether what they perceive is true or false.

This is the preface to what our Savior was about to deliver to his disciples. It will be a weighty, convincing affirmation, to separate their thoughts from prejudice, and to prepare them to receive that great truth.

2. In the assertion that follows: "*Sumferei humin, hina ego apelto.*" It is expedient for you that I go away." There are two things in these words: Christ's departure; and its usefulness to his disciples:

It is known what his departure will mean; his bodily presence will be withdrawn from the earth after his resurrection. The "heavens receive him, until the times of the restitution of all things," Acts 3:21. In respect to his Deity, and the exercise of his love and care towards them, he promises to be with them to the end of the world, Matt. 28:20. Of this he says, "Sumferei humin," "It is conducive to your good; it is profitable for you; it is for your advantage; it will provide the end you aim for." That is the sense of the word that we have translated "expedient." "It is for your profit and advantage." This, then, is what our Savior earnestly asserts, desiring to convince his sorrowful followers of its truth. His departure, which they so much feared and were troubled to think of, would turn to their profit and advantage.

3. It might be expected that they would accept this affirmation of truth. But because they want to know the basis for it, he gives them certainty and evidence for the proposition. He expresses it negatively and positively: "If I do not go away, he will not come; but if I depart, I will send him." I have spoken before concerning Christ's going away. I will now address the sending and the coming of the Comforter.

"*Ho parakletos*": Because the word has a number of meanings, many translations have retained the original word "*paracletus*," as the Syrian does. Some think it was a word used among the Jews (the Chaldee paraphrase makes use of it in Job 16:20). And among the Jews it signifies one who taught others in a way that delighted them in his teaching, that is, in a way that makes him their comforter. In Scripture it has two eminent meanings. It may either be an "advocate" or a "comforter." Our Savior is called "parakletos," meaning *advocate*, in 1John 2:1. Whether it is better rendered an advocate or a comforter here in John 16 is less clear.

Looking at the disciples' sorrow and trouble, and it seems to require the Comforter: "Sorrow has filled your hearts; but I will send you the Comforter." But looking at the words that follow, which mention the unique work for which he is sent, they seem to require that he be an Advocate, to plead the cause of Christ against the world, verse

8. I choose to interpret the promise by its occasion, which was the sorrow of his disciples. I prefer Comforter here.

Our blessed Savior declared who this Comforter is in John 15:26. He is "*Pneuma tes aleteias*," "the Spirit of truth." That is, he is the Holy Spirit who reveals all truth to the sons of men. Two things are affirmed about this Comforter:

    (1.) He will come.

    (2.) Christ will send him.

(1.) That he will come. His coming is conditioned on Christ going away: "If I do not go away, he will not come;" "If I do go (*eleusetai* [NT:2064]), he will come." So there is not only the mission of Christ, but the will of the Spirit in his coming: "He will come," his own will is in his work.

(2.) That Christ will send him. "*Pempso auton*," [NT:3992;846] "I will send him." Our Savior instructs his disciples by degrees in the mystery of his sending the Spirit. In chap. 14:16, he says, "I will pray the Father, and he will give you another Comforter." He goes one step more in verse 26, "But the Comforter, which is the Holy Spirit, whom the Father will send in my name." In 15:26, he says, "I will send him from the Father." And then here, absolutely, "I will send him." This business of sending the Holy Spirit by the Son was a deep mystery, which they could not handle all at once. Therefore he instructs them in it by degrees. Sending him argues for the Spirit's personal procession from the Son.

This is the summary: the presence of the Holy Spirit with believers, as their comforter, is better and more profitable for them than the corporeal presence of Christ, now that Christ has fulfilled the one sacrifice for sin that he was to offer.

The Holy Spirit is promised for two purposes:

    [1.] As a Spirit of sanctification for the elect, to convert them and make them believers.

    [2.] As a Spirit of consolation to believers, to give them the privileges of the death and purchase of Christ.

It is only in the latter sense that he is spoken of here. As to his presence with us in this regard, and the purposes for which he is sent, we will observe

    1. The source of his coming;

    2. How he is given;

    3. Our manner of receiving him;

    4. His abiding with us;

    5. His acting in us (chap. 2); and

    6. The effects of his working in us (chap. 3).

How we hold communion with him will appear from all of these.

1st. The *source of his coming* is mentioned in John 15:26, "*Para* *tou Patros ekporeuetai,*" "He proceeds from the Father." This is the fountain of his dispensation. There is a twofold *"ekporeusis"* [NT:1607], or "procession" of the Spirit:

(1st.) *"Fusike,"* or *"hupostatike,"* in respect to substance and personality.

(2dly.) *"Oikonomike,"* or dispensational, in respect to the work of grace.

In the first respect, he is the Spirit of the Father and the Son, proceeding from both eternally, and so he receives his substance and personality from them. This is not the business at hand. I will only say that, here lies the first foundation of all our distinct communion with him and our worship of him. But we cannot progress beyond the bare acquiescence of faith in this revealed mystery, performing what is due him solely on the account of his participation in the essence of God. And so I will not dwell upon it.

His *"ekporeusis"* or proceeding, mentioned here, is his dispensational proceeding to carry on the work of grace. It is spoken in reference to his being sent by Christ after his ascension: "then I will send him who proceeds from the Father," Jn. 15:26. When God was said to "come out of his place to punish the inhabitants of the earth," Isa. 26:21, it did not refer to any mutation in God, but to the work of punishment he would effect. The Spirit is likewise said to proceed in reference to a specific work, which is to testify of Christ. This cannot be assigned to him in respect to his eternal procession from the Father and the Son, but only in respect to his actual dispensation. It is also said of Christ, "He came forth from God," Jn. 16:30. The mention of the Father in 15:26, and not the Son, only reflects the gradual way by which our Savior reveals this mystery to his disciples, as mentioned earlier. He does refer to himself as sending the Spirit in John 16:7. This external relation of the Spirit to the Father and the Son in respect to his operation, proves his internal relation to them in respect to his personal procession.

Three things may be considered in the foundation of this dispensation, and in reference to our communion with the Holy Spirit:

[1st.] The will of the Spirit is in the work: "Ekporeuetai," "He comes forth himself." Frequent mention is made of his being sent, given, and poured out. It should not be understood to mean that this Spirit is an inferior, created spirit, a mere servant, as some have blasphemed. Nor does his personality principally represent the virtue of God, as some have fancied. He has *"idiomata hupostatika,"* personal properties, applied to him in this work. This argues for his personality and liberty. "Ekporeuetai," "He, of himself and of his own accord, proceeds."

[2dly.] The condescension of the Holy Spirit in this

dispensation, to proceed from the Father and the Son in this work. Taking on this work of a Comforter, as the Son took on the work of a Redeemer, will be discussed later.

[3dly.] The fountain of all this is discovered to be the Father. It is done so that we may know his works in pursuit of electing love, which is always ascribed to the Father. This is the order that is intimated here: First, there is the "*protesis*" of the Father, or the purpose of his love. This is the fountain of all. Then there is the "*erotesis*," the asking of the Son, John 14:16, which includes his merit and purchase. From this follows the "*ekporeusis*," or willing proceeding of the Holy Spirit. And this also testifies to the foundation of this whole discourse, namely, our unique communion with the Father in love, the Son in grace, and the Holy Spirit in consolation. This is where that fellowship of the Holy Spirit begins to which we are called. His gracious and blessed will, his infinite and ineffable condescension, is seen by faith as the foundation of all those effects that he works in us, and the privileges that we partake of by him. Our souls are uniquely conversant with him. Our desires, affections, and thankfulness are focused on him: more about this later. This is the first thing to consider in our communion with the Holy Spirit.

2dly. *The manner of his bestowing or communicating to us* from this fountain, that is, *how he is given*, should also be considered. It denotes three things:

(1st.) The *freeness* of it. Thus he is said to be **given**, John 14:16; "He will give you another comforter." The most frequent adjunct of the communication of the Spirit is that he is given and received as a gift: "He will give his Holy Spirit to those who ask him." A gift is free. The Spirit of grace is given of grace. The Spirit of sanctification, or the Spirit to sanctify and convert us, is a gift of free grace. In respect to consolation, the Spirit is a gift as well; he is promised to be given to believers. Hence, the Spirit is said to be received by the gospel, not by the law, Gal. 3:2. He is received of mere grace, and not of our own procuring. All his works are called "charismata," [NT:5486] meaning "free donations." He is freely bestowed, and he freely works. The different measures in which he is received arise from the fact that we have him by donation, or free gift. This is the tenure by which we hold and enjoy him, a tenure of free donation. That is how he is to be seen, to be asked, and to be received. In our communion with the Comforter, faith also draws together his will with the gift of the Father and Son. The one respects the distinct operation of the Deity in the person of the Holy Spirit, while the other respects the economy of the whole Trinity in the work of our salvation by Jesus Christ. The soul rejoices that the Comforter is willing to come to him, and is willing to be given to him. And seeing that all of this is the will of the Spirit and the gift of God, grace is magnified.

(2dly.) The *authority* of it. Thus he is said to be **sent**. Jn. 14:26, "The Father will send him in my name;" and 15:26, "I will send him to you from the Father;" and, " I will send him to you," 16:7. This mission of the Holy Spirit by the Father and the Son, reveals the order of the subsistence of the persons in the blessed Trinity, and the Spirit's procession from the Father and Son. It also reveals the order that is voluntarily engaged in by them to accomplish the work of our salvation. In his love for us, there is a very special way of condescending by the Holy Spirit to the authoritative delegation of Father and Son in this business. This speaks not of a disparity, dissimilitude, or inequality of essence, but of oneness in this work. The office of the Holy Spirit is to be an advocate for us, and a comforter to us. In respect to this office, he is sent authoritatively by Father and Son. This subjection or inequality in respect to his office, does not in any way prejudice the equality of nature that the Spirit has with Father and Son; no more than the mission of the Son given by the Father would prejudice his own equality of nature. The right understanding of many mysteries in the gospel, and the ordering of our hearts in communion with the Spirit, depend on this authoritative mission.

[1st.] Hence, the sin against the Holy Spirit is unpardonable. It has that color of rebellion put upon it that no other sin has. This is because he does not come or act in his own name alone, but in the name and authority of the Father and Son, from and by whom he is sent. Therefore, to sin against him is to sin against all the authority of God, all the love of the Trinity, and the condescension of each person to the work of our salvation. It is from the authoritative mission of the Spirit that the sin against him is uniquely unpardonable. It is a sin against the united love of the Father, Son, and Spirit. From this consideration, the true nature of the sin against the Holy Spirit might be investigated. Certainly it must consist in contempt for some operation of his, acting in the name and authority of the whole Trinity, and their ineffable condescension to the work of grace. But this is another consideration.

[2dly.] Because of this mission, we are to ask the Father and the Son to give the Spirit to us. Luke 11:13, "Your heavenly Father will give the Holy Spirit to those who ask him." Now the Holy Spirit, being God, is no less to be invoked, prayed to, and called upon, than the Father and Son, as I proved elsewhere. How, then, do we ask the Father for him, as we do in all our supplications, if we also pray that the Father himself would come to us, visit us, and abide with us? In our prayers that are directed to the Spirit, we consider him as essentially God over all, blessed forevermore. We pray for him from the Father and Son, as being under this mission and delegation from them. And, indeed, God has clearly revealed himself in the order of this dispensation to us. Thus, in our communion with the Spirit, we are to address him accordingly. That is, we not only address the person of the Holy Spirit himself, but properly we address ourselves to the Father and Son for him, which refers to this dispensation.

[3dly.] That is why such a great weight is placed upon not grieving the Spirit, Eph. 4:30. He comes to us in the name, with the love, and upon the condescension of the whole blessed Trinity. To grieve him for the purpose which will afterward be mentioned, is a great aggravation of sin. He justly expects cheerful entertainment with us, because of who he is and the work he comes to do. But when we also consider that he is sent by the Father and the Son, commissioned with their love and grace, to communicate them to our souls, this ought to instill unspeakable esteem with believers. And so the manner of his communication indicates that he is sent by authority.

(3dly.) He is said to be **poured out** or *shed on us abundantly*, Tit. 3:6, "*Hou ekseche-en* [NT:1632] *ef hemas plousios.*" This was the primary way in which he was communicated under the Old Testament. The mystery of the Father and the Son, and the matter of commission and delegation was not so clearly revealed then. "Until the Spirit be poured upon us from on high, and the wilderness be a fruitful field, and the fruitful field be counted for a forest;" Isa. 32:15. That is, until the Gentiles are called, and the Jews are rejected. In Isa. 44:3, "I will pour my Spirit upon your seed, and my blessing upon your offspring." Zech. 12:10 is an eminent example and always comes to mind. "And I will pour on the house of David and on the inhabitants of Jerusalem the Spirit of grace and supplication; then they will look on Me whom they pierced. Yes, they will mourn for Him as one mourns for his only son, and grieve for Him as one grieves for a firstborn." This expression of being poured out or shed is an allusion to water. It refers to all the uses of water, both natural and typical. I will not go into the particular association between them, but perhaps efficacy and plenty are the primary meanings.

This threefold expression of giving, sending, and pouring out the Spirit, gives us the three great properties of the covenant of grace:

First, it is free; he is given.

Secondly, it is orderly and sure. It comes from the love of the Father, by the procurement of the Son. This is where we get the Father sending him, and the Son sending him from the Father.

He is the gift of the Father's love, and the purchase of the Son's blood.

Thirdly, it is efficacious and plentiful.

3dly. The third thing to consider in the Spirit's purpose, is our *receiving him*. Mind what I first proposed of the Spirit: consider him as a Spirit of sanctification and a Spirit of consolation. Receiving him as a Spirit of sanctification is a mere passive reception, just as a vessel receives water. He comes as the wind on Ezekiel's dead bones and makes them live (Ezek. 37). He comes into dead hearts, and quickens them by an act of his almighty power. But now, as the Spirit of consolation, it is otherwise. In this sense, our Savior tells us that the "world cannot receive him," John 14:17, "The world does not receive, because it does not see him, neither does it know him: but you know him, for he dwells with you, and will be in you." It is the Spirit of consolation, or the Spirit *for* consolation, that is promised here. This is evident from the close of the verse, where he is said to be in them when he is promised to them. He was in them as a Spirit of quickening and sanctification when he was promised to them as a Spirit of comfort and consolation. He abides with them for that purpose. The power to receive the Spirit is denied to be in the world. It is ascribed to believers. Unbelievers cannot receive the Spirit because they do not know him. Believers can receive him, because they do know him. So there is an active power to be exercised in receiving him for consolation, but not in receiving him for regeneration and sanctification. This active power is the power of faith. In Gal. 3:2, they received the Spirit by the hearing of faith. In other words, the preaching of the gospel instilled faith in them, enabling them to receive the Spirit. Hence, believing is the qualification of receiving the Holy Spirit. "This he spoke of the Spirit, which those who believe on him should receive," John 7:39. It is believers who receive the Spirit, and they receive him by faith. There are three special acts of faith in receiving the Spirit:

(1st.) It considers the Spirit *as promised*. It is faith alone that profits from the benefit of the promises, "For indeed the gospel was preached to us as well as to them; but the word which they heard did not profit them, not being mixed with faith in those who heard it," Heb. 4:2. He is called the Spirit of that promise, "In whom you also trusted, after you heard the word of truth, the gospel of your salvation: in whom also after you believed, you were sealed with that holy Spirit of promise," Eph. 1:13. He is the Spirit promised in the covenant. And we receive the promise of the Spirit through faith, Gal. 3:14. So receiving the Spirit through faith is receiving him as promised. Faith looks at the promise of God and of Jesus Christ, of sending the Spirit for all those ends that he is desired. Thus faith depends on this promise, waits for it, and mixes the promise with itself until it receives him.

(2dly.) Faith acts by prayer. He is given as a Spirit of supplication, that we may ask him as a Spirit of consolation, Luke 11:13. Indeed, this asking of the Spirit of God, in the name of Christ, is the primary work of faith in this world.

(3dly.) Faith cherishes the Spirit by being attentive to his impulses, improving his acting according to his mind and will.

This is all I will say about our receiving the Spirit, sent of Jesus Christ. We do it by faith, looking at him as purchased by Jesus Christ, and promised of the Father. We seek him at the hands of God, and we receive him.

4thly. The next thing to consider in the Spirit's purpose is his abiding with us. This is expressed two ways in the Scripture:

(1st.) In general, it is said he will abide with us.

(2dly.) In particular, as to how he abides, it is by inhabitation or indwelling. I have spoken fully of the inhabitation of the Spirit elsewhere. He is said to dwell in us primarily, or perhaps solely, as a Spirit of sanctification or consolation. This is evident from the work he does. Because he is indwelling, he quickens and sanctifies us, Rom. 8:11. He dwells in us as if in a temple, which he makes holy by dwelling there, 1Cor. 6:19. "He will abide with you forever," John 14:16, There is a difficulty in this promise. His permanence in abiding relates only to sanctification, not to his role as Comforter. How is it that the Spirit of sanctification dwells in us forever, making it impossible to completely lose our holiness, and yet we may completely lose our comfort? A little to clear this up in our passage:

[1st.] He is promised to abide with the disciples forever, in opposition to the abode of Christ. Christ, in the flesh, had been with them for a little while. Now he was leaving them and going to his Father. He had been the comforter for a season, but he is now departing. In promising them another comforter, they might fear that he would only visit them for a little while too, and then their condition would be worse than ever. But our Savior says, "Do not fear that. This is the last dispensation. There will be no alteration. When I am gone, the Comforter will do all the remaining work. There is no other to look for. I promise him to you. He will not depart from you. He will always abide with you."

[2dly.] The Comforter may always abide with us, but he will not always comfort us. He is always with us for other ends and purposes, such as to sanctify and make us holy. This was the case with David, Ps. 51:11-12, "Take not your Holy Spirit from me." The Holy Spirit of sanctification was still with David; but he says, "Restore to me the joy of your salvation." That is, restore the Spirit of consolation that was lost when the promise was made good in the abiding of the Spirit of sanctification.

[3dly.] The Comforter may abide as a comforter, even when he does not actually comfort us. In truth, the essence of holiness requires that he cannot dwell in us without making us holy, for the temple of God is holy. But his comforting is an act of his sovereign will. And so he may abide, and yet not actually comfort us.

[4thly.] The Spirit often works to console us, even when we do not receive it. The well is close, but we do not see it. We refuse to be comforted. I told you that the Spirit as a *sanctifier* comes with power to conquer an unbelieving heart. The Spirit as a *comforter* comes with sweetness, to be received in a believing heart. He may speak, but we do not believe it is his voice. He may offer consolation, but we will not receive it. "My sore ran," says David, "and my soul refused to be comforted."

[5thly.] I deny that the Holy Spirit ever leaves a believing soul without any consolation. A man may be darkened and clouded; he may refuse comfort; he may actually find none, and feel none. But he has a radical foundation of consolation, which in due time will be realized. Therefore, when God promises that he will heal sinners, and restore comfort to them, as in Isa. 57:18, it is not that they were without any comfort, but that they did not have as much as they needed. It is not my present purpose to list all the ways by which men refuse comfort, and come short of the consolation that God wants them to have.

Being sent and given, the Spirit abides with believers, and does not leave them; but he shows himself in various ways in his operations.

213

CHAPTER 2

WHAT THE HOLY SPIRIT DOES IN AND TOWARDS US –

Having declared why and how the Holy Spirit is given to us as a Spirit of consolation, I come next to the following:

5thly. To declare what his acts are in us and towards us.

There are two general areas to consider:

(1st.) His various manners and kinds of acting, and

(2dly.) The particular products of his acting in us, in which we have communion with him.

(1st.) His various manners and kinds of acting.

[1st.] He is said "to work effectually," [NT:1754 *energein*]. 1Cor. 12:11, "All these work" (or effect) "that one and the self-same Spirit." This is said in respect to his distribution of gifts, but the same can be said for communicating graces and privileges. He does it by working. This is evidence of his personality, especially when we consider the words following, "Dividing to every man according to his will." To work according to will is the inseparable property of a person, and it is spoken expressly of God, Eph. 1:11. So in relation to 1Cor. 12:6, it makes his Deity no less evident. What he is said to do there is said of God himself: "There are various operations, but it is the same God which works all in all." In other words, "All these works are of one and the same Spirit, dividing to every man severally as he will." What we have from him, we have by his energetic working. It is not by proposing this or that argument to us. It is not by persuading us with this or that moral motive or inducement, leaving us to make use of them as we can. Instead, he works effectually to *communicate* grace or consolation to us.

[2dly.] In the same verse, it speaks of the manner of his working. He is said to divide or distribute to everyone as he will, *diairein* [NT:1243]. This act of distribution involves operation, choice, judgment, and freedom. One who distributes variously, does so with choice, judgment, and freedom of will. Such are the proceedings of the Spirit in his dispensations. To one, he gives one thing abundantly, to another, something else. To one, he gives one thing in one degree, to another, the same thing in a different degree. Thus, in his sovereignty, the saints are kept in constant dependence on him. He distributes as he will. Who should not be content with his portion? What claim can any make to what he distributes as he will?

[3dly.] This is further manifested by his giving what and when he chooses. They "spoke with other tongues, as the Spirit gave them utterance," Acts 2:4. He gave these tongues to them, freely. Whatever he bestows upon us is his gift. Hence, in the economy of our salvation, no one person prejudices the freedom and liberty of any other. So the love of the Father in sending the Son is free. Sending him in no way prejudices the liberty and love of the Son. He lays down his life freely. The satisfaction and purchase made by the Son in no way prejudices the freedom of the Father's grace in pardoning and accepting us. The Father and Son sending the Spirit does not derogate from his freedom in his workings. What he gives, he gives freely. And the reason for this is because the will of the Father, Son, and Holy Spirit is essentially the same. In the act of one is the counsel of all, and each freely participates in that.

This describes the general manner and kind of his working in us and towards us. Power, choice, and freedom are evidently denoted in the passages cited. It is not a unique work of his towards us that is declared here, but the manner in which he produces the effects.

(2dly.) What remains is to explain the foundation of the communion which we have with the Holy Spirit.

The Spirit being sent to us, and working in us, I will now take up the effects that he produces. I will not put them into any artificial order. Instead I will treat them as I find them lying scattered up and down in the Scripture. I will move from those which are more general, to those which are more specific. My aim and desire is not to be exhaustive, but to address only the most obvious ones.

I will speak of the Spirit principally (if not exclusively) as a comforter, and not as a sanctifier. Therefore, I must omit the great sanctifying work of the Spirit towards us all our days, his constant supplying of new light, power, and vigor in the grace that we receive from him.

Nor will I speak of those things which the Comforter effects in believers towards others, in testifying to them and convicting the world. These are promised in John 15:26, 16:8, where the Spirit is properly the believer's advocate. I will only speak of those effects that he works in and towards believers as their comforter.

215

CHAPTER 3.

THINGS IN WHICH WE HAVE COMMUNION WITH THE HOLY SPIRIT –

6thly. The effects of the Holy Spirit in us, or towards us, are the subject-matter of our communion with him. They are the things in which we hold unique fellowship with him as our comforter. The following effects are proposed:

1. The first and most general is that of John 14:26, "He will teach you all things, and bring all things to your remembrance, whatever I have said to you." There are two parts to this promise:

(1.) Teaching.

(2.) Reminding.

I will speak later of the first part, his teaching, when I address our anointing by him.

(2.) The first general promise of the Spirit as a comforter is that he will REMIND us of all the things that Christ spoke: "*Hupomnesei humas panta,*" [NT:5279,5209,3956] "He will make you mind all these things." This may be considered two ways:

[1.] In respect to the words he actually said. Our Savior promises his apostles that the Holy Spirit will directly remind them of the things he said, so that by his inspiration they might be enabled to write and preach them for the good and benefit of his church. Peter tells us in 2Pet. 1:21, "Holy men of God spoke as they were moved by the Holy Spirit" (that is, in writing the Scripture); "*hupo Pneumatos Hagiou feromenoi.*" [NT:5259,4151,40,5342] They were borne up by him, and carried beyond themselves to speak his words, and to write down what he dictated to them. The apostles might forget much of what Christ said to them. What they did retain by natural remembrance, was not a sufficient foundation for a rule of faith to the church. The word of prophecy is not "*idias epiluseos,*" [NT:2398,1955] 1Pet. 1:20, from any man's private motivation. It does not come from any private conception, understanding, or remembrance. That is why, Christ promises that the Holy Spirit will do this work, so that they might infallibly repeat what he delivered to them. Hence, the phrase in Luke 1:3, "*Purekoloutekoti anoten,*" [NT:3877,509] is better rendered, "Having obtained perfect knowledge of things from above" rather than "Having obtained perfect knowledge of things from the beginning." It denotes that the source of his understanding is such that he is able to give an infallible rule of faith to the church.

216

[2.] Reminding may be in respect to the comfort of what he said. This seems to be largely the intent of this promise. He had been speaking to them of things suited for their consolation. He gave them precious promises of the supplies they would have from him in this life, the love of the Father, and the glory he was providing them. The sense and comfort of these things is inexpressible, and the joy arising from them is full of glory. He says, "I know how unable you are to make use of these things to console yourselves. Therefore, the Spirit will restore them to your minds, in their full strength and vigor, for that purpose for which I speak them." This is one reason why it was expedient for believers to have the presence of the Spirit in place of Christ's body. While he was with them, the heavenly promises Christ gave them had little effect on their hearts! When the Spirit came, he made all things full of joy for them! This unique work, which belonged to the Spirit by virtue of his office, was reserved for him so that he too might be glorified. His work to the end of the world is to bring the promises of Christ to our minds and hearts. He gives us their comfort, joy, and sweetness, far beyond what the disciples experienced when Christ spoke the promises to them in person. Their gracious influence was being restrained, so that the dispensation of the Spirit might be glorified.

This is true of the next words in this promise, Jn. 14:27, "Peace I leave with you. My peace I give to you." The consequence of the Comforter being sent, to bring to mind what Christ said, is peace and freedom from a troubled heart. Whatever peace, relief, comfort, joy, and support that we receive from any work, promise, or thing done by Christ, all belongs to this dispensation of the Comforter. It would be useless to apply our natural abilities to remember, call to mind, or consider the promises of Christ. But when the Comforter undertakes the work, it is done to fit the purpose.

Afterward, I will discuss how we have unique communion with the Spirit in faith and obedience, and in the consolation that we receive from Christ's promises that the Spirit brings to mind. In general, what we obtain is this: our Savior Jesus Christ leaves the efficacy of those promises of consolation, which he gave in person to his apostles, to the Holy Spirit. In this we see the immediate source of all the spiritual comfort we have in this world, and the fellowship which we have with the Holy Ghost in that comfort.

Only here, as in the following particulars, what should be borne in mind is the *manner* of the Spirit's working this comfort, and the interest of his power, will, and goodness in his working. He comforts powerfully, voluntarily, and freely.

1st. **Powerfully**. Therefore, comfort from the words and

217

promises of Christ sometimes breaks in through all opposition into the saddest and darkest condition imaginable. It comes and makes men sing in a dungeon, rejoice in flames, and glory in tribulation. It will pass into prisons, racks, through temptations, and the greatest distresses imaginable. Why is this? *"To Pneuma energei,"* the Spirit works effectually. His power is in it. He will work, and none will stop him. If he will bring to our remembrance the promises of Christ for our consolation, then neither Satan nor man, sin nor world, not even death, will interrupt our comfort. The saints, who have communion with the Holy Spirit, know this to their advantage. Sometimes the heavens are black over them, and the earth trembles under them. Public, personal calamities and distresses appear so full of horror and darkness, that they are ready to faint with the apprehensions of them. This is where their great relief comes from, and the revival of their spirits. Their consolation or trouble does not depend on any outward condition or inward frame of their own hearts. It depends on the powerful and effectual workings of the Holy Spirit, to which they surrender by faith.

2dly. **Voluntarily**. He distributes to everyone as he will. Therefore, this work is done in great variety, both to the same person and to various people. For the same person, every promise brings sweetness when his pressures are great and heavy. Sometimes he may be full of joy or consolation in great distress. Other times, in the least trial, he may search the promise seeking comfort, but it is far away. The reason is, *"Pneuma diairei katos bouletai,"* the Spirit distributes as he will. And so with various people, under the same circumstances, some find each promise is full of life and comfort while others taste little of it all their days. And faith affects this whole business of consolation. It depends on the sovereign will of the Holy Spirit. It is not tied to any rules or course of procedure. Therefore faith is exercised waiting upon the Spirit for the seasonable accomplishment of the good pleasure of his will.

3dly. **Freely**. The variety in dispensing consolation by promises results from the freedom of the Spirit's operation. Hence, comfort is given unexpectedly, when the heart has every reason in the world to expect distress and sorrow. Thus, sometimes it is the first means to recover a backslider, who might justly expect to be cut off. These considerations apply to all the other effects and fruits of the Comforter.

In this first general effect or work of the Holy Spirit towards us, we have communion and fellowship with him. The life and soul of all our comforts is found in the promises of Christ. They are the breasts of all our consolation. Who knows how powerful they are in their bare letter, or when they are enhanced by considering and meditating on them? They sometimes break unexpectedly upon the soul with a conquering, endearing life and vigor. This is where faith deals uniquely with the Holy Spirit. It considers the promises themselves. It looks up to him, waits for him, considers his appearances in the word, and owns him in his work and efficacy. No sooner does the believer begin to feel the life of a promise warming his heart, than he knows the Holy Spirit is there relieving, cherishing, supporting, and delivering him from fear, entanglements, and troubles. This will add to his joy, and lead him into fellowship with the Spirit.

2. The next general work of the Spirit seems to be that in John 16:14, "The Comforter will *glorify* me; for he will receive of mine, and will show it to you." The work of the Spirit is to glorify Christ. From this we can see that the Spirit does not substitute himself for Christ, or say that he is everything in himself. That would not be the Comforter. His work is to glorify Christ, the one that sends him. It would be an evident sign of a false spirit if it did not glorify Christ; and such are many spirits that have gone abroad into the world. But what this Spirit will do to glorify Christ is to, "take of mine," "*ek tou emou lepsetai.*" What these things are is declared in the next verse: "All things that the Father has are mine; therefore I said he will take of mine." Our Savior is not speaking of the essence and essential properties of the Father and Son, but of the grace that is communicated to us by them. By, "my things," Christ means the fruit of his purchase and mediation, the basis on which he says all his Father's things are his. That is, he means all the fruits of election, the things that the Father, in his eternal love, has provided to be dispensed in the blood of his Son. He is saying, "The Comforter will receive these. They will be committed to him to dispense for your good and advantage, and for their appointed purpose." So it follows, "*anangelei,*" [NT:312] he will show them, or declare and make them known to you."

This, then, is how he comforts. He reveals to the souls of sinners the good things of the covenant of grace which the Father has provided, and the Son has purchased. He shows to us mercy, grace, forgiveness, righteousness, and acceptance by God. He lets us know that these are the things of Christ that he has procured for us. He shows them to us for our comfort and security. He effectually declares these things to believers, and makes them know them for their own good, and know them as the things that come originally from the Father. They were prepared from eternity in his love and goodwill, purchased for them by Christ, and stored in the covenant of grace for their use. Then Christ is magnified and glorified in their hearts. Then they know what a Savior and Redeemer he is. A believer does not glorify or honor Christ when he learns of the eternal redemption he has purchased for him. It is a unique effect of the Holy Spirit as our comforter. "No man can say that Jesus is the Lord, but by the Holy Spirit," 1Cor. 12:3.

3. He "sheds the love of God abroad in our hearts," Rom. 5:5. What is meant here is the love of God to us, not our love to God. The context is so clear that nothing can be added to it. The love of God is either of ordination or acceptance; it is either the love of his intent to do us good, or the love that gains us acceptance and approval by him. Both of these are frequently called the love of God in Scripture, as I have said. Now, how can these be shed abroad in our hearts? They cannot be in themselves, but only the sense of them. It is a spiritual apprehension of them. "*Ekkechutai*" [NT:1632] is "shed abroad." It is the same word that is used concerning the Comforter being given us, Tit. 3:6. God sheds him abundantly, or pours him on us; so he sheds abroad, or pours out the love of God in our hearts. The expression is metaphorical. What it indicates is that the Comforter gives a sweet and plentiful evidence and persuasion of the love of God to us. It is such that the soul is taken, delighted, and satiated with it. This is his work, and he does it effectually. It is an inexpressible mercy to give a poor sinful soul a comforting persuasion, an overflowing sense that God in Jesus Christ loves him, and delights in him, that he is well pleased with him, and that he has thoughts of tenderness and kindness towards him.

We have this in a unique manner by the Holy Spirit; it is his unique work. Just as all his works are mixed with love and kindness, they are mixed with this communication of a sense of the love of the Father. In this, we have unique communion with the Spirit, and by him we have communion with the Father in his love, shed abroad in our hearts. So not only do we rejoice in, and glorify the Holy Spirit who does this work, but in the Father whose love it is. We also rejoice in the Son, in taking his things and showing them to us. What we have of heaven in this world is found in this. It is the basis and manner of our fellowship with the Holy Spirit.

4. Another effect of his work in and towards us is this: Rom. 8:16, "The Spirit itself bears witness with our spirit, that we are the children of God." By nature, we are children of Satan, of the curse and wrath. By the Spirit we are put into another capacity. We are adopted as children of God. By receiving the *Spirit* of our Father we become the *children* of our Father. This is why he is called, "The Spirit of adoption," Rom. 8:15. Sometimes the soul questions whether it is a child of God, because some its old condition remains. When that happens, the soul gravely puts in its claim of adoption, with all the evidence it has to make good its title. The Spirit comes and bears witness in this case. This is an allusion to judicial proceedings about titles and evidence. The judge being set, the person puts in his claim, produces his evidence, and pleads his case. His adversaries endeavor to uncover

anything that might invalidate his claim and annul his plea. In the midst of the trial, a person of known and approved integrity comes into the court, and gives testimony fully and directly on behalf of the claimant. This silences all his adversaries, and fills the claimant with joy and satisfaction.

So it is in this case. The soul, by the power of its own conscience, is brought before the law of God. There a man puts in his plea that he is a child of God, that he belongs to God's family. To this end, he produces all his evidence, everything by which faith gives him an interest in God. Satan, in the meantime, opposes with all his might. Sin and the law assist him. Many flaws are found in the evidence. The truth of them is questioned, and the soul hangs in suspense as to the outcome. In the midst of this contest, the Comforter comes. By a word of promise or other testimony, he overpowers the heart with a comforting persuasion, suppressing all objections that his plea is good. He is a child of God. Therefore it is said of the Spirit, "*Summarturei toi Pneumati hemon*," he "bears witness with our spirit." When our spirits are pleading their right and title, he comes in and bears witness on our side. This enables us, at the same time, to demonstrate our filial obedience, kind and childlike. This is called "crying, Abba, Father," Gal. 4:6.

Remember the manner of the Spirit's working, mentioned before. He does it effectually, voluntarily, and freely. Sometimes the dispute is a long one. The cause is pleaded for many years. The law sometimes seems to prevail, sin and Satan seem to rejoice, and the soul is filled with dread about its inheritance. Perhaps the soul's own witness, from its faith, sanctification, and former experience, maintains the plea with some sense of comfort. But the work is not done. The conquest is not complete until the Spirit, who works freely and effectually, when and how he will, comes in with his testimony as well. He clothes his power with a word of promise. He makes all parties concerned pay attention to him. And he puts an end to the controversy.

In this, he gives us holy communion with himself. The soul knows his voice when he speaks, *nec hominem sonat*, not with a man's voice. There is something too great in it to be the effect of a created power. When the Lord Jesus Christ at one word stilled the raging of the sea and wind, all that were with him knew there was divine power at hand, Matt. 8:25-27. And when the Holy Spirit by one word stills the tumults and storms that are raised in the soul, giving immediate calm and security, the soul knows his divine power, and rejoices in his presence.

5. He seals us. "We are sealed by the Holy Spirit of promise," Eph. 1:13. "Do not grieve the Holy Spirit, by which you are sealed to the day of redemption," Eph. 4:30. I am not very clear in the certain

specific intent of this metaphor. I will give what I am persuaded of briefly. In a seal, two things are considered: (1.) its nature, and (2.) its use.

(1.) The nature of sealing consists in imparting the image or character of the seal to the thing that is sealed. To seal something is to stamp the character of the seal on it. In this sense, the effectual communication of the image of God to us should be our sealing. The Spirit actually communicates the image of God in righteousness and true holiness to believers, and seals them with it. To have this stamp of the Holy Spirit is to be sealed by the Spirit. It is evidence to the soul that it is accepted by God. In this sense, our Savior is said to be sealed of God, John 6:27. He carried the impress of the power, wisdom, and majesty of God in the discharge of his office.

(2.) The purpose or use of sealing is twofold:

[1.] It confirms or ratifies any grant or conveyance made in writing. In such cases, men set their seals on their grants to make them good and confirm them. When this is done, they are irrevocable. They also confirm the truth of the testimony given by someone by sealing it. This was the practice of the Jews. When someone gave true witness to a matter, the judges immediately placed their seals on it, to confirm it in judgment. Thus it is said that one who receives the testimony of Christ "has set his seal to it that God is true," John 3:33. The promise is the great grant and conveyance of life and salvation in Christ that is given to believers. So we may have full assurance of the truth and irrevocableness of the promise, God gives us the Spirit to satisfy our hearts of it. He is said to seal us by assuring our hearts of those promises and their stability. Although many expositors go this way, I do not see how this can be consistent with the meaning of the word. It is not said that the *promise* is sealed, but that *we* are sealed. When we seal a deed or grant, we do not say the man is sealed, but the deed or grant.

[2.] Sealing is also used to appropriate, distinguish, or keep safe. Men set their seals on what they appropriate to identify it as their own. They place a seal on what they desire to keep safe for themselves. Evidently, it is in this sense that the servants of God are said to be sealed, Rev. 7:4, Ezek. 9:4. They are marked with God's mark as his special ones. Believers are sealed when they are marked for God to be heirs of the purchased inheritance, and to be preserved until the day of redemption. Now, if this is the sealing intended, it does not denote a sense in the heart, but the actual security of the person. The Father gives the elect into the hands of Christ to be redeemed. Having redeemed them, in due time they are called by the Spirit, and marked for God. And so they surrender themselves to the hands of the Father.

If you ask, "Which of these two is meant by our being sealed by the Holy Spirit?" then I answer, both. We are sealed until the day of redemption when the stamp, image, and character of the Spirit, placed upon our souls, gives us a fresh sense of the love of God, and a comforting persuasion of our acceptance by him.

Thus, the Holy Spirit communicates his own likeness to us, which is also the image of the Father and the Son. "We are changed into this image by the Lord the Spirit," 2Cor. 3:18. Here, he brings us into fellowship with himself. Our likeness to him gives us boldness with him. We look for his work. We pray for his fruits. And when any effect of grace, any discovery of the image of Christ that is implanted in us, persuades us that we are set apart for God, then we have communion with him in that.

6. He is an earnest or deposit to us. 2Cor. 1:22, He has "given the earnest of the Spirit in our hearts;" chap. 5:5, "Who also has given to us the earnest of the Spirit;" Eph. 1:13, 14, "You are sealed with that Holy Spirit of promise, which is the earnest of our inheritance." In the two former passages we are said to *have* the earnest of the Spirit. In the latter, the Spirit is said to *be* our earnest. "Of the Spirit," then, is the *genitivus materiae* or material source. It does not denote the cause of it, but the subject. The Spirit is not the author of the earnest, but the earnest itself, as in the latter passage. Considering what is meant by the "Spirit" here, and what is meant by an "earnest," will give some insight into this privilege that we receive by the Comforter.

(1.) Trying to determine what grace, what gift of the Spirit, is meant by this earnest, serves no purpose. It is the Spirit himself, personally considered, that is said to be this earnest, 2Cor. 1:22. It is God who has given the earnest of the Spirit in our hearts. It is an expression directly corresponding to Gal. 4:6, "God has sent forth the Spirit of his Son into your hearts." That is, only the person of the Spirit can be called the Spirit of his Son. And in Eph. 1:14, he has given the Spirit as that earnest, the Spirit of promise. Giving us this Spirit gives us this earnest.

(2.) The word for earnest is "*arraton*" [NT:728]. Neither the Greek nor the Latin has any word to directly express what is meant here. The Latins have made words for it from what is expressed here in the Greek, *arrha* and *arrabo*. The Greek word is only the Hebrew *herabon* ['*eravon*], which some believe came from the Syrian merchants as a word of trade. It is rendered by some, in Latin, *pignus*, a "pledge." But this cannot be what is meant here. A pledge is property that someone gives or leaves in the custody of another, to assure him that he will give or pay him some other thing. It is in the nature of what we call a "pawn." What is meant here is a part of what is to come, and only a part of it, according to the trade use of the word from which the metaphor is taken. It is excellently rendered in our language an "earnest." An earnest is part of the whole price, or part of a grant given beforehand, to assure the person to whom it is given that at the appointed time he will receive the whole of what is promised to him.

To be an earnest, it is required,

[1.] That it is part of the whole, of the same kind and nature. We give so much money in earnest as a promise to pay the remaining money later.

[2.] That it is a confirmation of a promise. First the whole is promised, and then the earnest is given until the completion of that promise.

The Spirit is this earnest. God gives us the promise of eternal life. To confirm this to us, he gives us his Spirit. He is the first part of the promise, to assure us of the fulfillment of the whole. And so he is said to be the earnest of the inheritance that is promised and purchased.

Consider that he may be said to be an earnest on the part of God who gives him, and on the part of believers who receive him:

1st. He is an earnest on the part of God, in that God gives him as a choice part of the inheritance itself, of the same kind as the whole, as an earnest ought to be. The full inheritance that is promised is the fullness of the Spirit in the enjoyment of God. When that Spirit given to us in this world has perfectly taken away all sin and sorrow, and enabled us to enjoy the glory of God in his presence, that is the full inheritance promised. The Spirit given to us to make us fit to enjoy God in some measure while we are here, is the earnest of the whole promise.

God does it to assure us of the inheritance. Having given so many external assurances, such as his word, promises, covenant, oath, and the revelation of his faithfulness and immutability in all of them, he is also pleased to graciously give us one within us, Isa. 59:21, so that we may have all the security we are capable of. What can more be done? He has given us the Holy Spirit, the first-fruits of glory, the greatest pledge of his love, and the earnest of it all.

2dly. He is an earnest on the part of believers, acquainting them with the love of God, and with their inheritance.

(1st.) *The love of God.* Being accepted by God lets them know their favor in his sight, that he is their Father, and that he will deal with them as with children. Because they are his children, the inheritance will be theirs. He sends his Spirit into our hearts, "crying, Abba, Father," Gal. 4:6. And what is the inference for believers? Gal. 4:7, "Then we are not servants, but sons; and if sons, then heirs of God." The same apostle argues in Rom. 8:17, "If children, then heirs; heirs of God, and joint heirs with Christ." Being persuaded by the Spirit that we are children, the inference is, "Then heirs, heirs of God, and joint heirs with Christ." We have a right to an inheritance, and a superior claim to it. This, then, is the use we have of the Spirit, persuading us of our sonship and acceptance by God our Father.

And what is this inheritance of glory? "If we suffer with him, we will be glorified together." The Spirit is given to us for this purpose. 1Jn. 3:24, "Hereby we know that he abides in us, by the Spirit which he has given us." The apostle speaks of our union with God, expressed in the preceding words: "He that keeps his commandments dwells in him, and he in him." We know this by the Spirit that he has given us; the Spirit acquaints us with it. It is not that we have such an acquaintance, because he gives a sense of this as he pleases. But the argument is good and conclusive in itself. "We have the Spirit; therefore he dwells in us, and we in him." Because God dwells in us by his Spirit, our interest in him, our knowledge of his love, comes from that.

(2dly.) The Spirit acquaints believers with *their inheritance*, 1Cor. 2:9, 10. As an earnest, and being part of the whole inheritance, the Spirit gives us knowledge of that inheritance.

In all respects, the Spirit is so completely an earnest, given by God, received by us, that he is the beginning of our inheritance, and the assurance of it. To the extent we have the Spirit, we have perfect enjoyment of heaven, and evidence of its future fullness. Believers receive him and rejoice in him under this perception of him in the dispensation of grace. They rejoice in every gracious, self-evidencing act of his in their hearts. It is like a drop from heaven, and they long for the ocean of it. Not to treat every effect of grace this way, is to neglect the work of the Holy Spirit in us and towards us.

What remains is to differentiate between believers receiving the Spirit as an earnest of the whole inheritance, and hypocrites "tasting of the powers of the world to come," Heb. 6:5. A taste of the powers of the world to come seems to be the same thing as receiving the earnest of the inheritance, but it is not.

[1st.] There are no grounds to think that "the powers of the world to come" means the joys of heaven. They are not called that anywhere. Nor does it suitably express the glory that will be revealed and that we will partake of. It doubtless means the powerful ministry of the ordinances and dispensations of the times of the gospel.

225

[2dly.] Suppose that "the powers of the world to come" did mean the glory of heaven. There is still a wide difference between taking a vanishing taste of it, and receiving an abiding earnest from God. Taking a taste of the things of heaven, and having them assured of God as from his love, differ greatly. A hypocrite may have a great deal of joy and contentment in considering the good things of the kingdom of God for a season. But the Spirit, as an earnest, pledges them to be provided to us in the love of God and the purchase of his Son Jesus Christ.

7. The Spirit anoints believers. We are "anointed" by the Spirit, 2Cor. 1:21. We have "an unction from the Holy One, and we know all things," 1John 2:20, 27. I cannot fully examine this expression here. I have done it elsewhere. At the bottom of it are the use of unctions in the Judaic church, the meanings and purposes associated with it, and the offices to which men were consecrated to by it. It refers to the anointing of Jesus Christ, from which he is called Messiah (the anointed one), and the Christ. The whole performance of his office of mediator is also called his anointing, Dan. 9:24. Christ is said to be "anointed with the oil of gladness above his fellows," Heb. 1:9; which is the same as John 3:34, "God gives not the Spirit by measure to him." We, who have the Spirit by measure, are anointed with the "oil of gladness." Christ has the fullness of the Spirit, from which our measure is communicated. So he is anointed above us, "that in all things he may have the pre-eminence." Christ was anointed with the Spirit to his threefold office of king, priest, and prophet. By virtue of an unction, having the same Spirit dwelling in us as in him, we gain an interest in these offices of his. We too are made kings, priests, and prophets to God. It would take a long discourse to handle this topic, and my design is only to outline these things.

I will therefore fix on only one passage where the communications of the Spirit in this unction of Christ are enumerated, and by which we receive our measure from him and with him. By this unction, we are made partakers with him. Isa. 11:2, 3, "The Spirit of the LORD will rest upon him, the Spirit of wisdom and understanding, the Spirit of counsel and might, the Spirit of knowledge, and of the fear of the LORD..." Here are listed many of the endowments of Christ from the Spirit with which he was abundantly anointed. Primarily they are wisdom, counsel, and understanding. Because of these, all the treasures of wisdom and knowledge are said to be in him, Col. 2:3. This is only part of the equipping of Jesus Christ for the discharge of his office. Yet, it is such that, where our anointing for the same purpose is mentioned, it specifically effects such qualifications in us. In 1John 2:20, 27, the work of the anointing is to teach us. The Spirit in that work is a Spirit of wisdom and understanding, of counsel, knowledge, and quick

226

understanding in the fear of the Lord. The great promise of the Comforter is that he will "teach us," John 14:26, and "guide us into all truth," John 16:13. Teaching us the mind and will of God, in the way we are taught it by the Spirit, our comforter, is an eminent part of our anointing by him. There is a threefold teaching by the Spirit:

(1.) The Spirit teaches us conviction and illumination. So the Spirit teaches the world by the preaching of the word; as he is promised to do, John 16:8.

(2.) The Spirit teaches us sanctification. He opens blind eyes, gives new understanding, and shines into our hearts to give us a knowledge of the glory of God in the face of Jesus Christ. He enables us to receive spiritual things in a spiritual light, 1Cor. 2:13. He gives a saving knowledge of the mystery of the gospel, and this in some degree is common to believers.

(3.) The Spirit teaches us consolation. He makes the discoveries of the mind and will of God, in the light of the Spirit of sanctification, sweet, useful, and joyful to the soul. Here the oil of the Spirit is called the "oil of gladness;" it brings joy and gladness with it. The name of Christ discovered through the Spirit is a sweet "ointment poured forth." It causes us to run after him with joy and delight, Cant. 1:3. By our daily experience, we see that many have little taste, sweetness, or relish in their souls for the truths they savingly know and believe. But when we are taught by this unction, oh, how sweet everything is that we know of God! As we may see in the passage of John where mention is made of the teaching of this unction (1Jn. 2:20,27), it refers specifically to the Spirit teaching us the love of God in Christ, the shining of his countenance which, as David says, puts gladness into our hearts, Ps. 4:6, 7.

The Spirit teaches us about the love of God in Christ. He makes every gospel truth like wine well refined to our souls, and he makes the good things of God's love a feast of sumptuous things. He gives us joy and gladness in all that we know of God. This is the great preservative of the soul to keep it close to truth. The apostle speaks of the teaching we receive by this unction. It is the means by which we are preserved from seduction. Indeed, to know the power, sweetness, joy, and gladness of any truth, is the best insurance of the soul's constancy in preserving and retaining it. Those who find no more sweetness in the one than in the other will readily exchange truth for error. All the privileges we enjoy, all the dignity and honor we are invested with, our whole dedication to God, our nobility and royalty, our interest in all the advantages of the church and our approaches to God in worship, our separation from the world, the name by which we are called, the liberty we enjoy, are all branches of this anointing of the Holy Spirit; they all flow from its effect. I have mentioned only our teaching by this unction, a teaching that brings joy and gladness with it by giving us a sense of the truth in which we are instructed. When we find any of the good truths of the gospel coming home to our souls with life, vigor, and power, giving us gladness of heart, and transforming us into its image and likeness, then the Holy Spirit is at work pouring out his oil.

8. We also have adoption by the Spirit. Hence, he is called the "Spirit of adoption." That is, either he is given to adopted ones to assure them of their adoption, and to persuade them of the Father's adopting love, or else he gives them the privilege of adoption itself, as intimated in John 1:12. Nor is there a conflict with Gal. 4:6; for God may send the Spirit of supplication into our hearts because we are sons, and yet we may still be adopted by his Spirit.

9. He is also called the "Spirit of supplication;" for which he is promised in Zech. 12:10. How he effects that in us is declared in Rom. 8:26, 27; Gal. 4:6. For this reason we are said to "pray in the Holy Spirit," Jude 20. Our prayers may be considered two ways:

(1.) First, as a spiritual duty required by God. As such, they are wrought in us by the Spirit of sanctification, who helps us to perform all our duties by exalting all the faculties of the soul to spiritually discharge our respective offices in these duties.

(2.) As a means of retaining communion with God. Prayers are the means by which we sweetly ease our hearts in the heart of the Father, and receive refreshing tastes of his love. The soul is never more raised with the love of God than when it is taken by the Spirit into intimate communion with him in the discharge of this duty. In this role, prayer belongs to the Spirit of consolation, to the Spirit promised as a comforter.

Let me summarize the specific effects which he works in us and towards us. These effects are his bringing the promises of Christ to mind, glorifying him in our hearts, shedding abroad the love of God in us, witnessing with us as to our spiritual condition, sealing us until the day of redemption (as the earnest of our inheritance), anointing us with the privilege of consolation, confirming our adoption, and being present with us in our supplications. The wisdom of faith is to seek out and meet with the Comforter in all these things, not losing their sweetness by being ignorant of their author, nor coming short of the responses required of us.

228

CHAPTER 4.

CONSEQUENCES ON OUR HEARTS OF THE EFFECTS OF
THE HOLY SPIRIT –

Having discovered the way of our communion with the Holy Spirit, and examined the most noble and known effects that he produces, it remains to declare the general consequences of these effects in the hearts of believers. Now, as with the former, I will do little more than name them. It is not at all in my design to handle their natures, but only to show what regard they have to the business in hand:

1. CONSOLATION is the first of these consequences: "The disciples walked in the fear of the Lord, and in the consolation of the Holy Spirit," Acts 9:31, *"Tei paraklesei tou Hagiou Pneumatos,"* He is *"ho parakletos"* [NT:3875], the Comforter, and he gives *"paraklesin"*, [NT:3874] comfort. From his work towards us, and in us, we have comfort and consolation. This is the first general consequence of his dispensation and work. Whenever mention is made of comfort and consolation given to the saints in the Scripture, it is the consequence of the work of the Holy Spirit towards them. Comfort or consolation generally is setting and composing the soul in rest and contentedness in the midst of troubles. It results when the consideration or presence of some good in which it is interested, outweighs the evil, trouble, or perplexity that it has to wrestle with. Where mention is made of comfort and consolation, it is in relation to trouble or perplexity. 2Cor. 1:5-6, "As the sufferings of Christ abound in us, so our consolation also abounds by Christ." Suffering and consolation are opposed. Consolation is a relief against suffering. All the promises and expressions of comfort in the Old and New Testament are proposed as reliefs against trouble.

As I said, consolation arises from the presence or consideration of a greater good, that outbalances the evil or perplexity with which we are to contend. Now, all the sources of our consolation lie in the effects or acts of the Holy Spirit mentioned before. There is no comfort apart from them, and there is no trouble from which we may not have comfort by them. The only thing required to give a man consolation in any condition, is the presence of a good to render the evil with which he is pressed inconsiderable to him. Suppose a man is under the greatest calamity that can possibly befall a child of God, or a junction of all those evils enumerated by Paul in Rom. 8:35. Let this man have the Holy Spirit performing the works mentioned before, and despite all his evils, his consolations will abound. If he has a sense of the love of God all the while shed abroad in his heart, a clear witness within that he is a child of God and accepted by him, that he is sealed and marked as God's own, that he is an heir of all the promises of God, and the like, then it is impossible for him not to triumph in all his tribulations.

From this source of all our consolation come those descriptions we have in the Scripture of its properties and associations, such as,

(1.) It is abiding. It is called "Everlasting consolation," 2Thess. 2:16, "God, even our Father, which has loved us, and given us everlasting consolation;" that is, comfort that does not vanish because it arises from everlasting things. There may be some perishing comfort given for a short season by perishing things, but abiding consolation from the Holy Spirit comes from everlasting things: everlasting love, eternal redemption, and an everlasting inheritance.

(2.) It is strong. Heb. 6:18, "That the heirs of the promise should receive strong consolation." Just as strong opposition sometimes comes against us, and our trouble has strong bands, our consolation is strong. It abounds and it is unconquerable, "*ischura paraklesis.*" It is will make its way through all opposition. It confirms, corroborates, and strengthens the heart against any evil. It fortifies the soul, and makes it able cheerfully to undergo anything that it is called to. And that is because it comes from the one who is strong.

(3.) It is precious. The apostle makes this a motive for obedience, which he exhorts the Philippians to do in chap. 2:1, "If there is any consolation in Christ; if you set any esteem and value upon this precious mercy of consolation in Christ by those comforts, let it be so with you."

This is the first general consequence in the hearts of believers of those great effects of the Holy Spirit mentioned before. This is so large and comprehensive, comprising so many of our concerns in walking with God, that the Holy Spirit receives his name from the whole work he performs for us. Hence, he is the Comforter; just as Jesus Christ, from the work of redemption and salvation, is called the Redeemer and Savior of his church. Now, as we have no consolation apart from the Holy Spirit, all his effects certainly have this consequence of comfort in us, more or less. I dare say that whatever we have that does not bring consolation, at least in its root if not in its ripened fruit, is not of the Holy Spirit. How comfort ensues from his works varies with particular cases. The fellowship we have with him consists, in no small part, in the consolation that we receive from him. This makes us value his love; it teaches us where to apply in our distress, whom to pray for and to, and whom to wait upon in our difficulties.

2. PEACE is also a consequence of his work. Rom. 15:13, "The God of hope fill you with all peace in believing, that you may abound in hope through the power of the Holy Spirit." The power of the Holy Spirit is not only extended to hope, but to our peace in believing. It is connected to the promises in John 14:26, 27, "I will give you the Comforter." And then what? What follows that grant? "Peace," he says. "I leave my peace with you; my peace I give to you." Christ leaves or gives his peace by bestowing the comforter on them. The peace of Christ consists in the soul's sense of its acceptance by God in friendship. Christ is said to be "our peace," Eph. 2:14, by slaying the enmity between God and us, and by taking away the handwriting that was against us. Rom. 5:1, "Being justified by faith, we have peace with God." A comforting persuasion of our acceptance by God in Christ is the basis of this peace. It wraps together our deliverance from eternal wrath, hatred, curse, and condemnation, all sweetly affecting the soul and conscience.

And this is a branch from the same root as consolation. It is a consequence of the effects of the Holy Spirit. Suppose there is a man chosen in the eternal love of the Father, redeemed by the blood of the Son, and justified freely by the grace of God. He has a right to all the promises of the gospel. Yet this person cannot by his own skill, or arguments of his own heart, or by considering the promises, or considering the love of God or the grace of Christ in them, be established in peace until it is produced in him as a fruit and consequence of the work of the Holy Spirit. "Peace" is a fruit of the Spirit, Gal. 5:22. The savor of the Spirit is "life and peace," Rom. 8:6. All we have comes from him and by him.

3. JOY is also numbered among the consequences. The Spirit is called "The oil of gladness," Heb. 1:9. His anointing brings gladness with it. Isa. 61:3, He is "the oil of joy for mourning." "The kingdom of God is righteousness, and peace, and joy in the Holy Spirit," Rom. 14:17. They "received the word with joy in the Holy Spirit," 1Thess. 1:6. As Peter tells believers, "you rejoice with joy unspeakable and full of glory," 1Pet. 1:8. Giving joy to believers is eminently the work of the comforter. And he does this by the effects listed earlier. "Rejoicing in hope of the glory of God," mentioned in Rom. 5:2, carries the soul through any tribulation with glorying. It has its source in the Spirit's "shedding abroad the love of God in our hearts," verse 5. There are two ways by which the Spirit works this joy in the hearts of believers:

(1.) He does it directly, without any other acts or works of his, and without interposing any motivations, deductions, or conclusions on our part. As in sanctification, he is a well of water springing up in the soul, immediately exerting his efficacy and refreshment. In consolation, he immediately brings us to a joyful and spiritual frame, filling us with exultation and gladness. This is not the result of our reflexive consideration of the love of God, but because the Spirit gives occasion for it. When he sheds abroad the love of God in our hearts, and directly fills us with gladness (as he caused John Baptist to leap for joy in the womb), then the soul raises itself to consider the love of God, from which joy and rejoicing also flows. There is no reason given for this joy, except that the Spirit works it when and how he will. He secretly infuses and distills it in our soul, prevailing against all our fears and sorrows, filling us with gladness, exultation, and sometimes unspeakable raptures of mind.

(2.) He does it by intermediate means. By his other works, he gives us a sense of the love of God, and of our adoption and acceptance by him. The consideration of these things enables us to receive this joy. Consider his operations, the assurance he gives us of the love of God, the life, power, and security we have, the pledge of our eternal welfare, and it will be easily perceived that he lays a sufficient foundation for our joy and gladness. We are unable by any rational consideration, deduction, or conclusion that we can make from the things mentioned, to affect our hearts with the joy and gladness intended. Yet, it is no less the proper work of the Spirit to do it by those things, or to do it directly without them. This process of producing joy in the heart can be seen in Ps. 23:5-6. "You anoint my head with oil." And from this flows the conclusion that exultation will result, "Surely goodness and mercy will follow me." This effect of the Comforter can be found throughout Isa. 35.

4. HOPE, also, is an effect of the work of the Holy Spirit in us and towards us, Rom. 15:13. "Now may the God of hope fill you with all joy and peace in believing, so that you may abound in hope by the power of the Holy Spirit. "

These, I say, are the general consequences of the effects of the Holy Spirit upon the hearts of believers. If we consider all their offspring in exultation, assurance, boldness, confidence, expectation, glorying, and the like, it will become apparent how far our whole communion with God is influenced by them.

CHAPTER 5.

OBSERVATIONS AND INFERENCES CONCERNING THE SPIRIT –

This process being done, I would like to have gone on to show how we hold communion with the Holy Spirit, but there are some misrepresentations in the world in reference to this dispensation of the Holy Spirit, and in contempt of his true work. I cannot help but remark on them in this chapter.

Take a view of those who profess to believe the gospel of Jesus Christ, and yet condemn and despise the operations, gifts, and graces his Spirit, and his dispensations to his churches and saints. While Christ was in the world with his disciples, he made no greater promise to them than of giving them the Holy Spirit, neither in respect to their own good nor in carrying on the work he committed to them. He instructs them to pray for the Spirit from the Father, being as necessary for them as bread for children, Luke 11:13. He promises them the Spirit as a well of water springing up in them for their refreshment, strengthening, and consolation to everlasting life, John 7:37-39. The Spirit is to carry on and accomplish the whole work of the ministry that Christ has committed to them, John 16:8-11. And upon his ascension, this gift of the Holy Spirit forms the foundation of that glorious and plentiful communication of gifts and graces mentioned in Eph. 4:8, 11-12. Christ received from the Father the promise of the Holy Spirit, Act 2:33, and that made the greatest and most glorious difference between the administration of the new covenant and old. The whole work of the ministry relates specifically to the Holy Spirit; though that is not my present business to prove. The Spirit calls men to that work; they are set apart for him, Acts 13:2. He furnishes them with gifts and abilities for it, 1Cor. 12:7-10. So without this administration of the Spirit, the whole religion that we profess is nothing, and there is no fruit of the resurrection of Christ from the dead.

This being the state of things, in our worship of and obedience to God, in our own consolation, sanctification, and ministerial employment, the Spirit is the principle, life, and soul of it all. Yet the malice of Satan is so desperate, and the wickedness of men so great, that their endeavor has been to shut the Spirit out of all gospel administrations.

First, his gifts and graces were not only decried, but almost excluded from the public worship of the church in the past. This was done by imposing a laborious form of service, to be read by the minister. This is neither a unique gift of the Holy Spirit to anyone, nor part of the ministry at all. It is marvelous to consider what arguments

233

and pretences were invented and used by learned men, to defend and maintain it. They argued from the antiquity of such a service, its composition and approval by the martyrs, the beauty of its uniformity in the worship of God, etc. But the main argument they insisted on, and used all their eloquence to condemn, was the vain babbling repetitions and folly of men praying by the Spirit. Once this was pounced on, everything else fell before them, and their adversaries were rendered ridiculous. Such is the cunning of Satan, and so unsearchable are the follies of men. The sum of it all might be stated this way: "Though the Lord Jesus Christ has promised that the Holy Spirit will be with his church to the end of the world, to fit and furnish men with gifts and abilities to carry on the worship which he requires and accepts at our hands, yet the work is not to be done for that purpose; the gifts he bestows are not sufficient for that end, either as to invocation or doctrine. And therefore, we will not only help men to avoid it by our human directions, but we will exclude them from exercising those gifts of the Spirit."

Innumerable evils ensue in formally setting apart men to the ministry who never "tasted of the powers of the world to come," or received any gifts from the Holy Spirit for that purpose. If ensues from an external pompous worship, wholly foreign to the power and simplicity of the gospel; from silencing, destroying, and banishing men whose ministry was accompanied with the evidence and demonstration of the Spirit. What I aim to do is point out the public contempt of the Holy Spirit, of his gifts and graces, by such an administration of the church of God, which has been found even where the gospel has been professed.

Again, it is a sad thing to consider, and to recall, the growth of that contempt of the Spirit in private men and their ways. The name of the Spirit had become a term of reproach. To plead for, or pretend to pray by the Spirit, was enough to render a man the object of scorn and reproach from all sorts of men, from the pulpit to the stage. "What! You are full of the Spirit? Then you will pray by the Spirit. If you have the gift, let us hear your nonsense." Perhaps these detractors would think themselves wronged not to be considered Christians. Christians! Some have pretended to be leaders of the flock, mounted themselves a story or two above their brothers, claimed to have a rule and government over them, and made it their business to scoff at and reproach the gifts of the Spirit of God. If this is the frame of their spirit, what can be expected of non-believers? It is unimaginable what height of blasphemy a process of this kind rose to. May the Lord grant there is nothing of this cursed leaven still remaining among us! Is this the fellowship of the Holy Spirit that believers are called to? Is this the appropriate entertainment of the one whom our Savior promised to send to supply us in his bodily absence, so that we might not lose anything by it? One infinitely holy and blessed person of the Trinity has taken upon himself to be our comforter. It would be bad enough that men with such a stupid blindness, being called Christians, can look no further for their comfort and consolation than to be led by moral considerations that are common to heathens. But they are not content with this. They feel compelled to oppose and despise him as well! Nothing more reveals how few there are in the world that have a true interest in that blessed name by which we are all called. But this is no place to pursue this. The aim here is to prove the folly and madness of men in general, who profess to own the gospel of Christ, and yet condemn and despise his Spirit in whomever he is manifested. Let us be zealous for the gifts of the Spirit, not envious of them.

From what has been said, we may also try the spirits that have gone abroad in the world, and which have been exercising themselves ever since the ascension of Christ. The iniquity of the generation that is past and passing away was in open, cursed opposition to the Holy Spirit. God has been above those who behaved presumptuously. Satan, whose plan is to be exalted as god of this world, and not to be cast down by the providence of God, has now transformed himself into an angel of light. He can only pretend to be the Spirit. There are "seducing spirits," 1Tim. 4:1. We have a "command not to believe every spirit, but try the spirits," 1John 4:1. The reason given is, "Because many false prophets have gone out into the world," that is, men pretending to have the revelation of new doctrines by the Spirit. Paul intimates that men with such deceits were present even in the first church. He called on men not to be "shaken in mind by spirit." 2Thess. 2:2. The truth is, the spirits of these days are so gross, that anyone with the least discernment may find them out. And yet their delusion is so strong, that not a few are still deceived. One thing is evident to every eye: in pursuit of his plan, and compared to his former ways of acting, Satan has gone to extremes with his delusions.

Not long ago, his great design was to cry for ordinances without the Spirit, casting all the reproach that he could upon the Spirit. Now his design is to cry for a spirit without ordinances, casting as much reproach and contempt as possible upon them. Before, he wanted a ministry without the Spirit; now, he wants a Spirit without a ministry. Before, reading the word might suffice, without either preaching or praying by the Spirit; now, the Spirit is enough without reading or studying the word at all. Before, he allowed a literal embracing of what Christ had done in the flesh; now, he talks about Christ in the Spirit only, and denies that he came in the flesh. This is the character of the false spirit that we are warned of in 1John 4:1. The Spirit we are to hear and embrace is the Spirit promised by Christ, not the Montanists' *paraclete*, or the one Mohammed pretended to be, or the ones feigned by those in our day. So let us briefly try these spirits by some of the effects for which Christ promised to give us the Holy Spirit:

The first general effect, as observed, was to bring to remembrance the things that Christ spoke for our guidance and consolation. This was to the work of the Holy Spirit towards the apostles, who were the penmen of the Scriptures, and this is his work towards believers to the end of the world. The things that Christ has spoken and done are "written that we might believe, and believing, have life through his name," John 20:31. They are written in the Scripture. This, then, is the work of the Spirit which Christ has promised. He will bring to our remembrance and give us understanding of the words of Christ that are written in the Scripture, and he will do so for our guidance and consolation. But the work of the spirit which is abroad in the world, and perverts many, is to decry the things that Christ has spoken and which are written in the word. His business is to pretend new revelations of his own, to lead men away from the written word in which the whole work of God and all the promises of Christ are recorded.

Again, the work of the Spirit promised by Christ is to glorify him: "He will glorify me; for he will receive of mine, and will show it to you," John 16:14. It is to make the one who suffered at Jerusalem, and who then spoke to his disciples, glorious, honorable, and highly esteemed in the hearts of believers. He was to do that by showing the things of Christ to them (his love, kindness, grace, and purchase). This is the work of the Spirit. The work of the spirit that is gone abroad is to glorify itself, to decry Christ and render him contemptible, under the name of a Christ outside us, which it slights and despises. All it aims at is its own glory, its own honor, wholly inverting the order of the divine dispensations. Because the fountain of all being lies in the Father's love, the Son came to glorify the Father. He says, "I seek not my own glory, but the glory of him that sent me." The Son, having carried on the work of redemption, was now to be glorified with the Father. He prays that it might be so, John 17:1, "The hour is come, glorify your Son." And the glory he asks for is the glory he had before the world began, when his joint counsel was in carrying on the Father's love. That is why the Holy Spirit is sent. His work is to glorify the Son. But now, as I said, we have a spirit in the world whose whole business is to glorify himself. That is how we may easily know where he comes from.

Furthermore, the Holy Spirit sheds abroad the love of God in our hearts, as was declared. He fills us with joy, peace, and hope. He quiets and refreshes the hearts of those in whom he dwells. He gives them liberty, rest, confidence, and the boldness of children. The spirit of which men now boast is a spirit of bondage, whose work is to make men quake and tremble. He casts them into an un-son-like frame of spirit, driving them with horror and bondage, draining their natural spirits, and making them wither away. There is hardly anything that more evidently reveals this spirit is not the Comforter promised by Christ than this: he is a spirit of bondage and slavery, a spirit of cruelty and reproach towards others. He acts in direct opposition to the Holy Spirit in believers, and all the ends and purposes for which he is bestowed on them as a spirit of adoption and consolation.

To give one instance more, the Holy Spirit bestowed on believers is a Spirit of prayer and supplication. The spirit we are dealing with pretends to take men beyond such low and contemptible means of communion with God.

In a word, it is a very easy and facile task, to take all of the eminent effects of the Holy Spirit in and towards believers, and to show that the pretending spirit of our days comes in direct opposition to every one of them. Thus, Satan has passed from one extreme to another, from bitter and wretched opposition to the Spirit of Christ, to pretending to be the Spirit; but it is still for the same purpose.

I might give a number of other instances of the contempt or abuse of the dispensation of the Spirit. Those mentioned are the extremes to which all others may be reduced. I will not digress any further from what lies directly in my aim.

CHAPTER 6.

PARTICULAR COMMUNION WITH THE HOLY SPIRIT –

The way being plain for us, I will now show how we hold particular communion with the Holy Spirit as our comforter, who works out our consolation by the means mentioned. The first thing I will do is prepare for this by leading believers to a proper valuation of his work towards us, for which he is called our Comforter.

To elevate our hearts and fit us for this duty, let us consider three things:

FIRST, what he comforts us against.

SECONDLY, what he comforts us with.

THIRDLY, the principle underlying all of his consoling acts and operations in us.

FIRST. There are only three things in the whole course of our pilgrimage in which the consolations of the Holy Spirit are useful and necessary:

1. *In our afflictions*. Affliction is part of the provision that God has made for his children, Heb. 12:5, 6. The great variety of its causes, means, uses, and effects, is generally known. There is a measure of affliction appointed for everyone. It is a temptation to be wholly without them, and so in some measure their absence would be an affliction. What I am saying is that we need the consolations of the Holy Spirit in all our afflictions. It is the nature of man to try to find his own relief from his entanglements, by any and all means. Man's natural inclination is to manage himself under pressure. "The spirit of a man will bear his infirmity" Prov. 18:14; at least, he will struggle with it. There are two great evils, either of which generally takes hold of a man under affliction, and keeps him from properly managing them. The apostle mentions them both in Heb. 12:5, "Do not despise the chastisement of the Lord; neither faint when you are reproved." Men usually fall into one of these extremes; either they despise the Lord's correction, or they sink under it.

(1.) Men despise it. They consider what befalls them to be a light or common thing. They take no notice of God in it. They can deal with it well enough, looking at its instrumentalities and its incidental causes. They provide for their own defense and vindication with little regard to God or his hand in it. And the ground of this despising is because they accept assistance in their trouble that God will not mix his grace with. They focus on remedies other than what God has appointed. And then they completely lose all the benefits

238

and advantage of their affliction. So will every man who seeks his relief in anything but the consolations of the Holy Spirit.

(2.) Men faint and sink under their trials and afflictions, which the apostle further reproves, Heb. 12:12. The first ones despise the assistance of the Holy Spirit through pride of heart; the latter ones refuse it because they are dejected in spirit, and sink under the weight of their troubles. Who does not offend God by doing one or the other at some point? Had we not learned to take lightly the chastisements of the Lord, and to take little notice of his dealings with us, we would find that our times of affliction comprise no small portion of our pilgrimage.

The only way to properly manage ourselves under affliction, so that God may have the glory and we may derive the spiritual benefit of it, is by the consolations of the Holy Spirit. The only promise that our Savior makes to his disciples when he tells them of the great trials and tribulations to come is this, "I will send you the Spirit, the Comforter; he will give you peace in me, when in the world you will have trouble. He will guide and direct, and keep you in all your trials." And the apostle tells us it came to pass, 2Cor. 1:4-6. Under the greatest afflictions, the Spirit will carry the soul to the highest joy, peace, rest, and contentment. "We glory in tribulations," Rom. 5:3. This is a great expression. He said before, "We rejoice in hope of the glory of God," Rom. 5:2. But what if various afflictions and tribulations befall us? "Why, even in those we will glory," he says. But why would our spirits be so borne up under afflictions, as to glory in them in the Lord? He tells us in verse 5, that it is from the "shedding abroad of the love of God in our hearts by the Holy Spirit." This is why believers are said to "receive the word in much affliction, with joy of the Holy Spirit," 1 Thess. 1:6, and to "take joyfully the spoiling of their goods." This is my point: there is no management or improvement of any affliction, except by the consolations of the Holy Spirit. What is it worth to you to derive the benefit of all your trials, temptations, and afflictions? Learn to value the only thing that renders them useful.

2. Consolation is uniquely suited for *dealing with sin*, the second burden of our lives, and the greatest. In Heb. 6:17-18, an allusion is made to the manslayer under the law. Having killed a man unawares, and having brought the guilt of his blood upon himself, he quickly flees to the city of refuge for his deliverance. Our great and only refuge from the guilt of sin is the Lord Jesus Christ. In fleeing to him, the Spirit consoles us. A sense of sin fills the heart with trouble and disquiet, but the Holy Spirit gives us peace in Christ. A sense of sin gives an anticipation of wrath, but the Holy Spirit sheds abroad the love of God in our hearts. It is sin that Satan and the law use to accuse us of being objects of God's hatred. It is the Spirit who bears witness with our

spirits that we are the children of God. There is no single weapon or instrument that sin can use against our peace, that one effect or another of the Holy Spirit cannot defeat.

3. The consolations of the Spirit are also necessary during the whole course of *our obedience*, so that we may go through with it cheerfully, willingly, and patiently to the end. This will be more fully examined as I give directions for our communion with this blessed Comforter.

To summarize, in all our concerns of this life, and in our expectation of another, we stand in need of the consolations of the Holy Spirit.

• Without them, we will either despise afflictions or faint under them, and God will be ignored in his intent for them.

• Without them, sin will either harden us so as to disdain it, or it will drive us to neglect the remedies graciously provided against it.

• Without them, our duties will either puff us up with pride, or deny us the sweetness that comes with new obedience.

• Without them, prosperity will make us carnal, sensual, and content with these things. It will utterly weaken us for the trials of adversity.

• Without them, the comforts of our relationships will separate us from God, and the loss of them will make our hearts as wicked as Nabal's.

• Without them, the trials of the church will overwhelm us, and the prosperity of the church will not concern us.

• Without them, we will have wisdom for no work, peace in no condition, strength for no duty, success in no trial, joy in no state, life with no comfort, and death with no light.

Our afflictions, our sins, and our obedience, with their respective circumstances, are the focus of our lives. What we are in relation to God is found in them, and the due management of them. Through all of these there runs a line of consolation from the Holy Spirit, that gives us a joyful response throughout. It is a sad condition for those who have no such consolations. What poor alternatives they are forced to resort to! What giants they have to encounter in their own strength! Whether they are conquered, or seem to conquer, they have nothing but the misery of their trials!

The **SECOND** thing to consider, is putting a proper valuation on the consolations of the Holy Spirit. This may be divided into the love of the Father, and the grace of the Son. All of the consolations of the Holy Spirit consist in his acquainting us with, and communicating to us, the love of the Father and the grace of the Son. There is nothing in one or the other that he does not make a matter of consolation to us. Indeed, we have our communion with the Father in his love, and with the Son in his grace, by the operation of the Holy Spirit.

1. The Spirit communicates to us, and acquaints us with, the love of the Father. Having informed his disciples that they would receive the foundation of their consolation by the Comforter, our blessed Savior encloses everything in this, "The father himself loves you," (John 16:27). This is what the Comforter is given to acquaint us with: that God is the Father, and that he loves us. In particular, the Father, as the first person in the Trinity, loves us. For this reason, the Spirit is often said to come from the Father because he comes in pursuit of the Father's love. He comes to acquaint the hearts of believers with it, so that they may be comforted and established. By persuading us of the eternal and unchangeable love of the Father, he fills us with consolation. Indeed, all the effects of the Holy Spirit mentioned before tend to do this. You heard earlier of this love and its transcendent excellence. The Holy Spirit communicates to us everything that is desirable in it. A sense of this love not only relieves us, but it makes us rejoice with joy unspeakable and glorious in every condition.

He does not comfort our souls with more corn, wine, and oil, but by shining the countenance of God upon us, Ps. 4:6-7. A soul that has the Spirit might say; "The world hates me, but my Father loves me. Men despise me as a hypocrite; but my Father loves me as a child. I am poor in this world; but I have a rich inheritance in the love of my Father. I am limited in all things; but there is bread enough in my Father's house. I mourn in secret under the power of my lusts and sin, where no eyes see me; but the Father sees me, and is full of compassion. With a sense of his kindness, which is better than life, I rejoice in tribulation, glory in affliction, and triumph as a conqueror. Though I am killed all day long, all my sorrows have a bottom that may be fathomed, my trials have bounds that may be compassed; but the breadth, and depth, and height of the love of the Father cannot be expressed." If I compared all other causes and means of joy and consolation to how the Spirit comforts us with the love of the Father, I would discover their emptiness, and its fullness, their nothingness, and its being all in all. I would render the consolation of the Spirit glorious by such a comparison.

2. Again: the Spirit does this by communicating to us, and acquainting us with, the grace of Christ, all the fruits of his purchase, and all the desirability of his person, because we are in him. The grace of Christ refers to the grace of his person, and the work of his office. The Holy Spirit administers consolation to us by both of these things, John 16:14. He glorifies Christ by revealing his excellence and desirability to believers, as the "chief of ten thousand, altogether lovely," Cant. 5:10, 16. Then he shows them the things of Christ: his

241

love, grace, and all the fruits of his death, suffering, resurrection, and intercession. He supports their hearts and souls with these. As a result, he gives them whatever refreshes them in the pardon of their sin, delivers them from the curse and wrath to come, and conveys the hope of glory in their justification and adoption, along with the innumerable privileges that accompany these things.

The **THIRD** thing to consider is the principle underlying all of his consoling acts and operations. This leads us a little nearer to the communion I intended to direct us in. The principle which governs them is his own great love and infinite condescension. He willingly proceeds or comes from the Father to be our comforter. He knew what we were, and what we could do, and how we would deal with him. He knew we would grieve him, provoke him, quench his impulses, and defile his dwelling-place. And yet he would come to be our comforter. Failure to duly consider this great love of the Holy Spirit will weaken all the principles of our own obedience. If this truth abided in our hearts, what a precious value we would need to put upon all his operations and actions towards us! Indeed, nothing is valuable that does not come from love and good-will. This is the way the Scripture motivates us to a right and due estimation of our redemption by Jesus Christ. It tells us that he did it freely. He laid down his life of his own will. And he did it out of love. "In this was manifested the love of God, that he laid down his life for us," 1Jn. 3:16. "He loved us, and gave himself for us," Gal. 2:20. "He loved us, and washed us from our sins in his own blood," Rev. 1:5. Here the Scripture reveals our state and condition. We must consider that he undertook to do this while we were still sinners, enemies, dead, and alienated. Then he loved us, and died for us, and washed us with his blood. May we not also value the dispensation of the Spirit for our consolation from this? He proceeds from the Father for that same purpose. He distributes as he will, and works as he pleases. And how do we respond to him? We are froward, perverse, and unthankful. We grieve, vex, and provoke him. Yet in his love and tenderness he continues to do us good. Let us by faith consider this love of the Holy Spirit. It is the source of all the communion we have with him in this life. This is, as I said, spoken only to prepare our hearts for this communion; and it is such a little portion of what might be said! It suffices to say that the work in hand is among the greatest duties, and most excellent privileges, of the gospel.

CHAPTER 7.

GENERAL WAYS THE SAINTS ACT IN COMMUNION
WITH THE HOLY SPIRIT –

As I did in showing how the Holy Spirit acts in us, I will now describe how we respond to him in our acts of faith generally, and then in particular. There are three general ways the soul deports itself in this communion, all expressed negatively in the Scripture, but all including positive duties. We are not to grieve him, not to quench his impulses, and not to resist him. Then there are three things to consider about the Holy Spirit: his dwelling in us, his acting in us by grace or impetus, and his working in us through the ordinances of the word and the sacraments. All of these are for the same purpose.

Linking the cautions to the considerations, we are: 1. Not to grieve him, in respect to his person dwelling in us. 2. Not to quench him, in respect to the acting and impetus of his grace. 3. Not to resist him, in respect to the ordinances of Christ, and his gifts for their administration.

Now, because the whole general duty of believers in their communion with the Holy Spirit is comprised in these three things, I will handle them separately:

1. THE FIRST CAUTION directly concerns his person dwelling in us. It is given in Eph. 4:30, "Do not grieve the Holy Spirit of God by whom you are sealed until the day of redemption." There is also a complaint given of those who grieved the Spirit in Isa. 63:10. This is where this caution seems to be taken from. It is evident from the following indications, that these passages refer to the *person* of the Holy Spirit:

(1.) Its phrasing or expression uses a double article, "*To Pneuma to Hagion*," which indicates it is "that Holy Spirit" rather than "a holy spirit," and also,

(2.) The work assigned to him is, "sealing to the day of redemption," which is the work of the Holy Spirit. While the Spirit may work in non-believers, it is evident that the apostle means believers. He adds that unique privilege which only believers enjoy by the Spirit: he is the one who seals us to the day of redemption.

This caution, "Grieve not the Holy Spirit," is the first general rule of our communion with the Holy Spirit. The term "grieving," or affecting with sorrow, may be considered either actively, in respect to the persons grieving, or passively, in respect to the persons grieved. In the latter sense the expression is metaphorical. The Spirit cannot be passively grieved or affected with sorrow. That would imply alteration, disappointment, or weakness, which are all incompatible with his infinite perfection. Yet men may actively do what is *capable* of grieving someone who has affection for them, as the Holy Spirit does. If he is not grieved, it is no thanks to us, but to his own unchangeable nature. So there are two things denoted in this expression:

First, that the Holy Spirit has affection for us. He is loving, careful, tender, and concerned for our good and well-doing. Therefore our miscarriages are said to grieve him, just as a good, kind, and loving friend is apt to be grieved by the miscarriage of the one he cares for. This love, kindness, and tenderness of the Holy Spirit towards us is our primary regard in this caution; it is its foundation. "Grieve him not."

Secondly, that we do things that grieve him, even though he is not passively grieved. Our sin is no less in doing them, than if he were grieved in the same way we are. Now, how this is done, how the Spirit is grieved, is declared in the context of Eph. 4:21-24. The Apostle presses the progress in sanctification, and all the fruits of regeneration in verses 25-29. He lists a number of evils that are contrary to sanctification and regeneration. He gives the positive duty required of them. And then he follows with, "And do not grieve the Holy Spirit of God." That is, do not grieve him by coming short of the universal sanctification that our planting into Christ requires.

The positive duty included in this caution not to grieve the Holy Spirit, is that we pursue universal holiness with regard to, and because of, the love, kindness, and tenderness of the Holy Spirit. This is the general foundation of our communion with him. We consider the love, kindness, and tenderness of the Holy Spirit towards us. We consider all the fruits and acts of his love and good-will towards us. And then, because of these considerations, and because the Spirit is so concerned with our ways and our walk, we choose to abstain from evils, and to walk in all our duties of holiness. This is what it means to have communion with him. This consideration that the Holy Spirit, who is our comforter, is delighted with our obedience, and grieved by our evils and follies, becomes a continual motive and reason to walk closely with God in all holiness. It is the first general way that we commune with him.

Let us focus on this a little. We lose both the power and the pleasure of our obedience for lack of this consideration. We see the reason the Holy Spirit undertakes to be our comforter, and the ways and means by which he performs his office towards us. What an unworthy thing it is to grieve the one who comes to us on purpose to console us! Let the soul, in the whole course of its obedience, exercise itself by faith to think of this, and give it its due weight. Let it say, "The Holy Spirit, in his infinite love and kindness towards me, has condescended to be my comforter. He does it willingly, freely, and powerfully. Look at what I have received from him! In all my troubles, he has refreshed my soul! Can I live one day without his consolation? Will I disregard him in what he is concerned with? Will I grieve him by my negligence, sin, and folly? Let his love constrain me to walk before him, well-pleasing in all I do." This is what we have in general fellowship with him.

2. THE SECOND CAUTION is found in 1Thess. 5:19, "Quench not the Spirit." There are various thoughts about the meaning of these words. Some say it means the Spirit in others, or their spiritual gifts," which falls in with what follows in verse 20, "Despise not prophesying." Others say it means the light that God has put in our hearts." But where is that specifically called "To Pneuma," "The Spirit?" It is the Holy Spirit himself that is meant here. It is not referring to his person directly, but his impetus, acting, and operations. The Holy Spirit was typified by the fire that was always kept alive on the altar. He is also called a "Spirit of burning," Isa. 4:4; Matt. 3:11; Lk. 3:16. The reasons for that allusion are various, but I will not examine them now. Opposition to the activity of a fire is called quenching, like casting wet wood into a fire. Hence, opposition to the acts of the Holy Spirit is called "quenching of the Spirit." Thus, using the same metaphor, we are told to "*anadzoturein*" [NT:329], to "stir up with new fire," or "rekindle" the gifts that are in us, 2Tim. 1:6. The Holy Spirit is striving with us, acting in us, moving variously for our growth in grace, and bringing forth fruit that is fitting for the principle he has endued us with. "Take heed," the apostle is saying, "lest, by the power of your lusts and temptations, you do not attend to his workings, but hinder him in his good-will towards you; that is, hinder what lies in you."

This, then, is the second general rule for our communion with the Holy Spirit. It respects his gracious operations in us and by us. There are several ways by which the Holy Spirit is said to exercise his power in us. It is partly by stimulating the grace we have received, partly by giving us new supplies of grace from Jesus Christ, providing occasions for their exercise, and motivating us directly or indirectly by circumstance. All of these tend to further our obedience and our walk with God. All of these are to be carefully observed and noticed, considering the fountain from which they come, and the end to which they lead us. Hence, we have communion with the Holy Spirit when we can consider him by faith as the immediate author of all our supplies and assistance, all the relief we have by grace, all the good acts, motivations, and impulses of our hearts, and all the striving and contending we make against sin. When we consider all his works in their tendency to console us, and we are careful to cooperate in them for the end aimed at, and we treat them as coming from the one who is so loving, kind, and tender to us, then we have communion with him.

What is intended is that every gracious act of the blessed Spirit in and towards us, is to constantly be considered by faith as coming from him in a unique way. His mind and his good will are to be observed in that consideration. From this will arise care and diligence in improving every motion of his. Then reverence for his presence will ensue, with due spiritual regard to his holiness; and our souls will want to commune with him.

3. THE THIRD CAUTION concerns his work in the dispensation of the ordinance of the word. Stephen tells the Jews that they "resisted the Holy Spirit," Acts 7:51. How did they do it? Just as their fathers did it: "As your fathers did, so do you." And how did their fathers resist the Holy Spirit? "They persecuted the prophets, and slew them," verse 52. That is, they opposed the prophets in preaching the gospel, or in showing the coming of the Just One. The Holy Spirit is said to be resisted by contempt for preaching the word, because the gift of preaching comes from him. "The manifestation of the Spirit is given to profit." 1Cor. 12:7. Hence, when our Savior promises his disciples that the Spirit will be present with them to convict the world, he tells them he will give them a mouth and wisdom that their adversaries cannot resist, Luke 21:15. When this was accomplished in Stephen, it is said that they "were not able to resist the Spirit by which he spoke," Acts 6:10. The Holy Spirit sets up a ministry in the church, draws men apart to it, and furnishes them with gifts and abilities to dispense the word. Not obeying that word, opposing it, and not falling down before it, is called resisting the Holy Spirit. We are cautioned against this resistance through the examples given of the wickedness of others.

This encloses the third general rule of our communion with the Holy Spirit: in dispensing the word of the gospel, we are to see the authority, wisdom, and goodness of the Holy Spirit in furnishing men with gifts for that purpose, and the virtue of his presence with them. Obedience is yielded to the word in its ministerial dispensation because the Holy Spirit, and he alone, furnishes gifts for that purpose. When this consideration causes us to bow before the word, we have communion with the Holy Spirit in the ordinance of the word.

CHAPTER 8.

PARTICULAR DIRECTIONS FOR COMMUNION WITH THE HOLY SPIRIT.

Before I name particular directions for our communion with the Holy Spirit, I must give some cautions concerning his worship.

First. The divine nature is the reason and cause for all worship. It is impossible to worship any one person in the godhead, and not worship the whole Trinity. The schoolmen denied, on good grounds, that the object of divine worship is found separately in the persons of the godhead. That is, they denied that their relationship means each is a distinct object of our worship. This relationship belongs to the indivisible divine nature and essence of God. Therefore, praying to the Trinity, by repeating the same petition to each of the several persons (as in the Litany), is groundless, if not impious. It supposes that we can worship one person and not another, when in fact each person is worshipped as God, and each person is God. It is as though we could desire something of the Father, have it heard and granted by him, and then we turn to the Son to ask the same thing, and once more we ask it of the Holy Spirit. We would be doing this as three distinct acts of worship, expecting to be separately heard by each, and separately granted by each. That is misguided. All the works of the Trinity are indivisible.

The proper and specific object of divine worship and invocation is the *essence* of God, in its infinite excellence, dignity, and majesty, and as the first sovereign cause of all things. Now, this is common to all three persons, and it is proper to each of them. It is not given to God formally as a person, but as God blessed forever. All adoration regards what is common to all, so that, in each act of adoration and worship, *all* are adored and worshipped. The creatures worship their Creator, and a man, the one in whose image they were created, the one "from whom descends every good and perfect gift" Jas. 1:17, all describing God as God.

Secondly. When we begin our prayers to God the Father, and end them in the name of Jesus Christ, the Son is no less invoked and worshipped in the beginning than the Father. He is specifically mentioned in the close of the prayer, not as the Son himself, but as Mediator to the whole Trinity, or to God in Trinity. In the invocation of God the Father, we invoke every person of the godhead. And *because* we invoke the Father as God, every person is invoked.

Thirdly. This whole business is declared in the heavenly

247

directory we have in Eph. 2:18. Our access in our worship is said to be "to the Father," and this is "through Christ," or his mediation, "by the Spirit," or with his assistance. Here is the distinction of the three persons as to their operations, but not at all as to their being the object of our worship. For the Son and the Holy Spirit are no less worshipped in our access to God than the Father himself. What we draw close to God for is the grace of the Father, which we obtain by the mediation of the Son, and the assistance of the Spirit. So when we are led by the distinct dispensation of the Trinity, and every person in that Trinity, to worship any person (that is, to exercise our faith on him, or invoke him), we worship the whole Trinity; and we invoke every person by whatever name we use, whether Father, Son, or Holy Spirit. So this is what is to be observed in this matter: when any work of the Holy Spirit or any other person, which is appropriate to him, draws us to worship him, he is not worshipped exclusively; the whole Godhead is worshipped. We never exclude the concurrence of the other persons.

Fourthly. This being said, we are to distinctly worship the Holy Spirit. As in the case of faith in the Father and the Son, "Believe in God, believe also in me," John 14:1, this extends no less to the Holy Spirit. Christ called the disciples to have faith in him as he was accomplishing the great work of his mediation. The Holy Spirit, now carrying on the work delegated to him, requires the same. And their distinct operations are to the same purpose: "My Father works until this time, and I work," Jn. 5:17. The formal reason for worshipping the Son is not his mediation, but his being God, yet his mediation is a powerful motive. So too, the formal reason for worshipping the Holy Spirit is not his being our comforter, but his being God; yet his being our comforter is a powerful motive.

This is the sum of the first direction: the grace, activity, love, and effects of the Holy Spirit as our comforter, ought to motivate and provoke us to love, worship, believe in, and invoke him. All of this, being directed to him as God, is no less directed to the other persons. And we are moved to these things only by the fruits of his love towards us.

Presuming all of these things, let the saints learn to act out their faith distinctly on the Holy Spirit, as the immediate and efficient cause of all the good things mentioned. This means faith to believe in him; and faith to believe him in all things, and to yield obedience to him. I am speaking of faith, not imagination. The distinction of the persons in the Trinity is not to be fancied, but believed. The Scripture fully, frequently, clearly, and distinctly ascribes the things we have been speaking of to the immediate efficiency of the Holy Spirit. And so faith embraces him in the truth revealed there. It uniquely regards him, worships him, serves him, waits for him, prays to him, and praises him.

The saints do all these things in faith. The person of the Holy Spirit, revealing itself in these operations and effects, is the unique object of our worship. Therefore, when he ought to be uniquely honored, and he is not, then he is uniquely sinned against. In Acts 5:3, Ananias is said to lie to the Holy Spirit, not to God. In its essence this would denote the whole Trinity, but it specifically refers to the Holy Spirit. Ananias was to have honored Him specifically in that special gift of his which he promised; in not giving it, he sinned uniquely against the Holy Spirit. But this must be a little further divided into its particulars:

Let us emphasize every effect of the Holy Spirit as an act of his love and power towards us. Faith that notices his kindness in all things will do this. Frequently he performs the office of a comforter towards us. If we are not thoroughly comforted, we take no notice at all of what he does. Then is he grieved. Of those who actually receive and accept the consolation he tenders and administers, there are few who recognize him as the comforter, and rejoice in him as they ought to! For each work of consolation that the believer receives, his faith ought to resolve that, "This is from the Holy Spirit. He is the Comforter, the God of all consolation. I know there is no joy, peace, hope, or comfort except what he works, gives, and bestows. And so that he might give me this consolation, he has willingly condescended to this office of a comforter. His love was in it. And because of his love, he continues it. He is sent by the Father and Son for that end and purpose. By this means I partake of my joy, which is in the Holy Spirit. He is the Comforter. What price, now, will I set upon his love? How will I value the mercy that I have received?"

This applies to every effect of the Holy Spirit towards us, and in this we have communion and fellowship with him. Does he shed abroad the love of God in our hearts? Does he witness to our adoption? The soul considers his presence, ponders his love, condescension, goodness, and kindness, and it is filled with reverence for him. It takes care not to grieve him, and it labors to preserve his temple, his habitation, as pure and holy.

Again: our communion with him causes us to return praise, thanks, honor, glory, and blessing to him. This is because of the mercies and privileges we receive from him, which are many. We do the same with the Son of God because of our redemption: "To him that loved us, and washed us from our sins in his own blood, to him be glory and dominion forever and ever," Rev. 1:5-6. Are not the same praises and blessings due to the one who makes the work of redemption effective in us? The Spirit undertook our consolation with no less infinite love than the Son had when he undertook our redemption. When we feel our hearts warmed with joy, supported in peace, established in our obedience, then let us ascribe to the Spirit the praise that is due him, bless his name, and rejoice in him. This begins our next direction.

Glorifying the Holy Spirit in thanksgiving, in response to a spiritual sense of his consolations, is no small part of our communion with him. Consider his free engagement in this work, his coming from the Father for this purpose, his mission by the Son, his condescension in accepting it, and his love and kindness to us. The soul of a believer is poured out in thankful praises to him for these things, and it is sweetly affected with the duty to glorify him. There is no duty that leaves a more heavenly savor in the soul than this does.

Also, our communion with him lies in our prayers to him to carry on the work of our consolation that he has undertaken. John prays for grace and peace from the seven Spirits that are before the throne (Rev. 1:4, the Holy Spirit) whose operations are perfect and complete. This prayerful part of his worship is expressly and frequently mentioned in Scripture, and all other parts of worship necessarily attend it. The saints will be prepared for this duty if they consider which effects of the Holy Spirit they need, weigh all the privileges they enjoy, remember that he distributes them as he will, and that he sovereignly disposes of them.

How and in what sense this worship is to be performed has already been discussed. I have also shown the formal reason for this worship, and its intimate object. No small part of the life, efficacy, and vigor of faith is put into this duty. If we do not learn to worship him in every way that he is pleased to communicate himself to us, then we will come short of what we have been called to: confidence of spirit in dealing with God, and walking in the breadth of his ways. In these things, God deals with us, and walks with us, in the person of the Holy Spirit. And we meet him in that person, in his love, grace, and authority, by our prayers and supplications.

Again: consider the Spirit condescending to undertake this delegation or dispensation of the Father and Son to be our comforter. Ask the Spirit daily for the blessings of the Father in the name of Jesus Christ. This is the daily work of believers. They look at the Holy Spirit as the one who was promised to be sent, and by faith they consider him so. They know that in this promise is found all their grace, peace, mercy, joy, and hope. For these things are communicated to them by this promised Spirit, and by him alone. Therefore, if the joy of our living to God is considered, we will abound in asking the Spirit of the Father, just as children ask for daily bread from their parents. In asking for and receiving the Holy Spirit, and for which he is sent, we have communion with the Father in his love. In his grace, by which the Spirit is obtained for us, we have communion with the Son. And because of his voluntary condescension to this dispensation, we have communion with the Spirit. Every request for the Holy Spirit implies our embracing these things. O the riches of the grace of God!

Humbling ourselves for our sin in reference to him is another part of our communion with the Spirit. We mourn that we have grieved him in his person, quenched him in the impulses of his grace, or resisted him in his ordinances. Let our souls be humbled before him on this account. This is a main ingredient of godly sorrow. Thinking of it is as suited to affect our hearts with humiliation and indignation against sin as any other means.

I will close this whole discourse with some considerations of the sad estate and condition of men who are not interested in this promise of the Spirit, and do not have his consolation:

1. They have no true consolation or comfort without him. If they have affliction or trouble, they must bear their own burden. But they are much too weak for it, especially if God lays on his hand with more weight than ordinary. Men may have stout spirits, and great resolve to wrestle with their troubles, but because this proceeds from their natural spirit,

(1.) For the most part it is only an external solution. It is done with respect to others, so that they may not appear to be low-spirited or dejected. Their hearts are devoured with troubles and anxieties. Their thoughts are perplexed. They still strive, but never conquer. Every new trouble, every little alteration in their trials, puts them in greater distress. The resolve that bears them up has no foundation, and so they are easily shaken.

(2.) What is the best we can say of their resolve and endurance? It is contending with God, the one who has entangled them. It is a flea struggling under a mountain. Though on outward considerations and principles, they endeavor to have patience and tolerance, it is only contending with God, striving to be quiet under what God has sent on purpose to disturb them. God does not afflict men without the Spirit to exercise their patience, but to disturb their peace and security. Arming themselves with patience and resolve only maintains the hold that God wants to release them from, or else it makes them nearer to ruin. This is the best consolation they have in the time of their trouble.

(3.) They may promise themselves to have God's care, and gain relief from that. This is what they often do for one reason or another, especially when they are driven from other holds. But their relief is like a hungry man who dreams that he eats and drinks, and is refreshed; but when he awakes, he is empty and disappointed. It is the same with the relief they promise to receive from God, and the support they think to have from him. When they are awakened at the last day, and see all things clearly, they will find that God was their enemy, laughing at their calamity, and mocking them when they were afraid.

This is what it is like when they are in trouble. Is it any better in prosperity? Their prosperity in life is often great, and marvelously described in Scripture. They often have a quiet, peaceable end. But did they have any true consolation all their days? They eat, drink, sleep, and make merry, and perhaps heap up wealth. But these things make them little different from the beasts that perish! Solomon's material wealth is well known. He had the most of these things, far beyond what anyone in our generation experiences. The account he gives of them is also known: "They are all vanity and grasping air," Ecc. 1:14. Their consolation is a crackling of thorns under the pot, a sudden flash and blaze that begins to perish. So both adversity and prosperity slays men without the Spirit. Whether they are crying or laughing, they are still dying.

2. They have no peace. They have no peace with God, or peace in their own souls. I know that many of them, on false grounds and expectations, make a shift to quiet their soul. It is not my business here to show the falseness and unsoundness of it, but this is their state. Because true and solid peace is an effect of the Holy Spirit in the hearts of believers, those without him have no such peace. They may cry, "Peace, peace," when sudden destruction is at hand, but the basis of their peace is darkness, ignorance, treachery of conscience, self-righteousness, and vain hope. What will these avail them on the day the Lord deals with them?

3. I might say the same thing concerning their joy and hope. They are false and perishing. Those who think they have an interest in the good things of the gospel, and yet have despised the Spirit of Christ, should consider that. I know there are many who pretend to have him, but are strangers to his grace. Some will perish who, despite their false profession, treat the Spirit kindly, and honor him, even though he does not dwell in them with power. What will happen to those who oppose and affront him? The Scripture tells us that unless the Spirit of Christ is in us, we are dead, Jas. 2:26; we are reprobates, 2Cor. 13:5; we do not belong to Christ, Rom. 8:9. Without him, you have none of those glorious effects of the Spirit mentioned before. And you, who do not care whether he is in you or not, are ready to deride these effects in those who do have him. Are there any who profess the gospel, who have never once seriously inquired whether they have the Holy Spirit? There are those who consider it ridiculous to be asked such a question, who look at anyone who talks of the Spirit as false believers. May the Lord awake such men to see their condition before it is too late! If the Spirit does not dwell in you, if he is not your Comforter, then neither is God your Father, nor the Son your Advocate, nor do you have any portion in

the gospel. O that God would awake men to consider this, before their neglect and contempt of the Holy Spirit reaches a point of despising him from which there is no recovery! O that the Lord would spread before them all the folly of their hearts, so that they may be ashamed and confounded, and stop their presumption!

End

CPSIA information can be obtained
at www.ICGtesting.com
Printed in the USA
LVHW090109090323
741203LV00002B/162